Falling

with Wings

A MOTHER'S STORY

DIANNA DE LA GARZA

THE MOTHER OF DEMI LOVATO

WITH **VICKIE McINTYRE**

FEIWEL AND FRIENDS
NEW YORK

A FEIWEL AND FRIENDS BOOK

An imprint of Macmillan Publishing Group, LLC

175 Fifth Avenue, New York, NY 10010

Our books may be purchased in bulk for promotional, educational, or business use.

Please contact your local bookseller or the Macmillan Corporate and

Premium Sales Department at (800) 221-7945 ext. 5442 or by e-mail

at MacmillanSpecialMarkets@macmillan.com.

Library of Congress Control Number: 2017960403

ISBN 978-1-250-14333-4 (hardcover) / ISBN 978-1-250-14332-7 (ebook)

Book design by April Ward and Sophie Erb

Feiwel and Friends logo designed by Filomena Tuosto

First edition, 2018

1   3   5   7   9   10   8   6   4   2

fiercereads.com

There are only two lasting bequests
we can hope to give our children.
One of these is roots, the other, wings.

—JOHANN WOLFGANG VON GOETHE

Demi Lovato

Mom—

From my very first memory of you, I've watched you take on every role, whether it was as a mother, a sister, a wife, a daughter, or a friend, with unmatched resilience, grace, and strength. As a Dallas Cowboys cheerleader and a country music singer, you were on your way to achieving great success, but you gave up your passions to see that my sisters and I realized ours. You provided a pathway for us to achieve our goals and dreams, simply because you loved us.

You've been through hell and back many times over. Life has dealt you cards that would have had lasting impacts on anyone. But the one characteristic that I've never seen in you is that of a *victim*. Through all the challenges you've faced—many of which I, surprisingly, didn't know about until I read this book—you have always remained the hero in our lives. You've been a true survivor in every sense of the word.

What an incredible and inspiring journey you've had! I'm happy that the rest of the world will now get to see all the parts of you that my sisters and I love the most: your kindness, your loyalty, your strength, your charisma, your brilliance, and a heart that is constantly bursting with love and care for others.

You're our inspiration and our forever hero. Thank you for telling your story, and *our* story, like no one else ever could.

PROLOGUE

*T*here are days when you get out of bed and instantly know that everything is going to slide downhill. This isn't one of them. My certainty rests in the fact that my mood is as bright as the sun that's streaming through the window of my Los Angeles home. For the first time in months, I'm not rushing off to spend eight hours on another movie-studio lot or listening to my attorney go through the intricate details of one more contract. My only concern is getting to the airport to catch my flight back to Texas. *I'm going home!*

A proper southern girl always looks her best, but I linger longer than usual in front of the mirror, checking every last detail. *No mascara smudges, hair in place, just enough lip liner.* I've dreamed about this day for so long that I want everything to be perfect. Satisfied, I race outside, where the car service is waiting with a black, shiny sedan. Out of nowhere, a gusty breeze pushes past me, grabbing my long, red locks and pulling them in every direction. I laugh all the way to the street.

"Good morning, sir," I chirp to the driver. "LAX, please."

By afternoon, I'll finally be in my "safe place"—our family's house in Colleyville, Texas, a suburb of Dallas. A little over two years ago, my husband, Eddie, and I packed our bags and headed west to help our girls—Dallas, Demi, and Madison—pursue acting and singing careers in Hollywood. We left filled with optimism, our dreams pinned to the stars, though many told us we were crazy. Today, I finally get to say, "I told you so!"

So many amazing things have happened recently that sometimes I fear that at the stroke of midnight, I'll wake up to discover it's all a dream. My middle child and one of the two children from my first marriage—Demetria Lovato, better known as Demi—is on the cusp of becoming a legitimate star. Thanks to the Disney Channel and Hollywood Records, she's now a popular actress and promising new recording artist. The whirlwind of the past few years—filming *Camp Rock*, starring in her own television show, and opening concerts for the Jonas Brothers—has catapulted her into the limelight of fame. At the thought, I clasp my hands together to steady the rush of nervousness leaping from my stomach to my chest. Sometimes all the changes are too much to comprehend.

Happy as I am to be returning to Texas, it seems odd to be leaving without my children. My life has revolved around my daughters' needs for so long that I feel as though I've forgotten to pack something essential. But I won't exactly be alone. My good friend Lorna will be joining me so we can escort each other to our thirtieth high school reunion, just a day away. I have so much to tell her that I suspect we'll be talking and laughing past midnight, just like we did as teenagers.

As I open the door to our former home, the past rushes back to greet me. Each step across the marble entryway echoes in eerie stillness as I smile at the familiar landmarks of the life we left behind. The same assortment of framed pictures—mostly Monet look-alikes from Eddie's bachelor days—still clings to the walls. There are no pictures of my children anywhere in sight, an oddity that reflects my lack of zeal for home decorating, which ranks about number 257 on my priority list. It's sad to admit, but our home has changed little in its decor since the day my girls and I moved in back in 1996. A perfect example is off to my right, where the same eight wooden chairs stand like soldiers gathered around our table, guarding the Waterford crystal stored in a nearby hutch. "The showcase area," I murmur to myself. But I have no desire to stop, no desire to touch any keepsakes. My feet know where they're going. When I reach the formal living room—so often referred to as "the junkyard"—I finally feel the pull of gravity. Within seconds, I'm floating in an orbit of pleasant memories.

The oversize room—with its threadbare sofa, two Kool-Aid-spotted wingback chairs, and a mahogany coffee table marred by mysterious carvings that no one ever admitted to—was always the happiest, noisiest, most magical room in the house. For years, I joked that it was the boundary between where the serene and beautiful ended and the madness began, mostly because of a grand assortment of music equipment that is still squeezed into every available nook and cranny. There are two five-feet-tall Madison

Tower Speakers, two massive floor monitors, a gigantic Marshall 4x12 stack, a sixteen-channel cabinet mixing board, and a P80 Yamaha performance keyboard, all purchased by Eddie off eBay soon after Demi and Dallas got accepted into Linda Septien's Vocal Productions Master Class, which now seems like eons ago.

I shake my head, trying to decide if the conglomeration of equipment makes it look more like a storage room or a prop lot at Universal Studios. For sure, it's enough to make a bona fide hoarder anxious! Only the vaulted ceiling gives the room some spaciousness. But truthfully, the cramped conditions never bothered us because every inch was tailored to our dreams and every fiber quivered with our energy. I wistfully remember how a joyous confusion erupted every time the doorbell rang, causing each one of us to run and jump over obstacles like we were training to be Olympic hurdlers.

Now silent, it's hard to imagine that this room was once the epicenter of our family's existence. By day, the room was full of laughter and chatter; by night, things always disintegrated. That's when the cacophony of throbbing bass, screechy microphones, and high-pitched vocals always spiraled out of control. Negotiating peacefully wasn't exactly in our grab bag of strategies, so more often than not, we resorted to yelling at one another. I can still hear our passionate lines, like ghosts rising out of the darkness. . . .

"DALLAS!" Demi screams while leaning over the banister from upstairs and peering into the living room. "Tone it down! I'm trying to write music."

"But you had the room for two hours," Dallas fires back, waving a sequin-covered sleeve in the air and flushing as red as her lipstick. "Now it's my turn!"

Then we all brace for Dallas's next round of vocals that will be ten times louder than before. Madison, who never could fall asleep in a quiet room, is sound asleep on the sofa, oblivious to the drama around her.

"Y'all need to go to bed," I holler from the kitchen. "It's nearly ten o'clock."

But Dallas never goes down without a fight. "That's not fair," she wails. "I just got in here."

Eddie, who has work in the morning, intones his mantra from the master bedroom, "GO . . . TO . . . BED!!!"

"You heard Eddie," I echo from the kitchen, listening for the stomping on the stairs as Dallas resigns herself to the fact that the bargaining is over.

Well, almost over.

"You always take too long of a turn," Dallas hisses as she passes by Demi's room, unable to resist one more push back.

"Whatever," Demi growls before firing off a few guitar riffs for emphasis.

One, two, three, I silently count before bellowing, "Don't make me come up there."

It's the final benediction that finally ushers in some peace.

When the doorbell rings, my daydreams vanish. "Come in. Come in," I exclaim to Lorna, standing on my tiptoes so I can wrap my arms around her. "I have sooo much to tell you." We barely make it through the living room before I start babbling about my girls. "You'll never believe it," I tell her, "but Madison's role on *Desperate Housewives* was renewed for another season; Dallas is busy doing voice-overs, and Demi's in South America right now with Eddie on the *Camp Rock 2* Tour with the Jonas Brothers." Breathless, I grab Lorna's hands and gently squeeze her fingers.

"Damn, girl! When you gonna have time to sleep?" Lorna barks, throwing her hands into the air and shaking her golden hair as that old familiar grin seeps across her face. "You ready?" she asks.

"Right this way," I say, leading her to the kitchen. We're on a mission, and it's time to strategize. "Bless your heart," I sigh. "Your roots have got to be done."

"Then do it!" she demands.

"Well, I could," I reply, "but I just might turn your hair orange." We laugh, embracing the sweetness of each other's company—then promptly make a hair appointment for the next morning. "There is one thing I *can* do for you," I tease, waving a package of false eyelashes in the air.

Lorna tries to put the eyelashes on but fumbles, which makes us both a bit giddy. She struggles some more before looking in the mirror. "You look fabulous," I exclaim. We toast our success and chatter away, even contemplating whether we should hire a limo to take us to our class reunion. At times, we toss questions back and forth like handfuls of confetti. *What should we wear? How should we fix our hair? Who will we impress?* And, yes, we even admit that we hope to look better than any of the cheerleaders from back in the day. I sheepishly confess that I resorted to tanning and getting Botox, just so I could look "real good."

"Isn't that what you do before a thirtieth reunion?" I laugh.

Just as Lorna and I start talking about Demi's collection of memorabilia that I'm donating to our class auction, my phone pings. Glancing down, I notice it's a text from Demi. *Hmmm, wonder what she wants?* Texting between us isn't normal when she's busy on tour. And, though I haven't told anyone, our communication lately has been strained by a barrage of teenage angst that stretches between us like the Grand Canyon.

Demi's message sends a chill down my spine, causing my knees to buckle.

"What's wrong?" cries Lorna.

I struggle to breathe as the light in the room slowly dims. I try to talk but can't. As though trapped in a bad dream, I fight through the grayness and read the message one more time: "I'm sorry ahead of time." The words electrify every nerve in my body, telling me that Demi is in serious trouble. Oh, I've pretended that everything is wonderful to my friends and the media—and even to my relatives—but it's not. For the past few months, Demi has vacillated between cheerful and sullen, as though her moods are altered by the pull of a string. At times, the darkness in her eyes frightens me, and her late-night escapades aren't slowing down, either. It's clear that something is terribly wrong. A sudden flashback pushes my anxiety even higher.

A few weeks earlier, I had walked into Demi's bedroom to wake her so she could get to Hollywood Center Studios for the filming of *Sonny with a Chance*. I remember how peaceful she looked, but when I gently touched her, I froze. Next to her on the clean sheets was a bloody rag. I felt as though someone had slapped me in the face. "Demi, Demi! Wake up," I shouted, fearing she was dead.

She awoke with surprise, her eyes clouding with fear.

"Why? Why?" I cried, my hands shaking.

"I can't . . . I shouldn't," she stammered, her eyes wide and bristling with tears. "Oh, God, I won't do it anymore. I swear; I'm so sorry."

As we held each other tightly, I wanted to believe her. So did Eddie. But the problem wasn't new. Demi had started cutting her wrists long before that morning. Once we noticed, we had a family meeting and decided to hire a life coach, figuring that if Demi could sort through the issues behind the cutting, she would stop. And she did. Everything seemed fine until I saw those bloody rags that morning. Despite the alarms that went off in my head, we pushed the incident aside. There wasn't time for talking. As Demi raced to the studio out one door, I left through another to take Madison, my youngest, to the set of *Desperate Housewives*.

From then on, Demi's schedule was an endless blur of photo shoots, press interviews, fittings, and filming that left little time for discussions. The pressures of the industry consumed not only Demi, but me, too. As mother and schedule keeper, it was my job to maintain control and to not let anyone down. So many people—music representatives, television executives, castmates, and management— were depending on Demi to be strong and to do her job. Nothing was just a family matter anymore. Walking away wasn't an option.

A wave of regret tumbles over me as I realize I sent Demi off that terrible morning with nothing more than a hug and some silent prayers. Guilt claws at my heart. *How could I have been so naive? Why didn't I do more?*

"Oh, God, what have we done?" I cry, watching Lorna's eyes grow wider.

A slow tremor vibrates at my feet, then rises to my chest. My whole body aches as I recall a haunting dream. The hazy sequence involved Sammy, one of Demi's favorite makeup artists, who was carefully applying foundation and eye shadow to my daughter's face. As Sammy bent over to apply the finishing touches, I suddenly realized that Demi was lying in a coffin. The dream was so real that I jumped out of bed, tears streaming down my cheeks.

The dream, the bloody rag, and the text—they suddenly add up to one terrible conclusion: *My daughter's going to take her own life!* I grab my phone and frantically start punching in Demi's number.

"No answer?" I cry. *Was she in her hotel room? Did she take a handful of pills? Did she cut too deep?* Questions fly through my head so fast that I can't think.

"DIANNA!" Lorna shouts. "What's wrong? What's happening?"

Her words sound far away, a mere echo compared with the thoughts rising and crashing around me. *No, God, don't let her kill herself!* I try Eddie's number, again and again, but he doesn't answer, either. With my eyes closed, I mentally prod Eddie to rush into Demi's room and save her, but the pounding of my heart tells me I'm already too late. *No, no! Don't let this happen.* Suddenly a reel of memories begins to play, and I can see my sweet, young girls laughing and teasing one another in the backyard, then sitting at the dining-room table as I help them with their homework, and finally, huddling around the television as they watch and sing along to the happy theme songs for *Barney & Friends* and *Rugrats*. Each scene cuts through me like a bolt of lightning. *I'm losing my little girl.*

I try Eddie's number one more time.

"Hello," he answers, his voice too calm, too flat.

"Eddie!" I scream, "Where's Demi?"

"She's here . . . next to me," he says through clenched teeth.

Typically friendly and upbeat, Eddie's response unnerves me. Clearly, he doesn't want to talk.

"Is she all right?" I ask, trying not to panic though the look on Lorna's face tells me she, too, is worried.

"No . . . not really," he says, frustration tugging at every word.

"What's going on?" I demand.

"Not now!" he snaps. "I can't talk."

Oh, no, no, no. He did not just say that. And so emphatically, like I'm bothering him. "Oh, you're going to talk," I say. "You're going to tell me right now what's happening." Only then do I hear the raggedness of his breath.

"We're on the plane," he begins. "There was a fight, and she punched one of her dancers in the face. . . . It's serious."

What? She hit someone? My mind can't quite assemble the pieces of Eddie's story, but I know anything less than "Demi just killed herself" is welcome news. I look at Lorna and mouth, "She's okay."

"Eddie, don't worry," I say a bit too optimistically. "We can deal with this."

The silence on the other end of the phone isn't exactly golden.

The truth is I'm rattled to the core but relieved, too. Demi isn't dead, and that's enough to convince me that we'll work the matter out as a family. After all, that's what we always do. But I can already feel the weight of everything I've tried to hold together slipping from my grasp. I wonder if we've waited too long to realize the extent of our problems.

"This Hollywood dream isn't going so well," I finally confess to Lorna. "We're all having a hard time."

Once I start shedding my secrets, I can't seem to stop.

"The past few months have been hell. No one in my family knows, but Dallas just got out of a treatment center for drugs and alcohol. She's struggling to find her own identity in LA, and Madison is being bullied on the Internet about her weight, which according to the press is all my fault." I pause, twisting a tissue in my hands. "But it's Demi I'm most worried about. She battles depression a lot . . . and I'm pretty sure all those parties she goes to are full of drugs and alcohol."

Lorna has the kindest look on her face, which suddenly confuses me.

"What am I supposed to do, Lorna? My family means everything to me. All I've ever wanted to do is help them, yet I feel guilty nearly every waking hour because I don't know how to do that anymore."

With each admission, my perfect world begins to crumble. None of it is pretty, but hearing my own voice acknowledge our family's problems releases the knot wedged below my rib cage.

"Dianna, you've always put your children first," Lorna offers, but I shake my head.

I can no longer ignore that our family needs help, especially Demi, who is rail thin, exhausted, and in a very dark place. This latest crisis means that all of our previous attempts to help her—cutting back on her schedule, hiring life coaches, pep talks, and punishments—were nothing more than Band-Aids on a very serious wound. Now, it's time for surgery. But as the doubts and questions about what we can do begin to multiply, I start wailing like a baby.

Lorna watches as I pace back and forth, raving like a lunatic. "What did I do wrong? . . . How could this happen? . . . Doesn't Demi know how much we love and support her?" Then my mind does a U-turn. "Why did she hit someone? . . . Did that girl provoke Demi?" Exhausted, I mumble that Demi's career is probably over.

Lorna jumps up and grabs my shoulders. "Good Lord, Dianna! Everything *is* going to be fine. You've still got her! She's alive—everything else will fix itself."

Her words sting my heart, making me even more emotional. Five years earlier, Lorna had lost her own son, Trenton, in a Halloween prank that went terribly wrong. The tragedy was hard on us, too, because Trenton was like a brother to my girls. That's when it hits me—*Lorna never had a chance to save him*. We, at least, have a fighting chance to turn things around.

"We *will* be okay," I tell Lorna, trying to sound strong. "We *will* work this out."

But as I head toward my bedroom, one labored step after another, I know without a doubt that the magic is gone. There will be no happily-ever-after ending for our Hollywood success story, no magic wand to erase the mistakes. It will take more than faith to turn our lives around, but I know it's where I need to start. "Dear God," I whisper, "send us the help we need."

It's a simple, heartfelt prayer. Though I mean every word, I have no idea how long or how hard each of us will have to work to turn our lives around. Nor can I comprehend the emotional layers beneath our troubles or my own deteriorating mental health that is woven into our family's issues. Only one thing is certain—I won't be attending that thirtieth high school reunion that seemed so important a few hours ago. It's time to start a new chapter in our lives. Our family's survival depends upon it.

Beginnings

OCTOBER 1965 TO OCTOBER 1996

God didn't promise days without pain,
laughter without sorrow, or sun without rain,
but He did promise strength for the day,
comfort for the tears, and light for the way.
If God brings you to it, He will bring you through it.

—UNKNOWN

CHAPTER ONE

"From an early age, I wanted more . . .
I wanted to be a star!"

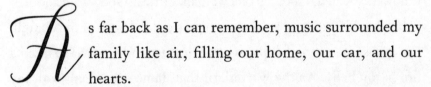s far back as I can remember, music surrounded my family like air, filling our home, our car, and our hearts.

"Stand up here," Daddy said one Sunday long ago, lifting me with his strong hands and placing me on a piano bench that was next to the pulpit at the Union Bower Assembly of God Church in Irving, Texas. "Steady yourself," he whispered before walking away.

It was 1965, and I was only three years old. Singing solo had been Daddy's idea. I was tiny, even for my age—the size of an insect compared to the grown-ups sitting in the rows and rows of pews in front of me—and the crowd looked immense to me. Although eager to please everyone, I suddenly wasn't sure I remembered all the words to the song Daddy had patiently taught me. My legs wobbled as my eyes blinked in the bright lights. Nervously, I slid my hands across the folds of my pale-blue dress, feeling the small, white bumps sprouting from the dotted-swiss fabric. When that didn't calm me, I shook my head, causing scarlet wisps of my pixie haircut to stick to my cheeks. After that, there was nothing more to do except stare into the eyes of the men and women in front of me. And that's when the magic happened.

Maybe it was their smiles. Maybe it was the eagerness in their eyes. But the longer we looked at one another, the more I enjoyed the attention. At the sound of the piano, I took a deep breath and began to sing. Don't ask me the name of the Gospel song or how I left the altar that day—those details are buried under time. What I do remember, quite vividly, is the shower of praise that followed. "Amen," shouted one woman. "Praise God," said another. "Hallelujah!" boomed a group of men from the back of the church. But it was the echo of applause swirling around me that sparked a fire in my belly. As the warmth of that flame spread upward, my sense of self grew taller and stronger, and from that day forward, I never doubted that singing was my God-given gift. And I never doubted that I would become a star. In my childhood imagination, I saw that piano bench grow and grow until it became a stage in front of thousands. The crowd's adoration was like manna from heaven and every crumb reinforced my destiny, which, in my optimism, meant I was going to be a singing sensation with fans around the globe.

I left no detail to chance. Our family's motto—"Practice makes perfect"—was put to good use. Every afternoon, I disappeared into my bedroom and stood in front of the full-length mirror, wrapping my little fingers around a hairbrush and belting out tunes until I forgot where I was. I loved watching myself, loved dreaming about the future. Although Gospel was the main soundtrack to our lives, popular music was there, too, and radio artists, such as Bobby Sherman and Tony Orlando, inspired me to think about hearing my own songs over the airways someday. My audiences may have been imaginary, but my ambitions were as real as the freckles on my face.

A few months after my church debut, my momma, Sue Dianne Emmons, and I were sitting on the porch as we listened to the radio wedged between us. Pots and pans—my collection of toys that day—were scattered around me, but my sole focus was on the lid to a large pot. As I fidgeted this way and that, trying to nestle myself into the shiny piece of metal, I stared at my mother as she put on her makeup.

Momma was young and naturally beautiful. That day, especially, she was very Annette Funicello–looking with her long, dark hair; stylish pedal pushers; button-up shirt; and white flats. Makeup made her glow like sunshine.

"Doesn't matter what you're wearing," she instructed. "You've got to make sure your hair and makeup are done."

Nodding solemnly, I stared at her intently. Then I studied how she brushed her hair with slow, even strokes and how, with a flick of her wrist, she could turn the ends up. How a bit of mascara could turn her eyelashes dark as charcoal. And how her lips turned a frosty pink with something that resembled a giant crayon. "It's called putting on your face," she told me. When she finished, Momma held up a small mirror, smiling at her handiwork. Before looking away, she caught my reflection, making her smile grow even wider. In that instant, an energy passed between us that made my skin tingle. Deliriously happy, I began to spin on the lid beneath me like a human top. Pushing harder and harder, I spun faster and faster, causing rays of sunlight to dance around me. Just as my momentum reached a crescendo, the number-one hit "Lil' Red Riding Hood" started to play.

Momma sang along. "Hey there Little Red Riding Hood, You sure are looking good," she trilled, cocking her head from side to side. "You're everything that a big bad wolf could want." Then looking right at me, her eyes bright with joy, she unleashed a comical howl, "Owoooo." Like magic, her voice, the song, and our happiness became an intimate conversation. You see, I knew this Little Red Riding Hood she was singing about, and I also knew about that big, bad wolf. "I mean baaaa. Baaa," she crooned, looking more beautiful with every note. Time slowed to a trickle as love devoured me.

As I grew older, whenever Elvis came on the radio or television, Momma would pause what she was doing and launch into her legendary Elvis experiences. No matter how many times I had heard the stories before, she'd retell them, always sounding a bit giddy. "Oohh, now there's a boy who loves his momma," she'd start, quickly adding, "Do you know I met him in my teens?"

Now I had heard these stories again and again, so, of course, I knew. In fact, I knew most of the details, such as how she had lived with her older sisters in Tennessee for a time in a house not far from Graceland, how Elvis was a good person because he started out in Gospel music, and how he was a fun-loving character who liked to play practical jokes. But I never said a word. How could I steal my momma's joy in reliving those experiences one more time?

"We'd wander down to Graceland and flirt with the security guards," she'd brag, "and eventually, they'd let us in." After she delivered this little tidbit, Momma's face always beamed like a schoolgirl who'd just found out she was voted prom queen. It made me wonder if living so close to "The King" had been a bit like handing my mother a diamond ring and telling her not to wear it. "That Priscilla, though," she'd add with attitude, "always got angry when we made too much noise. She'd give us a stern talking-to from her balcony, though we never paid much attention."

Elvis, who rented out the Memphian Theater to screen his own movies, often invited a group of friends to come along. My mother, friends with a friend who had been invited, always jumped at the opportunity to tag along. "Every time," she'd laugh, "he'd insist that everyone sit behind him so as not to obstruct his view." I got the feeling Momma was just fine with his request.

But popular music never dominated the airwaves at our house, mostly because of my father, Perry Hart. With his wavy, sandy-brown hair and bluish-gray eyes, Daddy may have looked like a movie star, but his heart lusted after God. Although he had a good-paying job at Central Freight Lines in Irving, it was his work with the church that he valued the most. As an ordained Pentecostal minister, he felt his true calling was to serve God. He fulfilled that duty by serving as the youth minister at Union Bower Church and leading praise and worship music with my mother. When Daddy finally invited me to sing along, it was like destiny tapping me on the shoulder.

CHAPTER TWO

"Faith was instilled in me as a young child."

To say our home was on fire for the Lord would be an understatement. There's nothing quite like a Pentecostal household where every day is treated like a Sunday and where faith, fire, and brimstone burn like an eternal flame. Talking about God, as well as the devil, filled our days.

"Everyone ready?" Daddy implored as we scrambled out of the house and headed to church. Seated behind the wheel, Daddy always started whistling. His happiness bounced off us the same way sunlight did from his gold wedding ring, making the entire car glow with heavenly light. Momma, always silent but smiling, clutched her favorite handbag, while I, alone in the back seat, hummed and stared at my shiny, patent leather shoes. We perfected the drill three times a week—twice on Sunday and again on Wednesday evenings.

Every church service was a feast for the senses. There was singing and shouting, crying and laughing, praying and praising, and often, all at once! Wide-eyed and spellbound, I sat amid the great drama—usually in the front row—watching the preacher in his black suit as he marched back and forth behind the pulpit, shouting about heaven and hell. Without fail, somewhere in his delivery, he'd raise his Bible to the sky in one hand and pound the podium with the other. I couldn't take my eyes off of him.

"All sinners," he'd cry, his voice so shrill it sent ripples of fear down my spine, "will be thrown into a lake of fire—FOR ALL ETERNITY!" Louder and louder he grew until I could barely stand it. When he started slinging sweat and spraying spittle like a madman, I'd hold my breath and close my eyes, hoping to stay dry. "Repent," he'd shout, a final crescendo that always ushered in a jubilant chorus of "Hallelujah" and "Amen." Then, his voice softening, he'd plead for everyone to accept Jesus and be saved. That was my cue to relax because I knew the music would soon return. When it did, I sang my lungs out.

Sometimes, in late spring or early summer, an entire week was devoted to worship. That's when we'd eat an early dinner and head out into the country to attend "brush-arbor" revivals. Although most children would balk at the idea today, I loved them because music was such an important component of the services. I remember how Momma, Daddy, and I would scan the fields from our car, hoping to spy the telltale signs that we had reached our destination: a wooden, tentlike structure with open sides and a roof piled high with dried grass and vines (thus the "brush-arbor" name). "There it is," one of us would shout, pointing to the wooden cross rising from the roof of the temporary shelter. Then we'd drive across the patch of grass, jostled by the bumpy earth, and walk hand in hand to find our seats.

There were no fancy chairs, no electricity. Paper fans and folding chairs were the norm. Yet, listening to those guitars strumming and voices rising in song, we eventually forgot about the Texas heat as we rode a wave of glory onto heaven's shores. It was pure bliss. And if church on Sunday mornings seemed loud, revivals were like Pentecostal churches on steroids! Some folks even took to dancing as they whooped and hollered. When it was time for testimony, one by one, each person would stand and share what the Lord had done for them that day. Some stories made me smile; some made me quiver in disbelief. And some made me as scared as a sinner in a cyclone. Regardless, it all pointed to one undeniable truth: God is great.

Every service ended with an altar call. "While every head is bowed and eyes are closed," our pastor urged, "raise your hand if you'd like to accept Jesus as your personal savior." Scared as I was of God's wrath, I never could resist peeking from at least one eye to see who raised their hand. In time, brush-arbor revivals would slowly become a relic of the past, but I've always cherished the memories of those nights when our faith seemed so strong and unshakable.

Although the Pentecostal world may seem strange, even frightening, to some, it was normal for me. Church was the neighborhood where we spent most of our days. I knew the people around me. I cherished their songs. And I was grateful for their love. It was there, in their midst, that I learned about prayer and scripture, as well as typical teenage things, such as how to pass notes to my girl-friends and how to flirt with boys. The rituals and faith of these people became my own, and the process of adopting their ways was as natural as taking bread from a basket being passed around the table. At least for a while.

By 1967, Momma, Daddy, and I had been leading the praise and worship services for nearly two years, faithfully standing together on the red velvet carpet at the front of the church. It was like being on stage, and I adored every minute of the attention. I thought of it as my training to become a star, but when my baby brother, Joey, arrived in August, the spotlight was no longer on me. A few weeks later, just as we started adjusting to being a family of four, Daddy crashed his motorcycle, and my world really turned upside down.

Daddy, scraped and bruised, hurt his back in the accident and could no longer work at the shipping company. Without a job or paycheck, our world became untethered. In a matter of weeks, the layers of our lives started to shed like dead skin. Pain, heartache, and sadness saturated our days. We lost our home. We sold our belongings. And we waved good-bye to the comfortable life we had known. Our car, packed with the few possessions that remained, would transport us into another existence.

"We're as poor as church mice," Momma sighed as we drove away. With my five-year-old face pressed against the back window, I watched as rows of houses flew by and sidewalks slowly gave way to pastures. Herds of cattle replaced people, and streetlamps were exchanged for stars. Eventually, we disembarked in a town called

DeSoto, in north Texas, that seemed as far away from our old neighborhood as the moon—and just as uninhabited.

But good Pentecostals never give up; instead, they get on their knees. "Dear Jesus," Momma pleaded, "we need food . . . we need healing . . . we need direction." The words poured out of her like tears. Daddy, still recuperating, stormed heaven as well, though his tone was more confident, more sure. "Amen," he boomed after every request, as though answers had already arrived. I watched and waited for their prayers to be answered. Through it all, we never stopped singing. And I never stopped dreaming.

No matter how bad things got, I could always escape to my imagination and drape myself in the pleasures of my future stardom. There, in my mind, I saw myself strutting on stage in fashionable clothes, reaching out to shake the hands of adoring fans, and belting out tunes to a captive audience. It was how I kept my dream alive, and with each vivid detail, I empowered myself to believe that my ambitions were not only attainable but that they were God's will for my life. My belly, though, still grumbled from hunger.

During one rough patch, we prayed repeatedly for food because there wasn't any money to buy groceries. "Heavenly Father, you know our needs," Momma prayed. While waiting for answers, we quoted scripture. Philippians 4:19 was a favorite: "But my God shall supply all your need according to His riches in glory by Christ Jesus." So, too, was Psalms 23:1: "The Lord is my shepherd; I shall not want." In my imagination, I prepared for God's riches. I tasted turkey and ham in my sleep and inhaled the delight of ripe strawberries when I awoke. If God were generous—and I fully expected him to be—I wanted nothing less than the rich, chocolate cake smothered in buttercream icing that I saw in my dreams. Every prayer made my mouth water.

One afternoon a neighbor knocked on our door. Anticipating our miracle, we ran to see our bounty. "Grew them myself," the woman proclaimed, handing my mother a box. "Bless you. Bless you," my mother gushed. One peek and I nearly fainted. Her blessing was nothing more than a dozen white turnips! To make matters worse, the woman reappeared, week after week, with another batch. And night after night, I'd struggle to swallow her abundance. We ate so many turnips that year, they came out our ears! Yes, I'll forever bless the woman, sent by God, who saved us from going hungry, but to this day if I smell a turnip, I get sick to my stomach. There's only one word to describe a turnip—and that's *nasty*. (Even Momma agrees with me on that one!)

Through it all, we never grew tired of thanking God for our music. It was, and would remain, the bright, shiny lining of our lives for many years to come. Without it, I shudder to think what would have become of us. One of the most profound lessons my parents taught me through those years was the blessing of singing through our tears. Every note of melody held the power of hope, joy, and prayer. It was our lifeline, and we held on with both hands, especially when our family's ship started sailing toward new horizons.

Barely settled in DeSoto, our family suddenly left for Colorado, where Daddy had been offered a ministry job. I started first grade there, but for reasons I never knew, we packed up the car and moved back to north Texas a short time later, hovering for a bit in the town of Blossom, where some of Daddy's kin lived. The Campbell Soup factory was about ten miles away, and Daddy quickly got hired. But that wasn't enough to keep us settled. By 1969, as I was entering second grade, we were on the move again. This time it was seven miles down the road to Detroit. *What exactly was my father looking for?* I wondered.

"These are good people with kind hearts," Daddy declared shortly after we arrived, which proved to be true enough, but I suspect the fact that my Granny lived there, not to mention that my Uncle Joe owned the Detroit Superette—the only store in town— may have helped to sway his decision.

And just like that, our nomadic existence came to an end. Before long, Daddy bought a small farm and started selling insurance. I'd like to say it was like being led into the promised land, but it wasn't quite like that.

CHAPTER THREE

"Pain is pain; it doesn't matter where it comes from."

wo things happened shortly after we moved to Detroit. The first was the birth of my sister, Julie. She was cute, tiny, and loud! My seven-year-old heart nearly burst with pride. Finally, I would have a sister with whom I could share my secrets, though it would be a few years before she'd understand what I was telling her. The second wasn't such a joyful event.

Although I had my music, a new baby sister, and loving parents, a thick fog of sadness descended on me at times that made me long for my grandparents and the cousins I had left behind in Irving. Even riding my new horse, Peppermint, or running through the open fields behind our house couldn't erase the homesickness that swept through my heart. In my childish wisdom, I decided there was only one solution: I'd run away. My plan had a few holes in it, but I didn't see them until it was too late.

If I could just reach the pay phone in town, I knew I could call my grandparents. "Please, come take me away," I intended to beg, never doubting that they'd rescue me. I set off at a good pace, but steps from home, I realized I couldn't use the phone in town because one of my neighbors would surely see me. And in our close-knit southern community, that meant someone would call and tell my momma.

No problem, I told myself. *I'll just walk the seven miles to the next town.*

There was no lack of determination on my part to get what I wanted. Two blocks from home, though, one entire family spotted me from their front porch.

"Hey, Dianna, where you goin'?" cried the mother, her teeth sparkling like stars against her dark skin.

"Oh, I'm just run'n' away from home," I told her, knowing that if I told a lie, I'd get into more trouble.

"Why, you best turn yo'self around and get back to your momma," she said, all the while shaking her finger like a stick as the crowd around her nodded in agreement.

So I did. I knew there was no use trying to get any farther; she'd just send one of her kids to find my mother. And unlike people today, my mother *never* would have told the woman to mind her own business. Keeping an eye on one another was a neighborly duty. And that duty cost me dearly. When Daddy walked through the door that night, I knew what was coming.

"Go to your room," he demanded.

It was a different era, one in which corporal punishment was the norm. In our house, it was also coupled with the biblical logic of

"Spare the rod and spoil the child." My momma even carried a paddle in her purse, so that all she had to do was pull it out and look at us and we'd know to straighten up. I was part of a generation that both loved and feared their parents. When we did wrong, we knew we were "going to get it!" And that day was no exception.

When Daddy would walk into my room, which was always full of other kids—neighbors, cousins, and eventually my other siblings—everyone would see the belt dangling from his hand and scatter. It's quite comical to look back on it now, but at the time, my mind went into complete panic mode. With that dear-God-please-help-me expression plastered on my face, the crowd of onlookers would stare back, all bug-eyed, before running for the doorway. The logjam, as they tried to exit, was a mass of waving arms and legs as each one pushed their way into the hall. No one wanted to stick around.

"You know this is going to hurt me more than it does you," Daddy always said.

Are you serious? I'd hear in my head. *I'm pretty sure it WON'T.*

One. Two. Three. With each strike, my mind revolted against what was happening. I was terrified. Outraged. And indignant. My father's good intentions to purge me of disrespect and misbehavior did nothing of the sort. Instead, my will to prove that I was in control, not my father, grew stronger. That didn't stop me from crying out in pain (often before the belt even hit my skin) in hopes that if I cried loud enough, Daddy would think I'd had enough punishment for one day. He rarely took the bait, so when he finished and walked away, I'd stare at his backside wondering why he disliked me so much. He didn't, of course. It was just my mind trying to make sense of two strong-willed people with opposite ideas about the parameters of discipline and obedience.

Ten minutes later, wounded and tearful, I'd be asked to come out of my room and join everyone at the table like nothing had happened. Then I'd listen to Daddy say grace over the food. "Lord, bless this food to the nourishment of our bodies . . ." My fiery temper simmered with resentment and the sting of disappointment grew more intense over time. I was Daddy's girl, and I didn't want that to slip away, yet my very existence seemed to plague him in ways that confounded me.

Not everyone reacted to the "whippin's" we got like I did. In fact, my brother Joey was once given the ultimatum of Daddy's belt or giving up his rifle for a year, and he didn't waste a second thinking about which was worse. "I'll take the whippin'," he shouted. But I would have parted with my right arm before consenting to my father's punishments.

Truth was, aside from his punishments, I adored my father. Still do. He has always been a good man—a loving, hardworking provider for his family—and I know he loved me as much then as he does now. But something about being punished flipped a switch inside my brain. By sixth grade, I was striving so hard to be good . . . be perfect . . . be loved . . . that eventually I developed an eating disorder. Those same inner mantras that pushed me to excel in sports, academics, and music also drove me to starve myself. Perfection became my goal, and every effort to attain it reinforced my thinking that if I just worked hard enough, I could earn the love and support—from my parents, from the community, and from God—that I so desperately wanted. Dinnertime seemed like a good place to start.

Always the last to finish eating, I had to clean up after everyone else was excused, which provided the perfect opportunity to brush most of my meal right into the trashcan. By my early teens, food was so distasteful to me that every morsel got stuck in my throat, making it difficult to swallow. As odd as it sounds, the minute someone said, "You're too thin," a choir of angels started singing in my head, confirming that I was on the right path toward being loved and admired by everyone around me.

My eating habits became my own dark secret, and one that I would carry with me for many, many years. Obscured in my darkness were factors I couldn't even imagine—such as genetic tendencies toward eating disorders that ran in my family and the poor example I'd be setting for my children in the future. Becoming aware of all that would take decades. And a good deal of therapy.

I still don't understand all the forces that drove me to stop eating at such a young age, but I do know that I felt compelled to be perfect. Perfection seemed to be the only way I could avoid my father's wrath and escape the clutches of hell. At the same time, though, I loved my independent spirit and pursuit of adventure. With no bridge to link such opposite pursuits, limiting my food intake offered me the sense of control I needed to juggle the yin and yang of my existence. It was a way of focusing on a solution rather than the problems that were causing so much anxiety. More important, it put me in the driver's seat of my life.

Before long, I viewed my eating restrictions as a badge of honor that boasted of self-control. With every lost pound, I felt more perfect . . . more admired . . . and more beautiful. Somehow, all my twisted logic got bundled into the hope that someday I'd look and act just like those glamorous stars filling the pages of the glossy magazines I liked to read.

Let me be clear. I don't blame my parents, the church, or God. It's just the way I was wired. No one forced or coerced me into an eating disorder. I chose that behavior to ease my own inner turbulence. It wasn't a wise decision. But without safe avenues to express the confusion inside of me, the stress eventually affected my thinking, my behavior, and my health.

Thanks to new research, the medical and social-service communities are finally beginning to recognize that traumatic events in childhood—everything from the death of a parent to living in poverty, from being punished to being bullied or witnessing domestic violence—can damage mental health and even change brain development.

But we didn't acknowledge this back in the '60s, '70s, or even '80s. Had it been a different time, someone might have suggested I seek professional help or at least talk about my feelings with my parents, but issues like that weren't discussed back then. It was all on me to find a way to deal with the troubling thoughts in my mind, and I did that by hiding, alleviating, and ignoring my emotions. *Act like everything is perfect*, I told myself. And I became quite good at it, no matter what was happening in my life.

CHAPTER FOUR

"It was like a baby parade—they just kept coming."

According to the church, children are a blessing from the Lord. And, my, oh my, how we were blessed. Two years after my sister Julie arrived, Kathy appeared, and the year after that, we welcomed Brandon, another brother. It was like a baby parade—they just kept coming. As the eldest daughter, my responsibilities multiplied with each new addition, especially after Momma decided she wanted to take some college classes and pursue a degree in home economics. Although I still had a dream of becoming a star, I threw myself into caring for my siblings like I was mother of the year. I soothed sore tummies, changed diapers, and prepared bottles like a pro. So familiar with my siblings, I learned to read their moods better than my parents. It was training I'd eventually put to good use.

Looking back, it's hard to picture all of us squeezed into a two-bedroom house, but that's how it was. Much like a dormitory, the girls slept in bunk beds on one side of the room while the boys slept on the other side. Thankfully, the bedroom door always stayed open, which afforded me the nightly pleasure of hearing Johnny Carson's voice floating through the air before I fell asleep as my father watched his show. It was a ritual I grew to love.

Although our family may have been constrained by tight finances and strict religious rules, we also enjoyed our share of good times. One thing is certain: Two adults and five children under one roof made life interesting. Every aspect of those growing-up years—the good as well as the bad—shaped and defined me in countless ways. By the time I was a teenager, the tapestry of my life was full of colorful threads. Sturdy, blue cotton strands, born from the grit of survival, reinforced with my parents' philosophies of "work hard, don't give up, and do your best." The bright red and orange patterns reminded me that love and laughter were sprinkled on our days to lighten the load. But it was the bold, purple threads of faith, spun from years of reading the Bible, praising God through music, and expecting miracles, that tied all the other components of my life together. For us, faith was more than just a set of beliefs, more than a set of rules. God was very real and tangible, especially when our prayers were answered in magnificent ways.

One evening when my brother Brandon was just a baby, he rolled across the kitchen floor in his walker. No one thought much about the deep fryer, sitting on the counter. As Brandon cooed and smiled, we clapped and made funny faces at him. Momma was behind the counter and so was Daddy. For a moment I was lost in the heady aroma of my mother's fried chicken, but something made me look at my father, just as he placed a quick kiss on Momma's cheek. The intimacy of the gesture made me flush with a warm, fuzzy feeling.

Someone, maybe it was Julie, suggested a silly game, and we all joined in. Voices fired from every direction. "Over here, Brandon." "No, no, over here," shouted another. But Brandon had other ideas. He ignored our pleas and headed straight for the electrical outlet, where a cord dangled like a magic snake. None of us could stop him before he gleefully pulled that cord, causing the fryer to topple over and unleash a stream of hot, bubbling oil that cascaded over his head and face.

Brandon screamed and so did my mother. Horrified, we watched as Momma grabbed our baby brother and wrapped him in a blanket, smothering and obliterating him from our eyes. All the while, her lips never stopped moving. "Dear Jesus," she said over and over, "protect my child." Daddy leaped into action, firing off directions. "Dianna, watch the kids," and "Momma, get in the car." His last words, as steady and calm as though he were talking about the weather, were for a miracle of healing.

Now, we knew as sure as we had five fingers on each hand that Jesus had turned water into wine and that he had fed five thousand people with nothing more than a loaf of bread and a few fish. We also knew that if miracles had happened in the days of the Bible, they could happen today, too. But saving my baby brother from scalding oil seemed a bit out of reach. While Momma and Daddy prayed their way to the hospital, we kids added our own pleas as we huddled together in the living room. I did my best to calm everybody down, while at the same time, I tried not to imagine how bad Brandon's face would look when they took off that blanket.

When my parents finally returned, they were still holding my brother in a blanket, though this time he was fast asleep. "The doctor's face was full of fear," Momma started. Then Daddy chimed in, "He warned us that Brandon's skin might fall off when they removed the blanket." But when the nurse unraveled my brother from his protective cocoon, his skin was as pink and soft as the day he was born. No burns. No blisters. "A medical miracle," declared the doctor.

Some years later, my other brother, Joey, had a God moment of his own, and I was his witness. While walking to school, Joey impulsively darted across the street and ran straight into a moving car. I watched as he sailed through the air, some five feet off the ground. When he landed, he cried out in pain. "God help him!" I screamed. "Don't let him die!" As I ran toward him, Joey suddenly jumped up and started darting in circles. He was in shock, dazed and confused, but I couldn't find a scratch on him. The doctor who examined him concurred, saying, "No concussion, no bleeding, and no scratches—he's one lucky boy." But we all knew that luck had nothing to do with it.

Faith was so ingrained in me that I never questioned if God was real. I just knew it was true, though *religion* is no longer a term I like to use. These days I prefer the word *faith* because to me it doesn't matter what religion you practice; it's faith in a higher power that's important. Call it walking with God, call it spirituality, or call it moonbeams—whatever. Positive attracts positive.

I'm not going to say that one religion is better than another. I just know which one works for me, and that's the tradition I was raised in—being a Christian. But if you believe in everything the

Bible talks about—like angels, miracles, and burning bushes—then you also have to believe in Satan. You can't pick and choose. Demons are part of the package, too.

Back before our family's music ministry really took off, we used to go to something called "a sing'n'," though it was pronounced more like "sang'n'" with our Texas drawls. Today, we'd probably call it a talent show or karaoke, and it came with all the fix'n's, like drums, pianos, and guitars. One particular night, the four of us—me, Daddy, and Momma, who was holding my baby brother in her arms—walked up to the door where there was a sing'n' under way. Loud voices and fervent praise floated in the air as we approached, but the closer we got to the door, the more violently I started to shake.

"What's wrong?" Daddy asked.

"I don't know. I don't know," I stammered, looking straight into my father's eyes. Now I had been to hundreds of church services before that night and had heard more than a few people speaking in tongues and loud voices. Yet, never once had I refused to go through a doorway. Frankly, that wasn't something my father would have tolerated, but that night, I couldn't control the sense of fear and dread that engulfed me. Daddy recognized that I felt something in my spirit, and he knew it wasn't something good.

"We need to go," he said, gently wrapping his arm around my shoulders and motioning for Momma to get back in the car. "The younger you are, the closer you are to God," he said as we drove away, "and who am I to question that?"

I still don't know why we weren't supposed to go in there that night, but the moment we walked away, the shaking stopped. Events like that happened throughout my childhood, solidifying my faith and training me to recognize when God was trying to tell me something. In the years ahead, it would be that voice, that feeling of connectedness to the spiritual world that would assure me that I was on the right path—though there would also be times when I didn't want to listen.

CHAPTER FIVE

"We find our purpose through our passions."

"Ladies and gentlemen, I introduce to you, the Harts."

How I loved hearing those words. By the time I entered seventh grade, Momma, Daddy, and I had started traveling all over northeast Texas to lead praise and worship services. Thanks to my grandparents in Irving, I was also taking piano lessons and practicing on the old upright that my parents had bought shortly after moving to Detroit. Although my cousins had taught me to play chords years ago, I was now broadening my skills enough to accompany our traveling trio and sing harmony with my mother. Sometimes during our performances, I even played the accordion.

We traveled for miles, often not returning until late in the evening, never refusing a request. It didn't matter if we were singing in front of small congregations or huge crowds; we threw our hearts into it. Sometimes the audience even took up a "love offering" to help pay our expenses, but payment wasn't really necessary. We sang because it was our gift and because we wanted to share our love for God and music. Even now when I hear songs by Gospel greats like Vestal Goodman, Dottie Rambo, and the Gaithers, artists that we frequently copied, my heart swells, just like it did in those days. Faith and music were so intertwined that it was hard to see the seam between the two.

For a while, I even saw myself becoming a Gospel star like my idol, Reba Rambo, but over time my taste in music slowly changed, especially after the whirlwind of adolescence ushered in bouts of rebellion and defiance. Once I discovered country music, I knew I was hooked. That's where my passion was, and that's the one that stuck. My new idol—Reba McEntire—took my dreams in a whole new direction. Barbara Mandrell and Tanya Tucker added fuel to the fire, and before long I was singing in every contest and talent show I could find, hoping someone would notice me. And how could they not, considering I copied the looks of all my favorite stars by sporting leather vests, fancy cowboy boots, and a palette of makeup? All of it struck a sour note with my parents' beliefs.

In my father's Pentecostal world, a world that had grown stricter over the years, there were rules about everything—especially for girls. I wasn't allowed to wear pants, apply makeup, have short hair, attend dances, or go to the movie theater. Christian music was acceptable; rock and roll wasn't. Drinking and smoking cigarettes? Well, that would send me straight to hell. And I do mean straight away.

Trying to adhere to all of Daddy's rules was like lighting a match to the combustion of teenage distress and rebellion rumbling inside me. To ease the anxiety I felt about trying to please my parents while also trying to please myself, my dieting efforts intensified. I also couldn't seem to resist experimenting with various enticing taboos.

One thing was certain: My worldly desires put me squarely in my father's crosshairs.

The summer before my freshman year of high school, our family moved yet again. This time it was back to Irving so my mother could attend Texas Woman's University in nearby Denton to finish her degree. Although Daddy worked long hours at a new job, we couldn't afford a fancy home, so we moved into government-subsidized housing that was close to the bus stop Momma needed to get to her classes.

Every day while she was gone, I was in charge of the younger kids, and in the evenings when Momma studied in the living room, I was the one who tried to keep everyone quiet. Although I resented my responsibilities at times, I also admired my mother's determination and stick-to-itiveness as she pursued her dream of becoming a teacher. A less resolute woman would have caved to the demands of raising five children, but not my momma. She set about to improve her life and the lives of her family and never complained about how hard she worked. Without ever saying a word, she showed me that chasing one's dreams requires the backbone of tenacity. Given the chance, I wanted to prove that I could do the same.

Although thrilled to be living near my grandparents again, I knew that moving back to the suburbs of Dallas wouldn't be an easy transition. Having lived in the country for so long, I was no longer familiar with city life, but the bigger problem was my parents' insistence that I dress ultraconservatively. As much as I loved my family and loved worshipping God, I completely rejected the Pentecostal dress code. My number-one priority became *not* being noticed for being different, and if that meant sinning, so be it.

Joey Miller, a redhead with freckles like me, appeared one afternoon outside our apartment complex like an angel summoned to duty. "You plan on wearing that to school?" he asked, lifting one eyebrow and smirking at my skirt and neatly pressed blouse.

"My dad won't let me wear pants," I sighed.

"There's *no way* you're gonna fit in at school," he chided, flopping his wrist up and down like a yo-yo as his index finger scrolled from my head to my toes.

Our friendship blossomed that summer, as Joey seized the role of fashion consultant. "Don't wear that barrette in your hair," he advised. "It makes you look like a Pekingese puppy!" Or, "Roll that waistline up a bit to make your skirt shorter." And, yes, he even encouraged me to wear a bit of makeup. After I saved some of the money my Paw Paw occasionally slipped into my hands, the two of us took off on covert shopping missions to scour every sale and bargain store in town. By the start of school, my forbidden wardrobe—pants, jewelry, and makeup—was so plentiful that I had trouble hiding it all. To make matters worse, I couldn't leave home wearing any of it. Not that it stopped me.

"Bye, Momma," I said on the first day of school, dressed in a skirt and blouse. I skipped out the door, taking the hands of my younger siblings Joey and Julie and telling them to walk faster.

"You don't want to be late," I scolded. As soon as I delivered them to their elementary school, I turned and started running. Clutching my books and swinging the bag that dangled from my fingers, I raced past mothers in their cars, scattered squirrels on the sidewalk, and squeezed my way through throngs of little kids, never stopping to say hello, never looking long enough to recognize anyone.

Once I reached the doors to the high school, I slipped into the hall bathroom. Ten minutes later, I was strutting down the hallway like a beauty queen in my forbidden pants and sleeveless top. A little blush and a touch of eye shadow made me feel even prettier. *Voilà! Now I fit in.* At the end of the day, I headed back to the bathroom to scrub my face and change into my "acceptable" attire. For an entire year, I continued the ruse without a single person questioning what I was doing. In fact, my new best friends, Lorna Bailey and Melody Mitchell, frequently complimented my outfits, which confirmed what I already knew—I was never switching back to the "old" me.

Appearance became so important to me during those years that my anorexia entered a new phase. Pretty soon, I was skipping breakfast and lunch as well as avoiding family dinners whenever possible. Once, I went three days without eating anything, just to prove that I could do it. *After all*, I told myself, *a star has to look perfect.*

My obsession with being fashionable also enticed me to consider changing my hairstyle. One morning, a pair of scissors gleaming like a shiny coin was too much to resist. *Just a snip here and there*, I told myself, hoping to give myself a more stylish, layered look. But each snip led to another. When I glanced at all the hair scattered on the bathroom floor, I gasped. *Why can't I get this right?* Ten minutes in, I knew my efforts to look better were going in the opposite direction. And, if I cut any shorter, my father would see it as sinful disobedience. There was only one person who could help me and that was Sharon, a bona fide beautician and friend of my mother's from church. She understood what was at stake.

"Oh, my," she said, sifting through my chopped layers, "I'll have to give you a neckline to fix *that*."

"Uh, sure," I replied, not really understanding what she meant.

"Take a seat," she said, pointing to an empty chair. When she finished, I looked like Dorothy Hamill, the Olympic skater. I was speechless. Not because I hated the look but because the siren in my head was blaring: *Daddy's gonna kill me!*

"What have you done?" he hollered the moment he saw me. "Sharon did this?" he fumed. "How could she?" As his tirade went on and on, I felt less and less anxious. Clearly, my father blamed Sharon, not me!

That evening, my parents left to do a visitation for the church, which often involved praying for the sick. Their absence became my opportunity. I sprinted to my bedroom, threw on a pair of skinny jeans, and wrangled into a velour V-neck pullover. As I stared at myself in the mirror, I started grinning from ear to ear. My new look was stunning! If anyone dared to stare in disapproval, I knew just what I'd say. "Close your mouth; you're going to catch flies." But my boldness didn't last. Before my parents returned, I was back in my regular clothes.

Although my relationship with the church was growing thinner by the day, there was no one I valued more dearly than Dorothy Marcantel, a big-busted, heavy-set lady with long black hair that was styled in a typical full-volume Pentecostal hairdo with teased layers and flipped-out ends. (That's right—you couldn't cut your hair, but you could tease the daylights out of it!) Dear Dorothy, played Gospel music like nobody's business, and she never looked at a piece of sheet music. She didn't need to. Rhythm and notes ran through her like currents of electricity, causing her body to rock and sway with every note. I have no doubt that it was God's grace that brought the two of us together.

Once a week, I'd walk up to her house and knock on the garage door that led to her studio. "Dianna," she'd exclaim, as if seeing me was a huge surprise. Then she'd draw her huge arms around my skinny waist and squeeze so sweetly that any troubles I'd brought with me would simply slip away. "You're just the person I need to brighten my day," she'd add, but we both knew it was really the other way around.

Whatever prayer line Dorothy had to God, it was wide open and full of guidance, because she always knew what I needed to learn and she knew how to make it fun. She was the only piano teacher I ever had that I didn't dislike.

"So what do you want to work on this week?" she always asked.

" 'The Entertainer,' " I replied on one visit, knowing I had worked so hard on the piece that I could play it from memory.

"Okay, show me," she said. I played flawlessly, hitting every note and keeping my hands in perfect position. The confusion on her face mystified me. "Uh, you should have turned the page two minutes ago," she said. "Someone memorizing again?" One afternoon, she finally sighed, "Dianna, if you're not going to read the notes, you're never going to learn them."

I figured that was the end of my piano lessons.

"It's time you learned to play by ear," she said, taking away the sheet music and promptly retrieving her hymnal. Then she began to teach me how to be a church pianist. I learned about every chord—major and minor, augmented and diminished—and I put them all to good use. Songs such as "Power in the Blood," "Victory in Jesus," and "I'll Fly Away" poured out of my fingers without me reading a single note.

Dorothy was such a gift to me, not only because she taught me a ton about music, but because she also nurtured my soul. Using love and laughter, she allowed me to see how faith can be more than a set of rules. To this day, I regret that I never made it back before she passed away to tell this beautiful woman of faith how precious she was to me during those teenage years. Thanks to her, I never completely shut the door on God, and I gained the confidence to strike out on my own.

Midway through my senior year of high school, when I was still seventeen, my aunt Jan told me about an audition at Six Flags Over Texas. "Great opportunity to sing seven days a week and earn money all summer long," she encouraged, even though my parents were sure to protest since the job involved working on Sundays. And they did.

"But you're the church pianist," Momma and Daddy argued

when I broke the news. In the end, my parents relented about the audition, mainly because they figured my chances of securing the job were slim to none since thousands of others would be auditioning as well.

To my family's surprise, I left the auditorium at Six Flags that January with the golden ticket in my hand. It was official—my singing career had started. I'd be expected to attend rehearsals immediately so that I'd be ready to sing when the park opened on weekends in the spring. By summer, I'd be singing six days a week. It was the opportunity of a lifetime and I wasn't about to walk away. And that's when the thin line running between my parents and me completely snapped apart.

"You know we can't support you on this," Daddy stated. "I depend on you to help me with Sunday services. Besides, you shouldn't be working on the Lord's Day—it's a day of rest!"

"It's my dream," I pleaded.

"If you take the job," he continued, "you can't live under our roof."

It was a strong ultimatum, and one that challenged my resolve. I'm sure they thought I'd buckle and stay, but they underestimated my passion. This was my shot at stardom, and I wasn't letting it pass. In my mind, my parents saw the job as something frivolous that I wanted, like an expensive new sweater or fancy car, but to me it was so much more. It was opportunity, training, and experience—all the things I needed to get better. The thought of refusing the job offer made my chest tighten so severely that I couldn't breathe. I figured when something hits you that hard, you really don't have a choice.

Standing face-to-face in a battle of wills, I finally declared, "I'm taking the job." My answer wasn't meant to hurt my parents. But I also didn't think about how my decision might affect my relationship with my parents in the future. And it did, for years to come. That night, though, there wasn't a shred of regret in my bones. I took my parents' silence in stride and made plans to live at my friend Melody's house until I could work out a better solution. Headstrong and resilient, I was ready to live out of the car my grandparents had bought me if I had to. Staying would surely kill the passion inside me, and I was more afraid of that than living on the streets.

A few nights later, without warning anyone, I picked up my bags and walked to the car after everyone had gone to bed. It was a cowardly move, but I couldn't bear the pain of saying good-bye to each and every person in my house. I figured it was better to just leave and patch things up later. But every step away from the front door was like wading against high tide. After my final look back, I made a silent vow: *Someday if I have a daughter and she wants to do something like I'm doing right now, I will be her biggest fan and cheerleader, regardless of my religious convictions.*

CHAPTER SIX

"After falling prey to his charm and wit, I agreed to go out with him one night after the show—and the rest is history."

Just as planned, I kept my job and moved in with Melody for a bit. Eventually, I landed at my grandparents' house and stayed until I finished high school. My parents and I didn't talk much during those first weeks of separation, but as we saw one another at family gatherings such as holidays and birthdays, we managed to start conversing about nonthreatening topics like the weather and my siblings. To show their support, my parents even came to my graduation, but we never talked about Six Flags or my future plans. Conversations about God were shunned as well. The wall between us had been breached, but it wasn't completely dismantled.

Keeping parts of my life secret from them seemed harmless at the time. *Why dredge up all the ways I had failed and disappointed them?* I reasoned. In hindsight, though, I wonder if what I read as disapproval was actually fear, especially since I had graduated before turning eighteen. Surely, Momma and Daddy had worried that I wasn't mature enough to handle the choices and obligations in front of me—something I, too, would worry about when my own kids became teenagers.

Of course, weighty issues like healing relationships weren't exactly on my mind. I was too busy enjoying my showbiz life, which was as exciting and wonderful as I had hoped it would be. It also was hard work. Every day, all summer long, I dressed up as a saloon girl and belted out old country standards while dancing across the stage with two other saloon girls and three cowboys who served as our partners. Each show was forty-five minutes long and, typically, we did five shows a day. Another crew performed the exact same show five times a day as well. Then, once a week, my crew did all ten shows to give the other group a day off and they did the same for us. But since I was designated as a "swing," I also had to learn the parts for all three girls and fill in if anyone got sick. The demands on my vocal cords were extraordinary.

My social life was equally demanding but for totally different reasons. Living in an apartment with fellow entertainers meant we all let loose when we could, indulging in many of those taboos that my parents loathed. We drank, we smoked, we stayed out late, and we dated without asking for anyone's permission. My first love, Russ, was actually someone I had met during the auditioning process, and we stayed together for several years, even after I left Six Flags. And one day while hanging out on the steps of the Southern Palace, another venue in the park, I met Lisa Morris, who worked on the lighting crew for that show. We became fast friends, which unbeknownst to me would turn into a lifelong friendship that would have important implications in the years ahead.

I loved my new life, and every aspect—from performing and making new friends to falling in love—was thrilling. Until it all came to a screeching halt. By mid-August, I completely lost my voice. Even talking was difficult. Without any formal training to teach me about protective measures, I had severely strained my vocal cords.

No longer able to earn a paycheck, I left the show and asked my parents if I could move back in with them. "Just temporarily, until I heal," I explained. After I settled into their home, which was now bigger and closer to Daddy's church, they never once said, "I told you so!" But we also didn't talk about what had transpired in the months I'd been away. We simply tried to make peace with a new beginning. I also started taking jobs wherever I could find them, which meant that for a time, I worked in a grocery store, alternating between running the register and handing out product samples. It was a far cry from the stardom I had hoped for.

I didn't sing for months. When my voice felt strong again, I started booking gigs at bars and restaurants and entered a few contests. But it was a secretarial job in downtown Fort Worth that finally allowed me to regain the independence I coveted. The timing was perfect, as my parents suddenly announced that God was calling them to do missionary work in Alaska. Although I cried as they drove away with a trailer hitched to their truck and my four siblings waving from their seats, I had no desire to join them. With the keys to my new apartment dangling from my fingers, it was time to embark on new plans for the future.

In the spring of 1982, as I continued my office job, I chose an alternate route to stardom—I auditioned to be a Dallas Cowboys Cheerleader (DCC). At the very least, I figured it would help me to develop my stage presence. In reality, it did much more than that. Making the squad turned out to be one of the most amazing experiences of my life, and I learned a lot about being a celebrity, even though no one really knew my name.

Considered the "Darlings of the NFL," we, as a squad, represented one of America's great football teams, and we worked constantly—not just getting ready for game days but also behind the scenes by visiting nursing homes and children's hospitals, as well as interacting with fans and responding to each and every letter they wrote. Thanks to Suzanne Mitchell, the first director of the squad, I quickly learned that there was more to being a celebrity than just performing. Learning how to treat fans with respect and how to be a role model in the spotlight were also important, wisdom that I'd one day pass on to my own girls.

Being a DCC required a massive time commitment. Prospective cheerleaders couldn't even try out unless they could prove that they already had full-time jobs or were enrolled as full-time students. Holding a position as a DCC was considered an extracurricular activity, not employment. Monday through Friday, I'd finish my eight-hour shift at the office, then log another four hours at practice each night. The dancing was incredibly hard for me, so sometimes if there was a break at work, I'd find an empty room and practice the routines on my own. For my efforts, I, like everyone else, got fifteen dollars a game before they took out taxes, which left a whopping $13.99.

But none of us did it for the paycheck. We did it because we loved our Cowboys. Each and every one of us had been raised on the virtues of our city's football team. We all had stories about spending countless Sunday afternoons from Labor Day to the Super Bowl in front of the TV, hopping and hollering when our team did well and watching in disbelief as our fathers threw shoes at the screen whenever the team messed up. Supporting "our Cowboys" was as ingrained in us as saying "Yes, ma'am" and "No, sir." The only downside to the experience was that it totally reinforced my ideas about needing to be skinny. I can still hear the team seamstress as I tried on my uniform for the first time. "My rule of thumb," she joked, "is that I will take this material up, but I won't let it out!" Whether she was serious or not, I'll never know, because I took her comment seriously. In my head, I heard that if my uniform got tight, I'd be in trouble. And there were rumors among the squad that suggested no one was immune from being benched if she gained too much weight. Although I had to eat to have the energy to perform, I also had to be responsible and eat as little as possible.

After the close of the 1982–83 football season, I had the opportunity to audition for Show Group, the elite group of DCCs who perform overseas for our troops. Instead, I signed on with Rick Fleetwood, a promoter out of Midland, Texas, who put me on as the front act for major country artists like George Strait, Reba McEntire, Conway Twitty, and Hank Williams, Jr. It was an exciting time filled with big moments, like the night I found myself onstage with Merle Haggard, watching him direct his entire band by merely looking at them, or the night in Amarillo, Texas, when I got to witness George Strait playing "Amarillo by Morning" just as his song first hit the charts. And I still have fond memories of standing offstage listening to Conway Twitty, microphone in hand, opening his shows with those smooth lyrics of his: "Hello, darlin' . . . Nice to see you . . . It's been a long time."

It felt like stardom was just around the corner, especially when my first album got regional airplay in the Southwest. In the small town of Clovis, New Mexico, I even had the honor of receiving the key to the city and having a day named after me—just don't ask me what day that was! When you're young and twenty-one, you don't realize all the details you'll forget or all the keys you'll misplace by the time you get to be my age. But I do remember that I was extraordinarily happy and considered myself to be the luckiest girl alive.

By 1984, the recession that had started a few years earlier was now taking aim at the music industry. Ticket sales slowed to a trickle and promoters decided that building concerts around multiple stars, rather than up-and-comers like myself, was a smarter strategy. With my career at a standstill, I gratefully accepted a gig in Ruidoso, New Mexico, at The Barn, one of the biggest country-western clubs in the Southwest. For the entire summer, I'd be the opening act. It was a step down from my touring days, but I was grateful for the steady employment. By autumn, I hoped to be back on the road. In the meantime, I'd sing like every note mattered and greet every fan with enthusiasm.

———

On a lovely June evening, just four years after I graduated from high school, Patrick Lovato walked into my life moments after I finished my first set on opening night at The Barn. As I hurried offstage, Ronnie McDowell, a well-known country singer at the time, prepared to take the stage. In the flurry of activity, I noticed two men backstage having an animated discussion. One was a gray-haired security guard, the other a fine-looking, dark-haired young man sporting a black leather blazer and gray Lucchese snakeskin boots.

The security guard suddenly turned and walked toward me. "There's a guy here who's a big Dallas Cowboys fan, and he'd like to meet you. Do you mind?" he asked, nodding his head in the direction of the younger man in the fancy boots.

"Of course not! Always in the mood to meet a fan," I exclaimed, knowing that the headliner on the marquee outside read: DIANNA HART, FORMER DALLAS COWBOYS CHEERLEADER.

"Hello," the young man said, offering me his hand, "I'm Patrick. Nice to meet you."

"Nice to meet you, too," I replied, noticing how his eyes sparkled when he smiled.

"Hope you don't mind how I bribed your security guard to meet you," he added, looking a bit bashful.

"He's not *my* security guard," I laughed, hoping we'd run into each other again.

My second set finished at about 2:00 a.m., a bewitching hour for musicians when euphoria, hunger, and tiredness all collide. I was surprised and pleased when Patrick reappeared and asked me out to breakfast. "Please," he insisted, "call me Pat like my friends do." Over coffee and eggs, we got to know each other. I learned he was a construction contractor from New Mexico who was eleven years my senior. *Maturity*, I thought, *that's a good quality*. He also told me that he was recently divorced and that he had a five-year-old daughter, Amber Devonne, whom he didn't get to see very often because he had a strained relationship with his ex-wife. *Poor guy*, I mused. *Bet he'd make a great dad*. As more and more people stopped by our table to talk to him, I also gathered he was well liked in the community. But I really couldn't believe my luck when he, a former musician himself, profusely praised my vocals. *When had I ever met someone who was handsome, mature, sweet, and interested in my career?* More important, I'd finally be in one place long enough to have a relationship.

By August, we secretly made our way to Vegas to get married.

Life was grand. I moved into Pat's condo in the mountains, drove his Cadillac whenever I wanted, and performed in local clubs at night. Being married was like wrapping myself in blankets of love. I mailed a letter to my parents in Alaska and told them about eloping with Pat, but our communication from that point forward became sporadic at best. It wasn't their fault. I figured that if I was such a big disappointment to them for pursuing country music—and now marrying someone who wasn't a churchgoer—it was probably best to let the distance between us become a natural barrier.

With my parents' eyes of disapproval so far away, every sinful temptation glittered like gold. Pat and I eagerly pursued a happy-go-lucky lifestyle, routinely partying after shows. It was a heady time of independence and experimentation. Together, we embraced the nightlife scene with all the passion and cash we could generate, often indulging in pot and cocaine. We also didn't shy away from occasionally smoking meth and trying crack. Thank God we didn't get hold of heroin, or we probably would have tried that, too.

Marrying when you're young comes with risks. Other than wanting to be a country-music star, I hadn't really thought about who I was as a person or what I even liked about myself. I certainly hadn't taken the time to sift through all the emotional baggage from my childhood. Add to that a compulsive need to please others as well as an obsessive quest to appear perfect, and I blissfully put my twenty-two-year-old self right on the path to disaster.

My parents and siblings never saw my wild behavior, though I suspect that my silence told them more than I realized. Even when we did exchange letters, which took weeks to travel such a distance, or when either of us splurged on expensive phone calls, we had little to talk about because we no longer had much in common. It would have broken their hearts to see me living such a reckless life, but I figured if I was damned for something as harmless as wearing makeup, I might as well enjoy all those other sins, too. It was that great paradox of youth—a time when you're happiest doing all the wrong things. And my naive self went about it full throttle. I loved with my whole heart, partied like I was a pro, and fueled my dream of becoming a star with enough optimism to launch a fleet of spaceships.

I don't know what saved me from becoming an addict, but I suspect that my parents, who never stopped dropping to their knees on my behalf, had something to do with it. So, too, did my dream of becoming a star, because once I noticed that drugs and alcohol affected my voice, I stayed away from them whenever I was performing. It didn't matter if there were only five people in the audience—I acted like I was onstage at the Grand Ole Opry, and I was always stone-cold sober. But the moment I stepped offstage, no rules applied. My wild side couldn't be tamed.

Looking back, I'm not proud of some of the choices I made or the chances I took, but growing up doesn't come with a handbook. Learning to navigate the boundaries of my own limits, professionally, socially, and emotionally, was a bit like walking a tightrope. Sometimes I could balance the risks and rewards, and sometimes I tumbled in free fall, hoping to survive. By God's grace, I did. But that didn't mean my path was easy.

Several years into our marriage, our blissful existence suddenly burst like a bubble. It all started one evening with a phone call. As I walked into the living room, I caught Pat in the middle of an angry conversation. His eyes darkened as his jaw tightened, causing me to freeze in fear.

"No," Pat said emphatically. "You got what you paid for." Then he hung up. Over the course of the week, the scene repeated itself with more calls, more denials. Pat refused to talk about any of it. "Customers always think they're right," he muttered before walking away. Eventually, I caught wind of the rumors circulating around town that suggested people were unsatisfied with his work. When checks started to bounce, I knew there was a real problem, but I stubbornly refused to condemn my husband. "It's no big deal," I assured him. "I'm going to be a big recording artist and support us both."

Things turned sour in a hurry. "Sorry, Dianna, but there's no money to hire you," said one club manager after another. Who could have guessed that a second recession would hit so soon? As I tried to keep doubt and anxiety at bay, my confidence crumbled like stale bread. Forget about all those times I had opened for big stars; I was still no closer to stardom then when I had started.

The horizon was muddled in darkness. Opportunity had vanished, and all that was left were the storm clouds of mounting debts. "How are we going to pay our bills?" I screamed one afternoon, throwing a fistful of papers in Pat's face. He merely looked at me and walked out of the condo, slamming the door behind him. "You're not helping matters," I shouted to an empty room.

Every argument pushed us further and further apart. To make matters worse, it was evident that Pat was spiraling into addiction. I wondered why one person could walk away from drugs and alcohol and another couldn't. Clearly, Pat was no longer just a recreational user. When I looked into his dark, brooding eyes, I trembled. *How bad would things get?* Each day was a crapshoot. Would the sweet, loving Pat show up, or would it be the quick-tempered drunk?

Mornings were Pat's good times. Often, he showered me with affection and offered to make breakfast. By afternoon, my sweet husband was gone. Literally. And once he walked out the door, I never knew where he was going. By evening, he'd stumble back home, cursing me as though his unsteadiness were my fault. "Please," I begged, "go to AA and get help." His answer was always the same—that silent stare, followed by a hasty retreat into another room, where he'd slam the door behind him.

Of course, I wasn't exactly the best wife to help Pat out of his darkness. I had my own issues, though I never acknowledged them. For starters, I didn't consider myself an alcoholic because I didn't crave alcohol, but when I did decide to have a drink, it never ended with just one. I'd get so drunk that I could barely stand up. It was a trend that had started when I was only seventeen and sneaking into bars with my girlfriends.

Back in high school, though, it wasn't just about drinking. There was a method and purpose to our misbehavior. After getting all dressed up, we girls would enter a bar, purchase drinks, and proceed to do "the walk"—a ritual that involved walking through the entire bar with our drinks in hand while surveying and flirting with all the cute boys. It never failed to attract enough young men that we never had to buy another drink all evening long. Of course, when you're only five feet tall and less than a hundred pounds, getting drunk happens pretty quickly. At the time, it seemed like a harmless way to let off steam and have a good time. Now that I was married, "the walk" wasn't much of a temptation, but escaping the turmoil of my marriage with a few drinks certainly was.

The bigger problem, though, was my nerves. At times, my hands shook and my heart raced as though I had just chugged a pot of coffee. All the anxiety I had felt in my childhood about getting punished and making mistakes was now spilling over into every little decision I had to make. *If I eat that, will I get fat? Should I wear the white boots or the red ones? Should I sing at this club or the one down the street?* Forget the big questions like *How were we going to pay our bills?* or *Where can I turn for help?* It was the trivial decisions that rendered me helpless. Entire days passed when I couldn't eat . . . couldn't think . . . couldn't move. *If I could just launch my career*, I told myself, *my problems would disappear.*

As Pat's drinking and drug use escalated, I began to wonder if I had strayed so far from God that I was now invisible. Shame kept me from asking for help, and pride dangled the promise that if I pretended everything was fine, our lives might magically get better. After all, I did believe in miracles. But instead of drifting closer to God, I slipped further away. Pat and I spent most of our days fighting, then we'd declare a truce and share a joint or two in the evening. Neither of us had a clue about how to turn our lives around. And with all the extra anxiety, I nearly stopped eating altogether.

The more our lives fell apart, the more I longed for home. Miraculously, one morning Pat strode into the living room and announced, "Pack your things; we're moving to Texas." I was ecstatic. Apparently the construction business was thriving in Irving, my hometown. We moved into a cozy apartment that felt like heaven. While Pat built houses, I landed gigs and entered every singing contest I could find. The change of scenery was good for both of us. Sobriety returned, and paychecks finally arrived with regularity.

Then, like a yo-yo unfurled, Pat suddenly couldn't hold onto a job again. His slurred words and glassy eyes said it all. The timing couldn't have been worse. "Honey," I told him, "I'm pregnant." My due date was early January 1988.

We certainly weren't trying to have a baby, but I was elated. So was Pat, and he valiantly tried to pull himself together. Every morning, he'd pepper me with sweet talk and offer to make breakfast, but by evening, another Pat appeared—the one who was cussing and scrounging for a fix. Booze, pot, cocaine—they were all on his shopping list. By the next day, he was repentant and doting on my every need. His Jekyll and Hyde moods confounded me, but my number-one concern was to protect my unborn baby. I started eating again, stopped using substances, and tried my hardest to dodge my husband's mood swings.

Sometimes I'd catch Pat staring into space, completely unaware that I was in the room. I often wondered if those episodes had anything to do with a terrible accident that had occurred during one of his construction projects, when a gas line exploded and an entire family was killed. He was cleared of all wrongdoing, but I suspected he drank to blot out the pain of those haunting memories. Had I known then what I know now, I'd have rushed him to a mental-health clinic, but post-traumatic stress disorder and bipolar disorder, two afflictions he most likely suffered from, weren't openly talked about. In fact, the term *mental illness* was reserved for those who were psychotic and needed to be placed in a mental ward because they were a threat to themselves or others. Hard as I tried, neither hope nor love seemed to cure him.

As my belly swelled, so did my courage. One afternoon while Pat was out of the house, I discovered a fifth of vodka tucked away in one of his boots and promptly poured it down the drain. When Pat returned, he exploded. His barrage of foul language and hatred made me shudder; yet I excused him like I always did. *Marriage is forever*, I reasoned. *Once our baby arrives, our lives will turn around.*

It all was a lie, but I wasn't ready to see the truth. Or talk about it. It was far more natural to pretend that everything was fine. We were two lost souls, miserable and isolated, who just kept running from one mistake to the next. And I do mean running. It turned out that Pat had a knack for scamming landlords, which meant signing a lease one day and running for our lives thirty days later when the rent was due. Our situation grew more desperate by the day. I reached a new low one afternoon while at the grocery store. "That's forty-five dollars and fifty cents," the cashier said. I smiled and handed her a check, knowing full well that our account was empty.

That same week, I pawned my wedding ring. It was a risky move, because I did it without asking Pat. And it was no ordinary ring. One evening before Pat had proposed, the two of us were simply holding hands and talking about the future. "What kind of ring have you always wanted?" he casually asked. In those days when Pat looked into my eyes, all I saw was goodness. He nodded and listened as I revealed every detail of my imaginary ring.

"It would be a gold filigree band encrusted in diamonds and rubies," I told him, "because rubies are my favorite gemstone, but the most amazing part would be the centerpiece—a large heart-shaped diamond."

He secretly gave those instructions to a jeweler and a few weeks later slipped that "perfect" ring on my finger. Afterward, we laughed, hugged, and celebrated for days. It was one of the most precious things I'd ever owned. Not only was it beautiful, it also was a reminder of those early days in our relationship, when Pat had been so kind and ambitious. Now it was gone.

The pawnshop only offered me a few hundred dollars for my ring. "If you can't pay back the loan plus interest," the shopkeeper had explained, "you lose it, and we can sell it." I wasn't sure if I should agree to the deal, but I knew I had to eat to have a healthy baby, and that required money. I could have reached out for help, but that was a foreign concept, especially considering that I wanted my life to appear perfect. Besides, how could I ask my parents for money when we were barely communicating? I took the pawn shop's offer and marched straight to the grocery store. When I told Pat about what I had done, I expected the worst, but he didn't get angry. In fact, he responded like any concerned husband, telling me, "Don't worry, we'll get it back."

Just as promised, Pat found contracting work the next month and managed to earn the three hundred dollars I needed to get my ring back. I rushed over to the pawnshop and laid my money on the counter. "Your ticket?" the man behind the counter growled. When I handed him the wrinkled receipt, he peered over his reading glasses and said, "Looks like you're a day late."

"What?" I exclaimed. "That can't be right!"

He pointed to the date at the bottom of the slip, and my heart sank. It was yesterday's date. "Can I still get it?" I asked.

"Sorry, honey," he said. "We sold it this morning. One of our employees had his eyes on it from the moment it came in. You missed it by a day."

His words haunted me for a long time. I knew that I had just lost one of the most beautiful things I'd ever owned in my life. Without that symbol of hope on my finger, the days grew bleaker.

The only bright spot was that for the first time in years I wasn't starving myself. Caring for my unborn baby was a priority. Living honestly, though, seemed completely out of reach. Running out of options, we moved into a friend's house and signed up for Medicaid and food stamps, even though Pat kept insisting that a small fortune from investments was due any day.

Why did I stay? Mostly because I wasn't a quitter. And, even if my marriage was in shambles, I wanted to pretend that everything was perfect. *Nobody likes a loser*, I told myself. Besides, I loved him, and I firmly believed that Pat would come to his senses once the baby arrived. I also prayed that my baby's impending birth, predicted to be on January 12, 1988, would heal the strained relationship between my parents and me. The very fact that they had driven all the way from Alaska to be back in Texas for the Christmas holiday and had chosen to spend their days visiting me made my spirit soar. I had no intention of spoiling their trip or ruining my expectations of reconciliation by sharing the sordid details of our finances or marital problems. Hope and optimism ruled my days.

But as my due date came and went, my mother's cheerfulness faded. "We can only stay a few days longer," she tearfully told me one afternoon. Days later, Momma and I hugged fiercely, both of us a puddle of tears as we said good-bye. "I wanted to be here for the birth of my first grandbaby," Momma sobbed before leaving. The moment touched me deeply, because I knew without a doubt that my parents loved me and that they cared what happened to me. I suspect that had I shared something about the problems Pat and I were facing in our marriage, they would have offered their help. But I didn't. It just wasn't the right time.

Late one night in early February, three weeks after my due date, pain exploded like a bomb in my belly.

"It's time to go," I shouted, shaking Pat awake.

"Go where?" he mumbled.

I grabbed my stomach as another contraction hit, a frantic moan filling the space between us. "Oh, you mean it's *time*," he cried, jumping out of bed and running toward the door.

"Slow down," I laughed. "Put some clothes on."

I called my two best friends from high school, Lorna and Melody, and told them to meet us at the hospital. Finally, we'd find out whether I was having a boy or a girl. Knowing ahead of time, I had decided, was like opening Christmas presents a week early, which left nothing to look forward to on Christmas morning. "I know it's gonna be a girl," I told everyone. "Well, it better be— what am I going to do with a boy?"

Hours later, my contractions weren't progressing. The fun and excitement were gone, and I was exhausted. My doctor's furrowed brow told me something was wrong. "Your baby's heart rate is dropping," he explained. "Think we need to do a C-section." Pat, his face flushed and full of concern, ran alongside the gurney as they wheeled me into surgery. "It's going to be okay," he said, clutching my arm. "The doctor says everything is going to be just fine."

I wasn't so sure. *God, if things go wrong, please save my baby! I'll gladly give up my life for hers.*

When I pulled myself from the haze of anesthesia, a nurse handed me a beautiful baby girl. She was chubby and charming with no wrinkles and no red marks. She was perfect in every way, from her round head to her rosy cheeks to her pudgy little legs. "There's a tiny, pink tutu dress that's going to look fabulous on you," I told her, having spied the outfit earlier in one of the ritzy shops in Highland Park. It was definitely out of my price range, but in that moment, I wanted only the best for my daughter—beautiful clothes, great opportunities, and supportive parents. The future suddenly looked more amazing than it ever had before. I had no plans to stop singing, but I also knew that if singing didn't work out, motherhood would be enough to make my life complete.

The revolving door of visitors never stopped. Grandparents, aunts, cousins, uncles, and friends paraded in and out of my room from morning to night. All the "oohs" and "aahs" made me feel like a rock star, but eventually, it just wore me out. I even got a bit testy when my aunt Jeanette questioned my name choice.

"Why'd you name your baby after a city?" she scoffed.

"I named her after a cute baby I met at the doctor's office," I explained. "Besides, the name fits." Then—perhaps it was the pain meds kicking in—I did something totally uncharacteristic. I told them, "If y'all don't like it, you can suck it!"

"Mmmm," my aunt sniffed. I never was clear whether she was rolling her eyes at Dallas's name or my directive to "suck it" because right at that moment, in walked a nurse. "Mind if we borrow your baby?" she said. "There's a siblings class on the second floor where we teach young children about their new baby brothers and sisters, and we'd like Dallas to be our model since she's the cutest!"

"Of course not, I'm honored," I said, knowing it was a confirmation of what I was already thinking: *My baby's gonna be a star!*

With Dallas out of my arms, exhaustion devoured me. Another nurse shooed everyone away and boldly wrote on a piece of paper: NO MORE VISITORS AT THIS TIME. The note stayed on my door the entire next day, which gave me plenty of time to dream about my daughter's future and how I could somehow get the money for that tutu!

When Dallas was a few months old, Pat sprang the news on me like we had won the lottery. "We're moving into a huge home in Plano," he said. Our meager possessions barely filled one room, but at twenty-six, I was eager to set down roots and rebuild our lives. Motherhood had its appeal, but my dream of stardom wasn't gone. My first priority, I decided, was to lose those extra pounds I had gained. The more I restricted my diet, the more pounds I shed. And there was no reason to feel guilty, because I was no longer breastfeeding Dallas.

Family life seemed to be off to a good start. Pat, who had left the construction business, was now home all day with us, and he wasn't sitting around brooding or drinking. Often, he tended to things that needed to be repaired or played silly games with Dallas. He also spent a good deal of time on the phone doing what he called "investment banking." I wasn't sure what that meant, but I hoped it would guarantee a steady income.

My hopes were dashed before the year was over. Tired of us not paying rent, the landlord eventually booted us out, and off we went to Grand Prairie. I was devastated. With our credit in ruins, we had to resettle in a tiny rental home that some poor soul was so desperate to lease, he skipped the usual background checks. The contrast between what we had left behind and what we now occupied was disheartening. Pat, never one to admit defeat, insisted we wouldn't be there long because "a big payout was due any day." A new normal ensued. While Pat worked on his "investments," Dallas and I spent hours watching Great American Country (GAC) on television, which featured twenty-four-hour country-music videos. I loved singing along, and on occasion, I'd pick up my baby and twirl her around to the most popular songs.

Dallas, who was approaching eighteen months, started pointing at the TV one day, saying, "Kint back, mommy! Kint back!" Over and over, she'd repeat the phrase, growing more and more adamant. I had no idea what Dallas was trying to say until Clint Black appeared on-screen, and she started grinning and waving her arms. Lord, she had a crush on him! And Pat thought it was adorable. When Pat learned that Clint was coming to the Dallas State Fairgrounds to perform that spring, he couldn't resist buying tickets to make his little girl happy.

The concert fell on one of the hottest nights on record, but we happily wiped the sweat from our faces because we had front-row seats, just inches from the edge of the stage. I didn't know how Pat had scored such great seats, but Dallas was so excited that I didn't care. As the music began, Pat hoisted Dallas up on his shoulders, where she giggled and bounced to every note. The only stitch of clothing she had on was a diaper, and the heat was causing the sticky flaps to come undone. Every few seconds, I'd stand on my tiptoes and slap the adhesive strips back into place, but they kept coming loose. All the while, Clint kept singing and waving at Dallas. Every now and then, he'd laugh at us. As the song went on, Clint's drummer eventually walked over and handed us two pieces of duct tape. Presto! Our problem was solved.

A few months later, we were evicted again. This time we didn't have anywhere to go.

I couldn't help but notice that all the moves and poverty of my childhood seemed to be replaying on a scarier, grander scale. When Patrick suggested we move to Albuquerque, New Mexico, for a few years to develop some of his family's land, I balked at the idea. "It's too far from my relatives," I pleaded. But in the end, living in a one-room house at the back of his parents' property was better than trying to survive on the streets of Texas.

"I'm happy to be here with you," I told Pat's parents, Frank and Vangie, as I jostled Dallas in my arms. Although my heart ached to be back in Texas, I knew we needed to make the best of things to keep our family together. *It's only temporary*, I reminded myself.

Of course, living with Pat's parents had its benefits, especially since their zest for life was so refreshing. Frank, one of the last surviving men from the Bataan Death March during World War II, quickly became our resident storyteller. Most evenings we'd gather around, fascinated by his tales. It was like learning about history without opening a book. Sometimes he even whipped out his harmonica, playing tunes like "You Are My Sunshine" and encouraging Dallas to sing along. It was in those quiet moments of tenderness that I began to believe our little family would survive.

CHAPTER SEVEN

"The Good Lord knows I tried to keep going on that tour—
I prayed and prayed, asking for His protection and loving hand
to keep me and the baby safe until we could get home."

Weeks after we moved to New Mexico, I learned that Pat's grand plans had once again fallen through. There would be no development of his family's land. Not that it surprised me. I'd had my doubts all along, but I never stopped hoping things would change. Pat once again searched for a job every morning, and came home empty-handed every evening. Somewhere between leaving the front door and returning, he always managed to find a bar. The only saving grace about our situation was Pat's parents. Without their assistance, we would have fallen apart.

As Pat's failures reached the breaking point, he devised one final plan to put us back on our feet. "Let me be your manager," he begged. "I'll put your career back on the path to success." I figured it was worth a try. *Lord knows we need the money.*

We made a few phone calls and discovered that the guys from Charley Pride's old band, White Buffalo, were interested in teaming up with me. "Sounds perfect," I said. Nearly everyone was from Dallas, and we had played together off and on over the years. Rick Webb, the bass player, was someone I really liked, and his friendship on tour would prove to be invaluable. The only non-Dallas member was Harold, a fiddle player from Oklahoma who shared lead vocals with me.

A few weeks before the start of spring in 1991, we hit the road on a wave of excitement, but the condition of our tour bus clearly portrayed our less-than-ideal circumstances. It was the oldest, most dilapidated, sorriest-looking, decomposing-dog-poop-white RV you've ever seen. And it was embarrassingly massive in size. Every time we chugged up a mountainside, we wondered if we'd have to hop out and give the old gal a push. One snowy evening when the RV slid off the highway around Helena, Montana, we found ourselves tipping sideways in a ditch as bears roamed around outside. I figured we'd all be dead by morning. When the AAA tow-truck driver finally showed up after daybreak, we greeted him like he was a beloved relative. With our enthusiasm rekindled, we clapped and cheered as the bus once again started chugging down the highway. I snuggled closer to Pat and whispered, "It feels so good to be back in a band."

Our tour—put together by Pat and a newly found booking agency—included cities in the United States and Canada. Some of our stops were at the nicest and biggest clubs around, and we saw amazing sights like Mount Rushmore, the snow-capped Canadian Rockies, and the neon flashes of the Northern Lights. Pointing such things out to three-year-old Dallas was exhilarating.

We even passed the time like normal families do—playing cards, telling stories, and listening to Dallas sing the same songs by day that I sang at night. I guess all those hours of listening to me practice were bound to rub off on her. Most clubs wouldn't even let Dallas enter the building, though there were two exceptions. In Texas, she was usually allowed to enter with Pat, and in Canada she was welcomed with open arms. In fact, they *loved* my little girl.

One night when we were in western Canada, my band took a fifteen-minute break between sets. It was a brisk night, so no one wanted to go outside, where snow still clung to the ground. Dallas, in a long-sleeved, one-piece denim jumpsuit and tennis shoes, was beside me listening to the DJ spinning songs. Like a mannequin come to life, she suddenly felt the beat of the music and started to dance. Everyone in the room started cheering her on. When a young, lanky cowboy sporting a big belt buckle loped by, he stopped and placed his ten-gallon black hat on Dallas's tiny head, causing the gigantic brim to obscure her eyes. But she never stopped grinning or moving. Like a pro, she flipped that hat into her hand and extended her arm to the audience. Every clink of coin that fell inside made her dance even faster. At the end of the song, she bowed to the gleeful crowd and returned the hat to its rightful owner—but not before she fished out the equivalent of about twenty-five US dollars. Of course, I promptly borrowed that money to buy groceries the following morning, though I got her plenty of candy to sweeten the deal.

From that moment forward, Dallas never shied away from performing. Over the next few months, she'd jump onstage whenever the opportunity presented itself, never needing my permission. One night, she belted out "God Bless America" with such conviction that it gave me chills, especially when she hit those big notes of "My home . . . sweet . . . home!" Completely uninhibited and confident, she'd always bow to the audience before walking offstage. Her natural instincts confirmed what my heart already knew—showbiz was in her future.

Those were the good days. We even handled the odd hiccups of life on the road without too much fuss, though none of us were prepared to have our fiddle player whisked away from us at the Canadian border for owing child support back in Oklahoma. Thankfully, he was able to go home, take care of business, and fly back without missing a show. Night after night, we played our hearts out, hoping against hope for a big break.

About six months into the tour, near the end of summer, we got what we asked for, though it was more literal in meaning. Instead of arcing to stardom, we started breaking apart. Late one night, I went out to the tour bus between sets to check on Dallas, but when I knocked on the door, no one answered. "Pat? You in there?" I cried. I tried again, but there was no answer. The silence made me panic. I ran back into the club and grabbed Rick.

"You gotta help me," I pleaded.

"I got you," he replied, motioning for me to follow him. Once we got to the bus, he fished out his key and unlocked the door. Pushing Rick aside, I raced down the aisle. "Dallas," I cried, spying her on a bed in the back of the bus, where she was playing with her toys.

"Mama!" she said, stretching out her arms toward me.

"Where's Daddy?" I asked. She stuck out her finger and pointed to another bunk. There was Pat, flat on his back and snoring with the stench of whiskey rising like mist around him.

"Patrick, wake up!" I screamed. "You're supposed to be watching Dallas."

"Huh?" he mumbled before rolling over and closing his eyes.

"Never mind," I hissed. "Now what am I supposed to do?"

Rick prodded me to pick up Dallas, and we left the bus. Then he headed straight toward a cute waitress and sweet-talked her into watching Dallas until the show was over. I put on a smile and sang like always, but I was seething inside. From that moment forward, I knew I couldn't trust Pat to be responsible for our child. But until we could figure out a plan B, he was in charge of Dallas while I went onstage. All I could do was hope that nothing terrible would happen.

Things got ugly pretty fast. No more nice clubs, no more adoring fans. And no one seemed to notice or care, except for me. We plugged along from one godforsaken town to the next, and night after night, the guys in the band partied after the closing song like we'd just been nominated for a Grammy. While everyone else downed shots of whiskey and lit up joints, I retreated to take care of Dallas. My mood quickly soured and so did Pat's. It seemed every detail of the tour that went awry became my fault. Pat cursed and shouted at me like I was the most incompetent human being to walk the face of the earth. The rest of the band, except for Rick, seemed to agree, which made arguing pointless.

By the time we pulled into a band house in South Dakota, my mood was as bleak as the landscape. My simmering discontent spilled into a heated argument after the show, which pushed Pat to storm off with two other band members. I looked at Dallas sleeping peacefully back in the bedroom, and my world snapped in two.

This is no life for my baby, and it's no life for me, either. It was all so clear: Turning my back on my dream would be tough, but staying would be toxic. I needed to go.

But I couldn't move. No matter how hard I tried, my feet, which felt like they were encased in concrete, wouldn't budge. As panic rushed in, my body started shaking. Every breath ushered in a wave of violent tremors.

"Rick," I shouted. "Help me!"

He took one look and knew something was terribly wrong. Racing through the house, he ripped a blanket off one of the beds. "Put this around you," he insisted. But I wasn't cold. "Breathe," he insisted. "Can you do that for me?" I couldn't. As my shivering continued, he whisked me into the kitchen and put me on a chair in front of the oven.

"Look at me," he said, taking my face in his hands. "Now breathe in and breathe out."

I focused on his commands until the shaking slowed. "D-d-do I ne-e-e-d to go-o to the hos-pi-tal?" I stuttered.

"No, I don't think so," he said. "But you need to listen to what I'm saying." He paused, gathering his thoughts. "Look, I want this job as much as you do, but I don't know if this is the best thing for you. The tour started off good, but now it's taking too much of a toll on you. Everyone can see it."

"I'm scared all the time," I confessed. "And Pat's drinking too much and getting meaner."

"End the tour and get him some help," he suggested.

But I didn't want to be the reason for the guys losing their jobs. They had families to support, too. And that's when I started praying in earnest. Surely God could figure out a solution. After ignoring him for years, I hoped he was listening.

My answer came in New Mexico, shortly after landing in a small desert town where we were scheduled to play in another bleak bar that was next to a seedy motel. It was beastly hot, and when I looked at our raunchy, mosquito-infested room that didn't have working air-conditioning, I knew I had to speak up. "Excuse me, sir," I said to the hotel owner, "our air-conditioning isn't working." His blank expression never changed. Just as I was about to repeat what I said, he cocked his head and fired back, "What do you want me to do about it?" When I asked if there was another room available, he walked away bellowing, "It was good enough for the last band, so it's good enough for YOU."

I spied Rick toward the back of the venue and hoped he'd have a solution. Walking to him with Dallas in my arms, I noticed a terrible smell and wondered what it was.

"Hey, Rick!" I yelled, "I—"

I never finished my sentence. The moment my shoe landed in something gooey, I started to slide forward. With one arm around Dallas, the other seesawed up and down as I lurched and wobbled trying to regain my balance. I did everything possible not to land in the sea of vomit surrounding me. Just as I started gagging from the smell, Dallas started wailing, "I'm hungry." And that was it—the moment when every broken promise, every dead end, and every frazzled hope welled up inside of me and exploded. "I'm done," I shouted. "I'm going home!"

"But we can't just take off; we have to play tonight," the guys sang in chorus.

"You can, but I'm not," I said, catching a glint of amusement in Rick's eyes.

"I'm going with *you*," Rick hollered, giving me the boost I needed.

With Rick in my court, the band followed. We hauled our belongings out of the hotel and threw everything onto the bus, including Pat, who once again was passed out from too much whiskey. "Let's get out of here," I cheered, urging Harold to get behind the wheel. One by one, heads turned as the manager started chasing the bus, but I told everyone to look away. "That guy should have given us a box fan when I asked," I snorted.

CHAPTER EIGHT

"He was kind and compassionate—until he drank.
Then he became a completely different person. That's when the anger
would come out—an anger that was violent and scary."

My journey through hell wasn't over. Once again we were back in New Mexico, living in the one-room cottage behind Pat's parents' house. Every day I prayed for help. Staying together still seemed important, though I had little understanding that the darkness consuming our lives was no match for prayer alone. Each day was like another spin of the wheel in Vegas. On Monday, we'd place our luck on getting sober and finding jobs in New Mexico, only to decide by Tuesday that our best solution would be to down a six-pack and head back to Texas. We never did hit the jackpot. The only goal we stuck to was staying married. I kept telling myself that two adults were stronger than one.

"Pat, please get some help," I begged often, but he always refused. One night he finally agreed to attend an AA meeting but insisted I come along. Since this was a new experience for both of us, we shuffled into the room trying not to look at anyone. Pat grabbed a chair closest to the exit and stared at the floor. Halfway through the session, he stood up and walked out. Curious, I followed, only to watch him head to the car and pull out a bottle of whiskey. By the time I pulled into our driveway, he was passed out.

Surely God can turn our *situation around,* I told myself. Drinking was the enemy, not my husband. That is until one evening in September.

It had been a fun day with my grandparents, who had driven ten hours to visit us, but as I stood alone in the driveway and watched them leave, weariness and homesickness blew through me like a cold wind. By the time I returned to the cottage, I was ready to pick a fight. Thankfully, Dallas had decided to join Pat's parents, who were headed to the nearby military commissary to buy food, because the moment I looked at Pat, anger poured out.

"Well," I snapped, "I hope your mom gets enough groceries for us, too, because there's no money in our account." Just for emphasis I pointed to our empty pantry shelves and slammed the doors shut.

"Well, since you walked off the job, you can't blame it all on me," Pat bit back.

"And if you didn't drink all the time, you might actually get a job," I screamed.

Then I saw it. Pat's eyes darkened and his body stiffened. Then my skin began to crawl. Before I could move, Pat picked me up and threw me. Rail thin from not eating, I launched into the air like a rocket. *My God, what's happening?* As I crashed onto the floor, my face smashed against a leg of the sofa, causing what felt like tiny fractures to ripple along my jawbone. Pain seared through my body. *God, please make him stop!* I jumped up and started to run. But as I reached for the screen door, I could feel Pat's breath on my neck. His rage shook the air.

"You're not getting away from me this time," he snarled.

I guessed he was about to body slam the heavy wooden door to keep me from leaving, so I pulled back but it wasn't in time. My left hand, which got stuck in the door, sliced open like a piece of fruit, causing my pinkie and ring fingers, just above the second knuckles, to rip away and fall to the floor.

"You cut off my fingers! You cut off my fingers!" I screamed over and over as blood spurted in every direction. My face, the floor, and even the walls were splattered in red.

"I'm so sorry, so sorry," Pat cried, stooping to pick up my fingers and running for the freezer.

A strange calm came over me as I realized that my hand didn't hurt. The pain would come later, but at that moment, I was in shock. I raised my injured hand above my heart and applied pressure to stop the bleeding. Then I walked toward the phone to call an ambulance, all the while thinking: *How can I dial without letting go of the pressure?*

"Get in the car," Pat yelled. "I'm driving you to the hospital."

At the emergency-room entrance, Pat jumped out of the car and started running like a madman, his arms flailing in every direction. He went charging toward a young nurse who was standing outside enjoying a smoke. "She got her fingers cut off! Help! Help us!" he wailed. The nurse's eyes went wide and her jaw dropped, causing the cigarette in her mouth to tumble to the ground. She looked as panicked as Pat did. And that fast, the two of them ran inside the hospital, leaving me behind. Shock must have been setting in, because I actually started laughing. "Think you forgot something," I muttered into the night air.

When Pat returned, he eased me into a wheelchair, and we raced down the hallway. "An accident," he said to every nurse we passed. "She had a terrible accident." By the time we reached the X-ray room, Pat was apologetic. "I never meant for this to happen," he pleaded, crouched by my side. "If you can forgive me, I swear on my life that I'll never let anything happen like this again."

I stared at him like he was a stranger.

My hand was throbbing so badly that I never even mentioned the pain in my jaw. I wouldn't know about the hairline fractures I had sustained until years later when a dentist, after taking X-rays, asked, "When did you break your jaw?" That evening in the hospital, everyone was focused on my fingers. As they wheeled me toward surgery, I was caught off guard when two policemen introduced themselves. Full of questions, they obviously had waited until Pat wasn't around. I listened but hesitated to speak.

"It was an accident," I finally said, forcing myself to look them in the eyes. "The wind caught the heavy door and smashed my hand." Skeptical, they asked me again. "That's how it happened," I stated. Too alone, too scared, and too confused, I refused to change my story or elaborate on the violent attack. If I didn't believe in second chances, what else was there?

In that moment—when I refused to acknowledge my husband's actions, when I excused his behavior, and when I lied for him—my life took a dangerous turn. No longer just a woman in a bad marriage, now I was also a victim—someone who had given away her voice and her power to the very man who had harmed her. Sadly, I was not alone. I'd eventually learn from agencies like the National Coalition Against Domestic Violence that every nine seconds in the US a woman is assaulted or beaten and one in three women are physically abused by an intimate partner. Sadly, the violence often happens in the very place where women should feel safe—at home. And many, like me, never report the incident.

Once the surgeon started putting my hand back together, all the chaos and turmoil of the past few years replayed in my head like a movie in slow motion. *What had I gotten myself into? Where had I gone wrong? Why couldn't I make it better?* But the one question that really haunted me was: *How could I keep this secret from my family?* There was no way I wanted to tell them that my husband had hurt me. That would be too humiliating and dangerous, as my brothers might retaliate and hurt Pat. To escape my thoughts, I stared at the drab walls around me as the doctor sewed me back together. First, he reattached my pinkie finger, a tedious process that required fusing all of the bones together. Then he moved on to my other finger, but quickly stopped. "Nothing I can do about that one," he muttered. "There's too much damage."

And just like that, as though he was removing a pile of dust, the doctor threw the remains of my finger into the trash. I didn't know what was worse—the throbbing pain from the tourniquet squeezing my arm; the disappointment that my one finger would never look normal; or the realization that a small, damaged part of me was discarded like garbage. As I stared at my hand, I wondered how significant it was that my missing piece of flesh was once the resting spot for my perfect wedding ring.

CHAPTER NINE

"Life had slapped me in the face,
and my new reality was simply trying to survive."

The next morning, Pat and I hung a pair of forest green curtains in the kitchen to replace the blood-spattered yellow ones. "A reminder of new beginnings," he declared.

But as fall descended on us, I wondered if we, too, were entering a season of slow death rather than rebirth. Life had slapped me in the face, and my new reality was simply trying to survive as a constant stream of nervousness trembled beneath my skin. I wanted to trust Pat, but I couldn't. He must have sensed my unease, because he made every effort to sprinkle kindness on Dallas and me.

Unless you've lived with an addict, there's no way to comprehend how charming and sincere Pat could be when he was sober and worrying that I might leave. He wasn't a monster. Sometimes he'd smile and pat me on the shoulder when I seemed depressed, or he'd make repairs on the house the moment I asked. He even splurged on new toys for Dallas on his way home from work. Small overtures, but I knew they were his way of showing me that he was honoring his promise to never hurt me again. Each act of tenderness was a lifeline. I held on as tightly as I could, because about two months after my night in the emergency room, I learned I was pregnant again.

It's easy to look back and wonder why I didn't leave, but another pregnancy made my life seem unmanageable. *How would I survive without a husband or an income?* In New Mexico, at least I had the support of Pat's parents. No one in my family even knew about our problems. I still worried that if I admitted my life wasn't perfect, no one would love me. The isolation I had created wasn't good for me, but I didn't know how to reach out for help. *If I unraveled the myth of our supposed happy existence, what would happen then?* Lying, manipulating, and keeping secrets seemed safer. The only positive step I took was to start eating again because I didn't want to harm my baby.

Months later, I walked into the kitchen one morning and all I could see was a mass of curly, dark hair. "Why, Ricky Mitchell," I exclaimed. "What a pleasant surprise!" I was overjoyed to see someone from Texas, especially since he was the brother of Melody Mitchell, one of my closest friends. "Your husband's business is doing so well that he asked me to lend a hand," Ricky explained. Just looking at him made me feel less homesick. Thankfully, Ricky's arrival reset something in my marriage, because for a long stretch of time, Pat's behavior improved.

Even though my husband's work was steady, we needed extra money with another baby on the way, so I sang on the weekends and took a temporary secretarial job at the largest Ford dealership in Albuquerque. It made me feel like I was taking some control over my circumstances, and it gave me lots of time to think about baby names. I was sure that I was having a boy, so I rolled a list of possibilities across my tongue. *Austin? Brooklyn? Fort Worth?* I needed a name that would sound cute with Dallas's name. Ultimately, I ditched the idea of using another city name and settled on *Dylan*. It sounded perfect.

But Dylan wasn't in any hurry to arrive. Those hot August weeks dragged on and on without any signs of labor. Two weeks past my due date, the Ford dealership firmly told me it was time to leave. "Go away and have your baby," they insisted.

I loved my job so much that I didn't want to leave, but I took their advice. The next morning, on August 20, 1992, Pat and I headed to the hospital, hoping they would induce me. Labor was so easy that I actually kept falling asleep. After a few quick pushes, the doctor held up my baby and announced, "You've got a little girl."

Whew! I thought. *At least I know what to do with girls.* But we hadn't picked out a girl's name. Pat's first question, of course, was a panicky, "What's her name?"

"Let me see what she looks like," I said, stalling for time. "I want something really special."

And special she was. As my baby rested in the arms of a nurse, I gazed into her tiny, dark eyes—all that was visible from her tightly wound blanket—and I instantly fell in love with her. She was like a bright star that suddenly had appeared from the darkness of my marriage. It made me teary with gratitude, though I still had no idea what to name her.

As the medical staff got me ready for visitors, I kept looking at the door to see who might arrive. It seemed so quiet compared to Dallas's birth that I bit my lip to stem the rush of disappointment welling inside me. "Well, slap me silly and bury my clothes," Ricky exclaimed as he walked through the door. "I hear we have a baby girl!" The nurse must have decided that his arrival was her cue to exit, because she suddenly stood up and walked toward Ricky. "Want to hold her?" she asked.

"Right now?" he quivered. Before either Pat or I could protest that we hadn't yet held her, the nurse laid my baby in Ricky's arms. "Nice to meet you," he said, his eyes welling with tears. Considering all that Pat and I had been through in the past few years and how utterly fragile and innocent my baby looked, I couldn't help but get a bit weepy, too. "Well, maybe I should let your daddy hold you now," Ricky said, and we all laughed. There was no pageantry, no parade, and no fuss that day, just the three of us with a lot of love in our hearts.

The last thing I remember before drifting off to sleep was listening to Ricky's long southern drawl. "Baaaby girl," he whispered, bending over the bassinette, "You are gonna be somebody reeeeal special in this world. I can feeeel it."

The next morning, a young nurse popped her head inside the room. "Ready for your baby?" she asked.

"Of course," I laughed, watching her slide the bassinet toward my bed. "Well, hello there," I cooed.

"You know they'll be discharging you soon," the nurse said. "Do you have a name picked out yet?"

"I'm working on it," I replied, hoping the entire staff wasn't ridiculing me for being so unprepared. Pat was still on his way to the hospital, so it was all up to me. "This might help," the nurse said, handing me a book. "You'd be surprised how many times I've pulled it out. Look it over while I give this little one a bath."

I scanned the A names, then the Bs, then the Cs. *Definitely needs a name that begins with D*, I decided. The list was long. *Daria, Delaney, DeeDee. No, no, no!* And then I saw it: DEMETRIA. *That's it! That's a name that sounds like strength! And I can call you "Demi" for short.*

It wasn't a moment too soon, as a cranky old nurse appeared. "I need a name for your baby right now, so I can fill out the birth certificate," she barked.

"Demetria," I said. "Her name is Demetria . . . um, Demetria Devonne," remembering the name of Pat's daughter from his first marriage, Amber Devonne, a sweet and beautiful girl I'd seen just a few times in the beginning of our relationship. Although neither Pat nor I still had contact with Amber, I loved the name. It was the perfect two syllables that would flow with Demetria. "You can put that on the birth certificate," I said, knowing Pat would surely approve.

"Such a strong name," the young nurse said when she came back into the room. Another nurse parked the bassinette by my bed and encouraged me to breastfeed before getting her ready for the photographer. But Demi didn't seem hungry, so instead, I dressed her in a little onesie I'd brought from home. *Thank you, Momma*, I whispered as I rolled a few locks of Demi's long, dark hair between my fingers, using a few drops of baby oil to make the cutest little curl on top of her head. It was a trick Momma had taught me with my baby sisters.

When Demi started fussing, I gently lifted her to my breast. "Shhh," I soothed. "You're about to get your picture taken."

Then I froze. The name tag said MARTINEZ. I summoned every ounce of breath I had and screamed, "WHERE'S MY BABY?" *My God*, I thought, *some other mother is probably breastfeeding my baby girl!* "Someone help me!" I screamed even louder. As time ground to a halt, I could hear myself yelling, could see nurses scrambling, but my baby was nowhere in sight.

A nurse grabbed the wailing Martinez bundle from my arms, assuring me that my own baby was fine. "Just a mix-up," she said over and over. But watching all the other nurses sprint to the nursery scared me even more. "I found her!" one nurse shouted from the end of the hallway. "She was in the Martinez bed."

"Oh, Demi, I'm so sorry," I said, taking her from the nurse. "I will never lose you again. Ever! I promise I'll always protect you."

"Let's leave them alone for now," the younger nurse said. "The pictures can wait."

As I cradled Demi's little body in my arms, I cried my eyes out. When I finally composed myself, I fed her and changed her into another outfit, as that little onesie never was returned. "Thank God we found you," I whispered in Demi's ear. Moments later, I flung open the door and announced, "We're ready for our close-ups!" But no one even looked in my direction.

"Oh, okay," I said, sarcastically waving a hand in the air. "We can wait."

The longer I sat there, the more impatient I became. "Someday," I sighed, staring into my daughter's eyes, "they'll all be begging to take your picture!"

CHAPTER TEN

"Every day I lived in fear until I finally left him."

"*I*'m moving back to Texas, with or without you," I told Pat one morning when Demi was eight months old. He looked at me like I was crazy. I didn't care. His cycle of drinking, drugs, and verbal abuse had returned, and it was endless. I still loved him and he most likely still loved me, but it was time to go before something more violent happened. I also knew that my daughters might be in danger, too. If I loved them as much as I said I did, I needed to protect them. Moving back to Texas seemed like a good first step.

There was another reason I wanted to leave, too. Ever since Demi's birth, depression had swallowed me whole, as though a dense fog had rolled in and refused to leave. I wondered if it was because I felt so lonely and far away from my family. My marriage didn't help my mood, either. From all of the fear, anxiety, and stress in my life, I only weighed about eighty-five pounds, soaking wet. Whenever I left the house, I'd look at other people on the street and wish we could trade places. It didn't matter if I saw business-women in heels or moms in sweatpants—I was sure their lives were happier than mine.

I never made the connection that Demi's birth might have some-thing to do with it. No one ever talked about postpartum depression at the time, but I struggled with it just the same. Sometimes, it got so bad that fierce bouts of sweating and shaking rendered me inca-pable of moving. At other times, scary thoughts hijacked my mind. More than once I saw myself tumbling over the edge of a cliff or falling down a stairwell. And I often had the fear that Demi would suddenly fall out of my arms and crash to the floor. I didn't want to hurt myself or anyone else, but those random thoughts had a life of their own. *Maybe if I can just return to my family and friends*, I reasoned, *these troubling thoughts will vanish*.

As I packed and loaded the Cadillac, I assumed I'd be leaving on my own. But at the last minute, Pat came trotting out of the house and threw a bag into the trunk before I pulled away. "Your grand-parents are hiring me to remodel their house," he happily explained. "Besides," he added, "you know you can't live without me. And who's going to hire you when you don't have a college degree?"

Pat's put-down pierced a few more holes in my shaky confi-dence. Ridiculing me had become his new sport, and my self-esteem plunged a little lower with every remark. As the four of us drove back to Texas, we said as little as possible. The moment I walked through the door to our tiny new apartment, I knew it would always feel more like a prison than a home.

For more than five long years, I had been putting up with Pat's verbal and physical abuse, but as long as we were together, I wanted to keep up the facade that we were happy. *How could I possibly split up our family and not feel guilty?* Besides, I felt it was important for my girls to know their father, even though I couldn't trust him to do normal fatherly things like watching them when I sang. His only responsibility when I worked was to drop the girls at my grandparents.

The turmoil between us waxed and waned like the moon. Just when I thought I couldn't live under the same roof as Pat for another day, I had an idea. "Let's see if I can get on *Charlie Daniels' Talent Roundup* on CMT," I announced. The show, hosted by the music legend and taped in Nashville during late fall in 1993, was already generating excitement, even though it wouldn't air until months later. The format consisted of daily singing competitions, Monday through Thursday. Each of the daily winners then squared off on Friday. By season's end, all the weekly winners vied for the chance to be the overall champion who'd walk away with a record deal. Pat, who had always wanted to manage me, thought the idea was brilliant. I made a few phone calls and before long, we dropped off the kids at my grandparents' house and headed toward Nashville.

It was a long drive, and as I sat and mulled the possibilities before me, I silently made a bargain with myself. *This is it*, I decided. *If I don't get the record deal, I am done. No more chasing dreams or putting up with Pat.*

Taping for an entire week of the show was actually done in one day, so in order to make it to the final competition, I had to win two times. If that didn't happen, my dream of stardom was officially over.

The first competition went well. I handily beat the other contestants by singing an original song that I had written. Friday's taping quickly followed, for which I sang another original song that someone else had written. As they started announcing names in the order that we had finished, everyone became still. One name followed another until just two of us remained on stage. But I wasn't the winner.

The drive home seemed even longer than our trip to Nashville. Neither of us said much, although Pat piped up a few times talking about future possibilities. His words were like static on the radio. I knew in my heart that my dream was dead. Surprisingly, it wasn't an awful feeling, because I had the best consolation prize—my girls! Instead of feeling, disappointed, I felt relieved. Now I could focus on being a mom. But, I also had to figure out a plan for the future that didn't include Pat.

Back at home, Pat doubled down on his criticisms of me. Sometimes his temper flared so violently that I thought he might explode. Fear trailed me like a shadow. So did guilt and shame. I wanted to make a new life for my girls and me, but I didn't know where to start. Still, I couldn't find the courage to tell anyone in my family about my situation, not even my grandparents. A Texan's honor is nothing to mess with, and I was afraid if I fessed up to the real cause of my damaged fingers, a brawl as fierce as the Alamo might ensue, especially since my Paw Paw's stash of guns would likely be involved. *No more violence*, I promised myself.

Then a strange ritual evolved. As soon as Pat left the house in the morning, I'd open the phone book and stare at the number for the Women's Shelter of Irving. For weeks, that's as far as it went. Then, one day, I dialed the numbers without even looking. "Hello," a woman answered. "Can I help you?" Too ashamed to speak, I hung up before saying a word.

Dial. Listen. Hang up. That became my pattern. As 1994 arrived, I finally mustered enough courage to stay on the line and ask a few questions. *"What would happen to my children?" "Am I doing the right thing?" "Who would protect me?"* The woman answered every question politely and encouraged me to find the strength to do what was best. "Not just for yourself," she said, "but think about what's best for your children." I hung up and started crying. Day after day, I repeated the sequence, often asking the same questions to see if the answers would change. The shelter's advice was consistent: "Don't tell anyone ahead of time; leave when Pat is out of the house; and take enough supplies to last two weeks." Then they warned me that my husband would probably go into a rage when he discovered I was gone. I started praying for a sign to know what to do.

Every day I thought about leaving. I couldn't eat. Couldn't sleep. Couldn't relax. I wondered how the tension was affecting my children, yet I couldn't find the energy to leave. Then one night Pat made it clear that I needed to go. It was early January, and I was in the kitchen with the girls painting some ceramics while Pat worked on our tax documents. My grandmother had owned a ceramics business for most of my life, so I knew how to use plaster of paris molds, as well as how to paint and glaze the fired clay. I even had a small kiln in my dining room. It was a great way to take my mind off my anxious thoughts.

"I need you to sign this paper saying we didn't earn any income last year," Pat demanded. "That's lying," I shot back. When I refused to sign the papers, Pat became as angry as a charging bull and reached for one of my plaster molds. Then he hurled it at me like it was a baseball headed for home plate. I ducked and stretched my arms out wide, trying to protect my girls, who were standing behind me, as it sailed over our heads.

No one uttered a word, but the tension in the room was electric. I quickly herded the girls into the bedroom and dropped to my knees. *Dear God, give me the courage to do what I need to do!* Time was running out. Sooner or later, Pat was bound to injure someone, and I couldn't bear the thought that it might be one or both of our kids.

I never talked about Pat's rages with my girls, so I had no idea how much the violence was affecting them. Years later, when Dallas and I were watching the movie *The Burning Bed* with Farrah Fawcett, she looked at me during one traumatic scene and said, "You know, I remember Daddy once grabbed a huge can of corn and reared back like he was going to hurl it at you. I jumped up and stood in front of you, screaming, 'No! Don't hurt her!' He stopped, but later that night Daddy got even angrier and smashed your jewelry box into pieces.

"You ran into your bedroom crying," she continued, "so I gathered all of my jewelry and gave it to you. I remember saying that you were too beautiful to be treated like that."

I had forgotten all about the incident until Dallas brought it up, making me wonder how many other things I had pushed out of my mind over the years. It broke my heart to realize that my girls had seen and heard so many things that must have terrified them, yet we never openly discussed any of it. I suppose growing up in a home where no one talked about troubling emotions or erratic behavior had subtly programmed me to be the same way. Even now when I try to talk about difficult subjects, finding the courage to do so is a bit like scaling Pikes Peak. Back in those early years of parenting, it wasn't even a thought.

As I made one excuse after another about not leaving, Demi suddenly got sick. I figured it was just a cold but worried that she couldn't breathe, so I made a doctor's appointment. Sitting in the waiting room, I was a bundle of nerves. Once I was ushered into the examination room, the doctor who had known our family for years took one look at me and said, "Give the baby to the nurse. I want to talk to you." The moment she walked out, his eyes got wide, his jaw tense. "I want to know what drugs you're doing, and I want to know now," he demanded.

"I'm n-n-ot on drugs," I stammered, realizing that my emaciated appearance made him suspicious. By then I couldn't even swallow food. I told the doctor I was planning to leave Pat and divorce him, though I didn't say when.

Living a lie was no longer possible. When I finally leveled with my grandparents about Pat's drinking and explosive temper, my Paw Paw was quick to speak. "You have to work this out for those girls," he urged, not wanting to believe that the man he loved like a son had treated me so badly. "They need their daddy," he insisted.

But my grandmother seemed to sense that I was telling the truth. "I trust you," she said, "and if you need to go to our lake house to hide, you can." Before I left, they both promised to keep my secret so Pat wouldn't find us.

A few days later on a brilliant February morning, shortly after Pat had left for work, I placed a note on the table, gathered the suitcases I had packed, and walked out the door. This time I meant it. I had no intentions of letting Pat find me, but if he did, I knew I wouldn't welcome him back.

CHAPTER ELEVEN

*"Every time I heard a sad country song, I'd cry my eyes out,
knowing I had split my family apart."*

I thought leaving Pat was enough to make my life peaceful again, but I was wrong. A couple of weeks into our stay at the lake house, the phone started ringing. And ringing. It was Pat. After calling various friends, my grandparents, and my cousins, he had finally figured out where we were hiding. "Why did you take my kids away?" he screamed at me, only to be in tears seconds later and begging, "Please come back! Please let me see my kids."

Sometimes pleasant, sometimes not, Pat's phone calls were as unpredictable as his paychecks had been. When he realized that his yelling and screaming would prompt me to hang up, he became more civil. Although he never tried to visit us while we were at the lake house, his pleas to see the girls continued. It tore me apart. I didn't want to badmouth Pat to our children or erase him from our lives, but I didn't know what boundaries to put into place, either.

"Why don't you move back into our apartment, and I'll move out?" he finally suggested. It wasn't the scenario I had imagined, but I also knew that I wasn't going to find a decent job while living in such an isolated location. The truth was that I needed to get closer to the city. In the end, I consented to his request, but I had two stipulations: One, he had to find an apartment of his own miles away from us, and two, he couldn't *ever* move back in with us.

The day I returned to our apartment, I knew the shelter had been right.

Evidence of Pat's rage was everywhere. Broken dishes. Trampled toys. Overturned furniture. I salvaged what I could and shuddered to think what would have happened had Pat found us sooner. I hoped and prayed that I hadn't made a mistake by agreeing to Pat's suggestion, but I also knew that because I had broken the silence about his abuse, there were plenty of people willing to come to my aid if I needed it. And that's when I finally decided to call my parents and admit to the shambles of my marriage.

It was a big step, and one that signaled I was finally ready to talk about my fears and failures, at least temporarily. Ever since Dallas's birth, my parents and I had slowly strengthened our bonds, and I wanted our relationship to deepen. I knew that wasn't possible unless I told the truth. Although they frowned upon separation and divorce, they never wavered about supporting me. "We never really trusted Pat," they eventually told me, "because he never asked us for our blessing on your union." In their eyes, that had told them a lot about his character.

Why did I waste so much time pushing my parents away? I suppose I had to mature enough to realize that they had made decisions for me based on what they thought was best for me, even if I hadn't agreed with them. Had I been able to see into the future, I would have seen similar storm clouds hovering above my own family in the years ahead.

Starting over as a single mom was hard. Dallas was ready to turn six and Demi was only eighteen months old, but I finally felt free. When my grandparents graciously offered to babysit, I eagerly set out to find a job. A real job. I still planned to do studio work and sing whenever I could, but my first priority was finding a job with good pay and benefits. The kids were depending on me, and I couldn't disappoint them.

My first stop was Westway Ford in Irving, Texas. It was the biggest, most well-known dealership in the area, mostly because of a catchy television commercial that starred the owner, Joe Tighe, who wore a white ten-gallon hat and green money-motif sunglasses as a catchy theme song played in the background. "Bah, bah, Westway Ford . . . West . . . Way . . . Ford!" the rousing lyrics proclaimed, which always made me smile. I had seen the commercials a thousand times and figured I'd see if they needed a receptionist. It was a shot in the dark, but since I had worked at another Ford dealership before Demi was born, I thought I had a chance. Besides, all the commercials made it look like a fun place to work, and I definitely wanted to put more fun back into my life.

I had called the dealership the day before and was told there wasn't a job available, but they suggested I stop by and fill out an application anyway. I happily put on my best Goodwill outfit and drove to the dealership while giving myself a pep talk. *You can do this, Dianna! There's a job that's meant for you.* But when I walked into the impressive showroom, I nearly retreated. I had never felt so timid or out of place.

"Can I help you?" quizzed a woman in her forties, eyeing me from head to toe.

"I'm here to apply for a receptionist job," I said, hoping to sound confident.

She pointed toward an office upstairs, refusing to smile. When I walked through that door, a more cheerful woman called me "honey" and asked the same question. "I'm looking for a receptionist job," I said again.

"What?" she exclaimed, her eyebrows jumping toward her forehead. "Well, aren't you an answer to prayer. I had to let one of my receptionists go this morning. When can you start?"

I was speechless. In my wildest dreams, I couldn't imagine that I—the ex-wife of a drunk, a failed country-music star, and the mother of two kids without a plan for the future—was the answer to anyone's prayers. The very thought made me soar with joy. Finally, we'd have insurance and food in the fridge. I actually had to restrain myself from skipping out of the office. As I bounced down the stairs, I barely noticed the handsome young man passing by me as he headed up the stairs. I'd later learn his name was Eddie De La Garza, who, instead of returning to his desk, raced into the main office to see if I had been hired. The stars above were already aligning to bring romance back into my life.

The hardest thing about going back to work was not being there for Dallas after school or for Demi, who spent her days at day care. Both were issues I had grappled with when I contemplated leaving Pat. I was especially nervous about Demi, because numerous reports were suddenly circulating about abuse at day-care centers across the country.

Mornings weren't easy. Day after day, I'd drive away from the day-care center in a pile of tears because I knew that I had always been there for both my babies . . . every second . . . every minute . . . and every time they had called my name. Now I had to trust strangers to do my job, and that reality pulled the plug on my emotions. Every morning, I'd bawl for a good fifteen minutes after I left the day-care center. Then I'd straighten my face and drive to work, all the while telling myself that I was doing the right thing. *This is how it's got to be. You're starting a new life now! Be strong!* But if a sad country song came on the radio, I'd be sobbing in seconds. The staff at Westway Ford must have looked at me most mornings and wondered why they had hired me.

A few weeks after I started working, I took a personal day and headed to the courthouse to get a divorce. If there was one thing I was adamant about, it was that Pat and I were *never* getting back together. Even his sporadic visits with the kids made me jumpy. For weeks, I'd been asking for advice from my friend Lorna, who had done the paperwork for her own divorce. "Oh, honey," she assured me, "I got this." She sent me her divorce paperwork with all the personal information covered over with Wite-Out and told me to "fill in the blanks." The judge couldn't have cared less about the sloppiness of my papers, but he adamantly refused to sign off on the measly five hundred dollars I had suggested for child support. "Way too little," he insisted. But I knew I'd be lucky if I got that much considering Pat's erratic work history. The more I pleaded that it was fine, the angrier the judge became. In frustration, he finally dismissed me with a wave of his hand. My court appearance was officially over.

I tearfully ran back to one of the secretaries. "If I don't get this done today," I wailed, "I won't have another personal day for weeks, and I'm afraid my husband's going to hunt us down and hurt me." With that news, she grabbed my papers, typed in the larger dollar amount, and marched back into the courtroom, boldly demanding the judge's signature. Thanks to that woman's help, I was finally and legally divorced. I couldn't have been happier. Life slowly righted itself, allowing our lives to regain a nice, steady rhythm. I even started going out in the evenings with my coworkers, and my girls seemed better off, too, quickly becoming social butterflies.

With my emotions on a more even keel, there was room for music to reenter my life. At first, I only attempted karaoke at the Big Apple, a local bar. A few coworkers went with me the first time, but eventually, I started drawing a following. Soon after, I joined a band called Starfire that played at weddings and corporate events to bring in a little extra money. And I continued to do studio work and sing backup whenever opportunities appeared. I knew I wasn't ever going to make the Top 100 list, but singing made me feel like I was sprouting wings and learning to fly again.

Even little details seemed to fall into place. Lisa Morris, a close friend from my Six Flags days who had worked behind the scenes operating the lights for another show at the theme park, reentered my life and volunteered to babysit when I needed help. Without her assistance, I never would have been able to keep singing. Little did I know that years down the road, she'd be the one to lend me a hand when the girls got busy with auditions and performances of their own. But the biggest surprise of all was when Pat finally started sending me child-care payments. That extra bonus made me feel like I had just won the Publishers Clearing House Sweepstakes!

Life was good. There was no yelling, no name-calling, and no violent tantrums. My self-esteem was gaining momentum, spurred on, in part, by the fact that I had quickly become "the face" of Westway Ford. My station was located right inside the main entrance, and it was my job to welcome everyone who entered, as well as to answer calls and make connections on the switchboard. Everyone seemed to appreciate how cheerful I was. I guess all that good karma opened my heart a bit, because one morning the other secretaries at work caught me staring at the cute, young guy in Finance, the same one I had seen on the stairs on my first visit.

His office was located directly across from my desk. That morning when Eddie stepped out of his office, standing with his hands on his waist and chin slightly elevated, he reminded me of a Greek god surveying his kingdom. I instantly fell in love with his broad shoulders, his perfectly groomed black hair, and his mysterious dark eyes. When he placed a pencil in his mouth and started gnawing on it, I had to suppress a giggle. It seemed everything about the man made me smile.

"Don't even think about it," my coworkers said in unison.

"Huh?" I said, finally looking away.

"He's bad news," said one woman. Another chimed in, "He'll ask a girl out, then break her heart." "Just forget about it," affirmed the older secretary who seemed wary of everyone.

Oh, well, I thought, *I'm divorced with two kids, and that's the last thing anyone wants. I'm not sure I'll ever be ready for another relationship.*

But it seemed like our paths always crossed. Eddie frequently stopped by my desk, and one day he invited me to lunch. "I'm going to the country club," he said. "Want to come along?" Another secretary also joined us, which I'd later learn was nothing more than a ploy to silence any rumors, because dating coworkers wasn't tolerated at the dealership. So excited about the possibility of going to a fancy country club, I jumped into the backseat of Eddie's car without hesitation. Halfway there, I looked down at my outfit and my heart sank. *Another Goodwill purchase!* To make matters worse, I noticed a run in my stockings that stretched from my knee halfway to my ankle. My cheery disposition suddenly failed me. *There's no way I deserve to be in his company*, I scolded myself. *I can't even afford a decent outfit.* Eddie, though, never seemed to notice. In fact, shortly after that lunch together, he even came to hear me sing.

Soon after, Eddie started pestering me about my car. "Let me help you buy a new one," he repeatedly suggested, a gesture that made my heart melt. I was flattered that he cared, but I simply couldn't bear to part with my 1982 Cadillac DeVille, otherwise known as "the ocean liner." It was the same set of wheels I had inherited after I married Pat. For nine steady years, through good times and bad, we had stayed together. Parting ways after traveling two hundred and fifty thousand miles together seemed like a betrayal.

But Eddie was persistent. "How about a brand-new, affordable Kia," he suggested. When I finally agreed, he quickly exiled the Cadillac to the back lot of the dealership, a sure sign it was destined to go to auction. It tortured me to see it there, so discarded and lonesome. My throat tightened, and my eyes sprang leaks every time I passed by. Then one morning, it suddenly was gone. My sadness didn't disappear overnight, but the more I drove my new car, the more I started to let go of the past. And the more I let go, the more I started to give myself permission to have a wonderful, new life. Slowly, my heart started to mend.

Just when I thought things couldn't get any better, Eddie made it clear one night at karaoke that my fantasies of a blossoming romance were going nowhere. "I'm not interested in settling down," he explained. "Besides, having kids is serious." It broke my heart that he wasn't ready to welcome my family into his life, but I figured if we stayed friends, he might change his mind someday.

The girls at work saw his remarks as the perfect opportunity to keep my options open. "You have plans on Sunday morning?" they asked, flashing the biggest smiles I'd ever seen. "Why?" I wanted to know. Turned out rumors were flying that Troy Aikman, star quarterback for the Dallas Cowboys, was attending Fellowship Church, which at the time was a newly formed group of believers meeting in an old movie theater in Irving. We all agreed that attending church would do us good, though our motives were clearly tied to Troy's single status!

It would have been cool just to lay eyes on Troy, but it never happened. What did happen was my daughters fell in love with Fellowship Church and kept asking, "Can we please go back?" Although we didn't go steadily, I took the girls when I could and even attended events like their annual Easter egg hunt. Eventually, the growing church moved its services into MacArthur High School. Each visit drew us in a little more until we suddenly started calling it "our church."

About the same time, I finally secured another apartment—one that wasn't tied to the turmoil of the past and one that I could pay for on my own, even though it wasn't in the best part of town. Nevertheless, I was happy to have our own place. Hoping to work my way up the Ford food chain, I figured we could eventually move somewhere else. Then, right before Christmas, after two years of steady employment and promotions, I got laid off.

My self-esteem plummeted and so did my resources. If losing my paycheck wasn't enough, Pat suddenly stopped sending child support, too. Christmas wasn't going to be so merry after all. All the expectations I had for my life seemed to be in tatters. I started wondering if I wasn't worthy of success . . . wasn't meant to be happy . . . didn't deserve a second chance. But I also knew I couldn't sit and marinate in self-pity, so I went straight to Kelly Services, a placement agency for temporary jobs. In a matter of days, I went from the aftermarket department at the car dealership to the switchboard at J.C. Penney. It wasn't exactly fulfilling work, especially because I would only be there for a few weeks. And my temporary status seemed to make me invisible to all the other employees. Loneliness crushed my spirit.

One afternoon as I watched everyone head to a holiday party

that I clearly wasn't invited to, I felt so ostracized that I went to the parking lot and sobbed. There—in my car, surrounded by crumpled tissues—I had an epiphany: I was depressed! For the first time in my life, I not only recognized the feelings of bleakness and isolation running through me, but I named those feelings. And I understood where the feelings were coming from. Yes, I was suffering. Yes, I felt like I had lost out on something in life. But I also felt empowered by my own awareness. For once, I hadn't pushed my feelings away or tried to ignore them. A short time later, a few friends offered to help me pay the rent and supplied some hand-me-down gifts for the kids, which helped my bleak feelings to trail away like smoke in the wind. What I failed to see was that barely eating had become an unconscious habit.

There was one bright spot about my job at J.C. Penney. It was the time of year when the store put their spring catalogue together, and as I manned the switchboard, mothers kept asking me for directions to the photo-shoot area. Day after day, I'd linger at the door watching all those kids parade around in their cute little outfits. It unleashed a bubble of envy inside me that grew stronger by the day. I couldn't help but wonder if my own adorable children could do the same thing. Cute clothes. Bright lights. The glamour of being in a magazine. *What could be more wonderful or exciting than that?* And I knew just the person to help me.

I called my cousin Pam, whose own children were in the modeling business at the time. "Finding representation is important," she said. So, I dished out the money for a photo shoot, put packets together with my kids' pictures and all the important stats—height, weight, and age—written on the back, and mailed everything to the top modeling agencies in Dallas. *Surely someone would love my daughters enough to offer us a contract!*

But no one ever did, at least not then. Although my first attempt to get my girls into the modeling business hadn't worked out the way I had planned, it wasn't enough to stop me—or my young girls—from dreaming about the future. "There will be other opportunities," I told them. And I firmly believed it.

After Christmas, Kelly Services sent me to work for Texas Commerce Bank in Richardson, and they also suggested I take classes to upgrade my computer skills so I could secure a better-paying job. I took the job and their advice, which resulted in a better-paying position—administrative assistant to the head of training, at the downtown office.

My confidence returned and so did Eddie. He finally seemed to be warming to the idea of getting closer to my girls. Sometimes I'd spend the weekend at his house, and sometimes after he finished his shift at work, he'd swing by my apartment.

"Dianna," he asked one night, "don't you think your neighborhood is a bit sketchy?" I laughed and brushed away his concerns, knowing full well that I had witnessed a robbery once from my own balcony. "It's all we got," I told him, "and we're making the best of it." His concern for me, as well as for my girls, proved his heart was opening a bit further. One night, he even tiptoed into the girls' bedroom while they were sleeping and drew a cartoonlike dog's face on their blackboard and signed his name. The gesture touched me deeply.

That August, Eddie called me from Sturgis, South Dakota, where he was spending the week with a few buddies at the Harley motorcycle rally. "Throw a few things together, and I'll fly you out tomorrow morning so you can join me," he pleaded. "Eddie," I protested, "I have kids to think about and a job I love. I can't just leave on the spur of the moment." The loneliness in his voice startled me. "What's going on?" I asked.

"Every guy here has his girlfriend along except me," he pouted, "and when I wasn't looking, someone put a teddy bear on the back of my bike . . . and that made me think of you." *Well*, I thought, *the infallible player has finally met his match!* Then he surprised me again by suggesting I move in with him when he returned. "Just get some stuff and stay at the house for a while and see how it goes," he said. "I can even decorate the spare bedrooms to make them more . . . well, more girlie." I told him I'd think about it.

And for a few weeks, that's all I did. In the meantime, Pat called around mid-August, wanting to stop by so he could take Demi shopping for a birthday present. Her fourth birthday was just days away. "She'd love that," I said, suggesting he stop by later that day. They left and quickly returned. Pat walked Demi to the doorstep, then hastily retreated to his car. "I got to go," he shouted over his shoulder. As he drove away, Demi burst into tears. Apparently Pat had asked enough questions to figure out that I was dating someone else, and he wasn't happy about it. In the months ahead, I'd learn just how angry he really was.

Shocked and frustrated, I called Eddie in tears. "Bring the kids over to my house right now," he insisted. "I'll throw Demi a party!" And he did. By the time we showed up, Eddie was standing there with a silly grin on his face, a bouquet of Barbie dolls in his arms, and a party hat on his head. Lisa was there, too, holding a cake. It was one of the sweetest gestures anyone had ever done for us, and I knew right then that we had turned a big corner in our relationship. After all, how many bachelors drop what they're doing to run to Toys"R"Us and shop for Barbies?

After that, I started spending more and more time over at Eddie's, but I still refused to give up my apartment. "My goldfish lives there!" I exclaimed, as though a bite-size piece of orange sushi stood in my way. "I'll move in when it dies." We were a bit like Lucy and Ricky Ricardo in those days. I'd stay with Eddie for a bit, only to run back to my apartment every time we had a fight. Then I'd sit by the phone waiting for him to call and apologize so I could run back over. Our relationship was so different from my previous one that I had trouble sorting through all my emotions. And wouldn't you know it, that little goldfish was like the Energizer Bunny—it kept going and going! By late October, I finally turned off the electricity, picked up my goldfish, and moved in for good.

And that's when our family compass started pointing in a whole new direction.

The Colleyville Years

OCTOBER 1996 TO JULY 2008

"Love will find a way, anywhere we go . . ."

—"LOVE WILL FIND A WAY" BY TOM SNOW AND JACK FELDMAN

CHAPTER TWELVE

"Eddie was my knight in shining armor. I had been a
single mom with two kids living in the ghetto, and he
came along and took us all in, giving us a new life."

*M*oving in with Eddie was like winning the lottery. I had never felt so lucky. If my life were a movie, it's the scene where I'd cue the angels to sing in the background. Really, it was that magical. But if you've never struggled to pay your bills or tried to break free from negative patterns, you probably can't appreciate how powerful an influx of love and financial stability can be. It was like entering my own fairy tale. I wanted to bottle up all that positive energy and keep it with me for the rest of my life.

It's no surprise that Colleyville became my "safe place." For starters, we were no longer confined to a two-bedroom apartment. Instead, we roamed about Eddie's four-bedroom house like it was our castle. Though "playground" might be a better word. Within days, the one-time bachelor's pool table became a tent for the girls to hide under and the double staircase in the middle of the house was transformed into a giant slide, perfect for anyone brave enough to ride the bumps in a sleeping bag. Kool-Aid and chocolate-milk stains started sprouting on the white carpet, while crayon marks dotted the walls. Eddie accepted every change with grace and humor. Well, almost. He wasn't exactly calm when he learned about a hole I had made in one of the solid wood beams running across the formal dining room ceiling because I wanted to hang a piñata for someone's birthday! But not even that could interfere with the strong bonds that held us together. When I reminded him of a question that I had posed years before about why a bachelor like him would live in such a large house, he grinned and said, "I built it for the day when I'd have a family just like this one."

Not exactly wealthy, the girls and I felt rich in so many ways. We waved good-bye to our secondhand clothes and bought preppy new outfits. We went to the beauty parlor for decent haircuts and splurged on trips to the movies. On Christmas morning, the girls got their first bikes to ride through our safe, new neighborhood. It was as if that "perfect life" I had always dreamed of had suddenly materialized. I didn't have plans to quit my job, but I was grateful, just the same, that Eddie so willingly wanted to take care of us.

I certainly didn't marry Eddie for his money, though. What was most attractive to me was his brain. I loved that he was smart. Being handsome, as well as sensitive and ambitious, was an added bonus. One of my greatest joys was, and still is, having intelligent con-versations together. It reassured me that no matter what came along in our lives, he could figure it out because he was that smart. Little did I know that we'd have so much to figure out as the girls got older. Of course, I also thought that our safe and perfect life in Colleyville would last forever.

One of the first hiccups we encountered happened shortly after we moved in. Wanting to "give Dallas her own space," Eddie cleaned out the spare bedroom and brought in a set of white wicker furniture. But Dallas refused to sleep there, telling us the room was haunted. Although Eddie and I had suspected as much, we never shared our suspicions with the kids. As stranger and stranger things started to happen, we couldn't deny it any longer.

One morning, the kids and I searched high and low for a specific pair of Eddie's socks, turning every one of his drawers inside out, only to find those very socks an hour later, neatly folded and lying on his bed. Another time I was awakened at 2:00 a.m. by something licking my hand. Startled, I awoke to see Trump, our black cocker spaniel, gnawing at my fingers, which wouldn't have been so strange, except he was an outside dog. Every evening I'd check on him before bed and lock the door behind me. Then there was the morning I awoke to find my downstairs bathroom sparkling clean after I had told myself the night before that the mess could wait until morning—and I was the only one in the house all night! But it was the voice wafting from the closet between Dallas's and Demi's rooms that set all our nerves on edge.

One afternoon, Demi finally identified our mysterious houseguest. I was in the kitchen sorting through some newly purchased picture frames when Demi passed by. Inside each frame, there was a typical generic photo, but one in particular caught Demi's eye. "Oh, that's Emily," she said, staring at the black-and-white photo of a young pioneer-looking girl wearing a long dress, button-up boots, and a hat. "I see her upstairs in Dallas's room sometimes," she added.

Her words made the hair on my arms stand on end. It certainly was all a bit freaky, especially after we learned that our house sat on a piece of land that was once part of the Trail of Tears, but we gradually got used to Emily's presence. After all, it's hard to get upset with a ghost who pitches in to do chores! In time, we even enjoyed sharing our ghost stories with visitors, but no one ever did volunteer to spend the night in that bedroom with the cute, white wicker furniture. Not Dallas, not Demi, and not even Madison when she came along.

Perhaps it was the ghost who poked our spiritual curiosity, because shortly after accepting Emily's presence among us, the girls started begging to go to Fellowship Church again. Since the church had expanded and moved closer to us, I agreed to take them. Pastor Ed Young was so popular that he often spoke at four different services to accommodate the crowds who wanted to hear him. It was easy to understand why. "We had so much fun," the girls shouted after every trip. I had to admit, I loved the place as well.

Although I had never stopped believing in God through the years, going to church hadn't been a priority. Even after discovering Fellowship Church, I couldn't seem to go consistently. Mostly, it was because I felt I couldn't live up to God's standards. If all those fiery sermons in my youth had taught me anything at all, it was that one sin or one bad thought would send me straight to hell. And who needs to be reminded of that? But my perspective slowly started to change. With all the love I felt at home and at church, I started to think about rededicating my life to a spiritual path. Before making a commitment, though, I decided to take membership classes to find out more about the church's beliefs.

One Sunday morning, listening to their teachings, I heard the most amazing words: "You don't have to be perfect to please God." *What? I don't have to be perfect?* My mind reeled. As I listened some more, I began to realize that I wasn't a failure in God's eyes, because everyone sins. Everybody does wrong. It's part of being human. And that's when I decided it was time to invite Jesus back into my heart. So I prayed the Sinner's Prayer, just like I had years ago, but with a new understanding of what it meant, knowing this time I wasn't backing out of the deal. It was time to deepen my relationship with God.

Funny thing was, it also deepened my relationship with my girls. Riding in the car one afternoon, Dallas, Demi, and I decided it was time for the three of us to get baptized together. A few weeks later, standing single file and squinting in the bright sunlight, we waited for our turn to be immersed in the pool behind Fellowship Church. A few relatives—Eddie; his sister, Debi; and her daughter, Bryanna; as well as my sister-in-law, Kerissa; and our cousins, Aris and Braeden—watched from the crowd around us. As we neared the water, the girls started giggling with excitement. I smiled and reached to squeeze their hands. Then—*whoosh*—it happened. The Holy Spirit's presence was upon me. In a rush of God's glory, I felt like an army of angels suddenly wrapped their arms around me.

That day would mark the start of a spiritual awakening in each of us that would continue to deepen over the years in surprising ways. But on that day, I was simply happy to be part of a vibrant faith community. It felt good to be going to church again.

Life was changing in other ways, too. As Christmas season approached, the girls and I were sailing down the highway when we heard about a contest sponsored by a local radio station. "Give us your best imitation of Elmo's laugh," the radio announcer urged, "and the winner gets a Tickle Me Elmo doll!" Considering not a single store could keep the toy in stock, we decided to give it a try. We drove to the designated parking lot at a local mall where a large tent had been erected and the station's bus was parked. As a small crowd of shoppers gathered to watch, Demi stepped up to the microphone and gave it her best shot, throwing off a deep, hearty laugh. A few onlookers nodded in approval, but it was Dallas who nailed it. When it was her turn, she stood in front of the crowd, composed and confident. Before starting, she took a deep breath and paused to look at everyone. When Dallas opened her mouth, a trail of high-pitched syllables flowed out that trembled and vibrated like a silly monkey trying to attract attention. It went on and on, earning the coveted prize. "We have a winner!" the radio host shouted as people applauded. The thrill of it all triggered something inside of us.

Later, as the girls were watching Nickelodeon, the station announced an interesting challenge: Create a character and present it at an open audition. The temptation was too much. Both girls went to work, writing sketches and practicing. Although nothing came of the audition, neither wanted to stop trying. They had caught the audition bug.

When an open audition for *Barney & Friends* was advertised that summer in the *Dallas Morning News*, Dallas insisted we go. "Remember how much fun we had a few years ago at the *Little Rascals* audition?" she squealed. And I did. Dallas had thought she'd make the perfect Darla. Of course, so did I. And she nearly got the part; at least that's how we saw it. She earned a callback on that first try, and the young boy standing next to us—one with hair so thickly gelled that it stood straight up in the air—actually landed the role of Alfalfa. "It's a sign," I said. "Good things are on the horizon." That flurry of hope was once again stirring, telling me that my baby was going to be a star.

The one prerequisite for the *Barney* audition was a mandatory age of six, because reading was required. Dallas was nine, so that wasn't a problem, but Demi was only five. Because she was going to have to spend the day with us anyway, I figured Demi should try out, too. "It'll be good experience," I told her. "And if someone asks, just tell them you're six." Besides, the initial audition wouldn't involve scripts.

The hours before an audition were always the same—rising early, ironing outfits, fixing hair, and adding the right accessories for that "cute factor." In our case, that usually meant brightly colored bows in the girls' hair. Our number-one priority was always to arrive early so we wouldn't have to wilt in the Texas sun, but the line at KD Studio that morning was already long when we got there. Even so, it was thrilling to stand with thousands of others hoping for a chance to be discovered. It would be a Cinderella story if it happened, and we were eager to give it a try.

Once the girls were handed numbers, the butterflies set in. Fear, nervousness, and excitement rattled around inside us, making us as giddy as kids on Christmas morning. As the line slowly inched forward, we dreamed out loud about landing a part, which got Dallas so excited that she couldn't stand still. *Please God*, I prayed, *if she's ready, let her get the part.* When someone finally called their names, my girls went running. Always the cheerleader, I shouted after them, "You can do it! I know you can!"

Dallas later told me that she refused to be separated from her sister. "We played charades a lot," she said, "like, pretend your dog is on a leash and it just got loose or act like your best friend just invited you to a sleepover." It was a way to spot the kids with big personalities and lots of self-confidence. Then, one by one, each girl entered a room and sang "Twinkle, Twinkle, Little Star." By the time my girls came back outside, they were exhausted, but they still managed to talk nonstop the whole way home. Oh, how I hoped that we'd hear something positive.

About a week later, the phone rang. Dallas's eyes grew wide and her hands started to shake. But it was Demi they were interested in.

"Oh, my," I said. "What do we do now?"

Dallas, who had started to worry that she was too old to appear on *Barney* without getting teased by her classmates, looked relieved. She also knew the next phase would involve a script. "Let me work with Demi," she begged. "I'll get her ready."

Looking back, I can see it was the first glimmer of Dallas's true passion, which is coaching. Dallas worked with Demi for days, creating a series of emoji-like characters that helped Demi remember her lines. When we returned for the second audition at Las Colinas Studios between Dallas and Fort Worth, we were starstruck to see the giant sneaker on the lot that had been used for the 1992 comedy *Honey, I Blew Up the Kid*.

Things started off well as Demi rattled off her part like a pro, but when new lines were tossed into the mix, the judges quickly caught on and dismissed her. The ride home was rather quiet, except for one comment that made my heart soar. "I want to keep doing this," Demi stated rather boldly, which prompted Dallas to chime in, "Me, too!"

I was happy to oblige.

"Dianna? You there? Pick up the damn phone," Pat ranted on the message machine. His explosive tirades never ended without a string of obscenities. "Bitch . . . whore . . . slut . . ." The list was endless, and the longer it went on, the uglier it got. Pat's contact with me came in spurts. Sometimes he'd call every few days, sometimes every few months. The downward spiral of his attitude seemed to stem from my decision to move in with Eddie. *Would the madness ever end?* I wondered. The uncertainty of when and where he'd let loose rattled my nerves.

Shortly after celebrating our first Christmas together, Eddie and I went out one evening after asking Jenna, who was like an older sister to our girls, to come over and babysit. Halfway through our meal, she called. "I answered the phone, and it was Pat," she rambled. "He screamed at us and said he's coming over to get his kids. I don't know what to do!"

"Not while we're not there," I exclaimed, telling her to take the girls to an upstairs bedroom. "Pretend like you're not there—lock every door, every window, and turn off the lights."

By the time we got home, Jenna was trembling. "We were upstairs, and Dallas was able to peek through a window and see him," she said. "He was pounding on the door and yelling all kinds of garbage, like 'I know you're in there' and 'I have a right to see you.' Then he got really mad and yanked the Christmas wreath off the front door and threw it in the yard."

Apparently, Pat stormed back and forth across our property, cussing and screaming, until he finally got back in his Trans Am and peeled out of the driveway, leaving tire marks on the concrete driveway that are still visible today. It was behavior that would continue off and on for years. It was clear that although I had left Pat and had an official divorce, he wasn't out of my life. And that meant I wasn't out of danger and neither were my kids. Over time, our contact with each other became less frequent because it was the only way I could protect my family from his volatile behavior.

It wouldn't be until June 22, 2013, when my tumultuous relationship with Pat finally ended. That's when Pat's brother, Francisco, called to let me know that my ex-husband had passed away from a heart attack in Albuquerque, New Mexico. The girls took it especially hard, mostly because they had missed out on making a lot of happy memories with him. For me, the news was mostly relief. Finally, I wouldn't have to worry about his bizarre behavior. At the same time, I also felt sad. I knew Pat's life could have meant so much more had he gotten professional help for his issues. To this day, regardless of all our ups and downs, I am forever grateful to him for giving me my amazing daughters Dallas and Demi.

CHAPTER THIRTEEN

"I didn't push them to be what I never became. It wasn't like that at all.
They wanted to do it. This was now their dream."

I tried my best to be the perfect mother. Rising a full two hours before my kids, I still washed and styled my hair and applied makeup each morning like I was stepping on stage. Looking good and being skinny were essential to my self-esteem. Although I felt happy and secure in my new life, I was still tormented by the need to look and be perfect. God might love me as I was, but other people surely wouldn't.

While Eddie worked nearly sixty hours a week, I juggled a full-time job, singing gigs on the weekends, and all the extras, such as cooking, cleaning, volunteering at church, and raising my girls to be the most well-behaved children on the planet. You could say I was one of those Stepford Wives—minus the cooking part. I couldn't—and still can't—cook a decent meal to save my life, but I made sure the kids got fed each night, though my go-to meal was generally boiled frozen vegetables tossed in butter with grilled-cheese sandwiches.

I also supervised my girls while they finished their homework and patrolled what they watched on television like I was Mother Teresa. I wanted to be that perfect mom. Most nights I drifted off to sleep in an exhausted haze of satisfaction, pleased that I was keeping everything under control. But the veneer on my ideal world started peeling away one afternoon in the fall of 1997, after a call from the school. "Demi had a little accident today in her kindergarten class and needs a change of clothes," the nurse explained.

"What?" I cried in alarm. "She's never wet her pants before!"

I left work and rushed home to find Demi another outfit. When the nurse called again the following afternoon, I really panicked. *What's wrong with my baby?*

Anxious and worried, I took Demi to the doctor, but the pediatrician assured me she was fine. Nevertheless, the phone calls continued. Afraid I'd lose my job for leaving so often, I started packing extra clothes in Demi's school bag, all the while convinced that something was terribly wrong. Almost two weeks after the calls started, Dallas finally set the record straight.

"Remember that Saturday when we all were watching a movie and you were cleaning?" she asked. I nodded, remembering that I kept looking up at the television in between dusting and vacuuming. There were clowns, balloons, and a pin-the-tail-on-the-donkey scene, as I recalled. *Looks okay*, I had reasoned. "Well," Dallas stuttered, "that was a Stephen King movie called *It*, and I think it frightened Demi."

"Whaaat?" I exclaimed. "I'd never let you watch something like that!"

"But you did," she insisted. Then she told me about the scene where a clown is hidden in the sewer pipes and surprises someone by pulling him down the drain. When I asked Demi about the movie, she admitted that she was fine using the bathroom at our house, but every time she got near the school restroom, she imagined a clown ready to drag her into the pipes and trap her underground. "So I wouldn't go in," she said. But holding her bladder all day was impossible.

We then had a long talk about what was real and what wasn't, which finally calmed her fears, but I felt awful for weeks knowing that I had stood in the same room with my girls and had failed to protect them. Vowing never to let my kids down again, I silently berated myself for being such a terrible parent. What I failed to see was that my unreal expectations were more damaging than my mistakes.

Ever since my girls were born, they'd watched me perform in bands, so I shouldn't have been surprised when Demi decided to sing at the school talent show. But her song choice seemed unusually ambitious for a five-year-old.

"Next, we have Demi Lovato singing Celine Dion's 'My Heart Will Go On,'" announced Coach Allen, the popular physical-education instructor serving as emcee. "Good luck," he murmured, motioning for Demi to step up to the microphone that rose several inches above her head. No one attempted to adjust it for her.

The cafeteria was full of kids and parents, some of whom were seated on the floor because all the chairs were taken. As the music began, my heart skipped a beat, especially when I caught two mothers looking at each other with raised eyebrows as if to say, "Really? A five-year-old singing that song?" I could only hope that Demi, adorable in her pigtails and pink ribbons, was oblivious to all of it.

I couldn't believe how nervous I was for my daughter. Not because I wanted her to hit every note perfectly but because I wanted her to feel good about the experience. As though my presence could help her, I mouthed the words right along with her. "Every night in my dreams, I see you, I feel you . . ." But something was wrong. Although Demi's mouth was moving, there was no sound. *Oh, dear! Louder, sweetheart, you need to sing louder!* But my mental cues were no help. One little boy in the front row definitely wasn't impressed. "Your microphone's not on!" he whined loudly. One giant tear after another rolled down Demi's cheeks, which broke my heart, but Demi never stopped singing. As I debated whether to whisk her to safety, I suddenly saw Demi's posture change. Defiantly, she pulled her shoulders back and looked right at that little boy, pouting her lips and tossing her head, as if to say, "In your face—I'll show you!"

And she did. It wasn't an amazing performance, but before the song ended, someone at least turned up the volume on the microphone so we could hear her. Hardly anyone her age had even entered the talent contest, and surely someone with less courage would have run off the stage in humiliation. But my daughter stood her ground, and I couldn't have been more proud of her.

By Christmas, a more confident Demi started emerging.

Every December, Fellowship Church put on a children's Christmas musical that drew huge crowds. It was a professional endeavor, complete with lights, set changes, ornate costumes, and original music. With my former cheerleading experience, I figured I could lend a hand with some of the choreography, especially since I finally had taken Eddie's advice and quit my job to be a full-time mother. Although Dallas was busy with cheerleading at the time, Demi decided she wanted to be a part of the musical, too. After her audition, she was given the role of Scribe Three, which involved a chorus number with other scribes. It was a small part. Or so we thought.

During one rehearsal, the scribes practiced their scene, over and over. They alternated between looking at the scrolls in their hands and breaking into song about the messages the scrolls carried as a lofty-looking pharaoh stood nearby. Brecca Preston, the director of the show and someone I had always admired because she had done numerous TV commercials, wasn't pleased with the pace of the scene. "It's not working," she sighed. "It's too slow." Everyone went still as Brecca mulled over possible solutions.

"Demi," she finally said, "I want you to sing this entire verse alone." Although Demi was one of the youngest members, she was also the loudest—a fact that hadn't gone unnoticed. By the time Demi finished belting out her lines, Brecca was smiling and clapping like a cheerleader. "Yes!" Brecca cried. "This scene is no longer about all of the scribes. Now, it's about one particular scribe." And that's how Demi earned her first solo in the spotlight.

On opening night, Demi, tiny as she was, marched onto that huge stage like she was seven feet tall. Her bobbed hair bounced with every step, and when she looked into the eyes of the audience—several thousand of them—there wasn't a trace of fear on her face. Wearing a mauve, crushed-velvet tunic that my grandma had made, she marched left, turned right, and dramatically waved her arms at all the right times, never missing a beat as she sang her heart out. I was so nervous for her that I couldn't breathe, but the moment she hit those really high notes of her solo, I knew she had nailed it. The audience knew it, too, and burst into applause. Her little, itty-bitty part had suddenly become a focal point of the show.

After the final curtain call of the weekend, Kelly Fuller, a teacher from school, stopped by to congratulate Demi. "That's it," she exclaimed, throwing her hands in the air. "You're going to be a star someday." My own mind was looping in the same direction. My aunt Jan, standing next to Brecca, nodded in agreement. "You know," she said, her eyes lighting with excitement, "Demi is so talented, and Dallas looks like a young Natalie Wood—have you ever considered entering the girls in Cinderella pageants?" Brecca got so excited about Aunt Jan's idea that she chimed in, "Now why didn't I think of that?"

My heart leaped as well because as a child I had longed to do beauty pageants, but we simply couldn't afford them. *Could we now?* I wondered as my girls twirled in joy over the idea. Poor Eddie, though, didn't know what to make of our excitement. All the details about entry fees, costumes, and weekend trips made his eyes glaze over. In the end, though, he knew that entering Cinderella pageants would make us happy, so he gave us his blessing. "But please," he cautioned, "don't spend too much money!" As the girls and I hugged and cheered, Eddie grinned at our enthusiasm, but he had no idea that our lives were about to veer in a direction that was so far removed from his male-dominated car kingdom that it would make his head spin.

CHAPTER FOURTEEN

"Lord, if you don't think we need to win
this year, then that's okay with me."

I thought Cinderella pageants would be the bridge my girls needed to break into show business—you know, impress the right judge who'd have the influence to get them a movie or television contract. But over the years, I began to realize that the pageant world was its own entity with no overlap into the entertainment world. It was hardly wasted time, though, especially considering everything we learned about showmanship and how we bonded as a family during those years.

My cousins Pam and Gina helped us prepare because they had competed when they were young. Their mother, my aunt Jan, helped as well, which seemed only fitting because throughout my childhood, I had enviously watched her drive all over Texas so my cousins could compete in pageants, audition for commercials, and work modeling jobs. Now that she was excited to work with my girls, it felt like life had come full circle.

"Cinderella isn't just about looking good and wearing fancy outfits," Pam said, pacing back and forth like an NFL coach on game day. "Qualities like poise, confidence, character, and humility are just as important."

Demi and Dallas both nodded their heads.

"You'll have to learn to stand in front of a panel of judges with clipboards in their hands as they ask random questions and listen to your answers," Gina piped in, "and you'll have to learn to walk like a model."

"Cool," Dallas grinned.

"There's a talent portion, too," Pam added.

"Thank God," I interjected, knowing my girls were never going to be six-foot-tall models and talent would give them a leg up against the competition.

The first preliminary pageant wasn't until the fall, but Pam insisted we start preparing right away. There were outfits to buy, techniques to learn, and regulations—like finding ankle socks with the perfect width of lace—to understand. Talent, which could be anything from dancing to singing to lyrical ballet routines, had to be showcased in less than three minutes or contestants were disqualified. It would take months to sort it all out. What I didn't expect was how much fun we'd have in the process.

"Let's start by learning to master the Cinderella modeling technique," Pam said one afternoon. From then on, all of us would meet in someone's living room after school, and we'd mark four giant *X*s with masking tape along an imaginary *T*-shaped runway. Each *X* represented the spot where contestants needed to demonstrate a modeling stance known as "pretty feet," which is best described as placing the right ankle in front of the left as the left foot points toward ten o'clock and the right points toward noon. We all toppled over like drunken flamingoes on our first attempts, but eventually, we got the hang of it.

To improve timing, I even ordered music that had the appropriate *ding*s and *buzz*es to signal when each girl should start and finish. I figured it was the best way to train my girls to get their bodies and brains comfortable with the system. Although it was a lot of work, they loved every minute of it. "Look what I can do!" Dallas, then eleven, boasted after she mastered her "pretty feet." Demi, not yet seven, immediately insisted on another turn, refusing to be outdone by her sister.

Pam, always trying to keep the mood festive, often ended our work sessions by delighting my girls with a few back handsprings from her Junior Olympic gymnastic days. Aunt Jan supplied a different kind of joy by turning our shopping trips into scavenger hunts. "Let's go," she'd cheer as we jumped into the car and raced to all the thrift stores around Dallas, searching for the perfect competition-worthy dresses, shoes, socks, and matching hair barrettes.

"Would you look at this," Aunt Jan exclaimed one day as she held up a frilly white dress. "It's perfect for Demi." But all I saw was the bright red stain on the front. "Oh, don't you worry about that," Aunt Jan scoffed. "Just needs a little OxiClean." And it did. That four-dollar dress from The Salvation Army turned out to be Demi's most-winning Partywear dress, and not even Eddie could complain about the price.

"So what do you girls want to do for talent?" Pam finally asked.

"That's easy," Demi piped up. "I want to sing."

"Of course, you do." Pam smiled. "I saw you at your Christmas play—but Dallas, what do you want to do?"

Dallas paused for a beat, then chimed in, "I can sing, too."

The room grew eerily quiet. Pam cocked her head before speaking, "Really?" she said. "Can you sing something now?"

"Sure," Dallas answered. "I'll do 'Somewhere Over the Rainbow.'"

I was stunned. Dallas had stopped singing when she was five years old, during a very volatile time with Pat. Ever since, I had wondered if fear or bad memories had prompted her to go silent.

"Some . . . where . . . over the rain . . . bow," she started, sounding a bit shaky. When I glanced at Pam, she was as rigid as a statue. "There's a land that I've heard of," she continued, gaining momentum. The more she sang, the stronger she got. *That's it, Dallas!* I silently cheered. *Just let it come from your heart.* As she gave her song a big Broadway finish, we all jumped to our feet, cheering and clapping. Not because it was perfect, but because she had found the courage to do it.

"Where have you been hiding that voice?" Pam exclaimed, causing Dallas to get a bit bashful. "Whew," Pam added, "thought I was going to have to choreograph a cheerleading routine or something."

Well, what do you know? I mused. *I have two really good singers in the family!*

By the time September rolled around, we were more than ready for the one-day preliminary competition held in Garland, Texas. With less than twenty girls competing, I figured that both my girls had a good shot at winning. And there were lots of opportunities to win something. Cinderella awarded titles for everything from Beauty to Personality to Talent, but every girl hoped to be the Overall Winner, who was then expected to compete in the five-day state pageant held in June.

Before the competition, Dallas was so nervous that she wouldn't even let me in the room while she practiced. I even caught her writing the lyrics to her song on her hand, only to watch those words melt in the heat onstage. Yet, she managed to sing just as beautifully as her younger sister did. Watching them both gave me such a rush of pride and emotion that tears filled my eyes. Proud as I was, though, I didn't expect them to win top honors on their first try. But they did! Demi was crowned Cinderella Miniature Miss and Dallas walked away with the Cinderella Miss title. The very next week, we started planning for the five-day state competition in June.

I didn't leave empty-handed, either. Although college scholarships, cash prizes, and trophies were the coveted prizes, Cinderella organizers also encouraged parents and contestants to network and develop friendships. The term *Cinderella family* was taken very seriously. Not exactly a church mouse, I jumped into the fray with both feet and became fast friends with Kris Smalling, whose daughter, Ashton, competed and won the Cinderella Tot division that same day.

A tall blonde, exuding beauty and calmness, Kris was a walking encyclopedia about pageants because she had competed years ago with my cousin Pam. She also had a bit of experience with show business, as her son, Ayden, was already working in the entertainment industry and her daughter was busy auditioning. I was impressed to learn that both children were signed with Kim Dawson Agency, the largest and best talent agency in Dallas. With all that experience behind her, I peppered Kris with questions faster than a sneeze through a screen door!

"What kinds of songs do the judges like best?" *"How much makeup is too much?"* *"What's your advice about doing interviews?"* My questions were endless. After all, it was a competition, and I wanted my girls to have a good shot at winning. Kris always tried to calm my craziness with her devil-may-care attitude. "We just come here for the fun and camaraderie," she always said. "I simply throw things together last-minute and get in the car and go." When I looked at her skeptically, she said, "Really, Dianna. I don't let it ruin my life."

But hard as I tried, I still got a bit neurotic about everything, even losing sleep over silly details such as how to pack our suitcases without getting anything wrinkled. Kris's attitude was certainly healthier, but I was wired completely differently. Being competitive was in my blood, which is why I listened to Kris's suggestion that we seek out Ms. Gayle Burkett at the state pageant. "She's legendary for helping contestants with hair and makeup," she said.

Ms. Gayle wasn't hard to find. Of all the rooms in the hotel, hers was the noisiest and most crowded, filled with girls of all ages waiting for her services.

"You wanna be one of *my* girls?" she boomed as we stood wide-eyed in her doorway.

"Yes, ma'am, we'd like that very much," I said, staring at the sight in front of me. Ms. Gayle was large in every way—in stature as well as personality—and she worked assembly-line style on each and every girl, wielding a can of hairspray in one hand and flourishing a cigarette in the other.

"Now that's perfection," she barked after shellacking one girl's meticulously coiffed hair until it was as stiff as a plank of wood. "Honey," she added, "don't wash your hair all week, 'cause it holds better that way."

Apparently, Ms. Gayle's legacy was hair that didn't move . . . all day . . . all week . . . all month, if needed!

Ms. Gayle was indeed one of a kind. Although we quickly realized that we didn't need her help to win, the pageants just wouldn't have been the same without her. You see, behind that big, loud voice was an even bigger heart—and a wicked sense of humor. "Let us pray," she began every session. If anyone looked confused, as my girls did on that first visit, she'd give them a few extra cues. "Kneel down, child," she'd laugh. "That's it, facing me." Only then did she start applying makeup.

Ms. Gayle's operation ran like a well-oiled machine, starting at 5:00 a.m. and going right to competition time. Sometimes she'd cut it so close that we moms were as nervous as long-tailed cats in a room full of rockers! Yet we always managed to make it to the stage in time. Besides making our girls pretty, Ms. Gayle loved to share her infinite wisdom regarding all things. Sometimes it was a bit of gossip, but mostly, it was advice. "Eyelashes should be applied by gluing them *underneath* the lash line," she explained one day. "That's what makes them pop!" If someone had plucked her eyebrows too thin, she'd explain how to do it differently, and if one of the girls was dating someone she didn't like, she'd talk about that, too. Above all, we loved the way she conveyed to each and every girl that she was special inside and out. "You're absolutely gorgeous," she often gushed. And if someone needed a little extra convincing, she'd wrap her arms around her and say it again. Ms. Gayle did more for everyone's self-esteem than winning ever did.

That first Cinderella state pageant was like a merry-go-round that kept spinning faster and faster. Thankfully, Aunt Jan came along to help, or I might have keeled over at some point. Each of the five days grew more intense, and by Friday, we all were a bundle of nerves. Although I wanted my girls to win, putting the outcome in God's hands only seemed right. "Lord," I prayed, "if you don't think we need to win this year, then that's okay with me." But that didn't mean I wasn't nervous for my kids.

When Dallas started vomiting that final morning, I knew we were off to a rocky start. "Oh, honey," I said, wrapping my arms around her. "You need to lie down and rest. You don't have to compete if you're not up for it."

At that point in my life, I was just a regular mom. If my kids were sick, then rest was needed. I wasn't worried about losing our money or not competing. Over the years, my attitude would change when contracts and paychecks were at stake, but things were different during those pageant years. To my surprise, Dallas rallied and insisted she wanted to compete.

An hour later, Aunt Jan and I were throwing costumes on the girls and wishing them luck. By evening, I was the one feeling so nervous for my girls that I thought I'd be ill. Surrounded by my new Cinderella family, I sat in the audience, holding hands with those around me, just like the girls did onstage as everyone waited for the winners to be announced. When the list of semifinalist names for Miniature Miss were announced, I nearly leaped out of my seat when I heard Demi's name. When she made top five, my heart rate tripled. As we waited for the final announcement of the Overall Winner, I stared at my youngest daughter in her gorgeous white dress—the very one from the Salvation Army—and I went rigid.

Oh, dear! Please don't let the judges see! Her feet were anchored to the floor. Her makeup glowed. Her smile never wavered. But her tiny right hand kept reaching toward her hair. First, it was a few scratches on the back of her neck, then it was a swipe across the side of her head. Before long, she was digging at her scalp.

Oh, God! No! No! No! It was more than bad timing. I knew then that all those rumors about a head lice breakout were absolutely true. And that's when my insides started quivering louder than the drumroll.

"The winner is . . . Demi Lovato!" I clapped and cheered like everyone else, but my mind was at war. *What do I do? Should I run to the drugstore? Should I act like I didn't notice?* Since there was no such thing as a quick exit, as there were after-parties and meetings that would keep us busy until 3:00 a.m., I tried to enjoy the moment and pretend everything was fine. But my hands never stopped shaking.

A few minutes later, Dallas won her division, too. The roller coaster of Dallas being sick, Demi getting lice, and both girls winning was a wild ride for all of us. Our family always tried to turn bad situations around into something positive, so for years afterward whenever one of the girls felt sick before an audition, we'd laugh and say, "You know that's good luck." Though I have to admit that I never found anything redeemable about getting head lice.

"Because they won, they have to compete in the international pageant or give up their crowns," I told Eddie at home. When I explained that the event was scheduled for early August, he frowned. "What should we do?" he asked.

First, there was the issue of money. Pageants aren't cheap. The entry fee for both girls, just for the state competition, had set us back $1,300—and that didn't include the extras like social events or Ms. Gayle's services. The next pageant would be more costly, especially since it was in Las Vegas.

But there was another problem that was even more perplexing. Eddie had proposed to me back in December and I was knee-deep in planning a summer wedding. I had chosen a cake, a dress, and invitations. *How was I supposed to fit in a trip to Vegas, too?* "This is too much work," I finally sighed. "How about we just get married in Vegas after the pageant?" When Eddie agreed, I made one stipulation: "It has to look and feel like a real wedding. No justice-of-the-peace affair."

We decided the groomsmen needed to wear tuxes and the bridesmaids would wear black cocktail dresses. Our guest list included family and friends from Texas as well as our pageant friends. For the first part of the week, we could focus on the pageant. Then, since many of our guests were arriving early, they could stop by the final ceremonies on Friday evening and watch the girls. On Saturday, we'd get married at the chapel in the Flamingo hotel. After that, we'd all depart in limos and head to our reception. It was the perfect plan, especially since I thought my girls were going to win it all like they had at the state pageant.

From June to August, we put the finishing touches on the girls' competition clothes and continued to work on their talent and modeling skills. Day after day, Demi practiced singing, "You're Never Fully Dressed Without a Smile," complete with choreography, and Dallas belted out her perfected version of "Somewhere Over the Rainbow." In between giving them pointers, I'd try on my wedding dress and imagine what it would feel like to look at Eddie, my knight in shining armor, and say, "I do." By competition time, I was running on pure adrenaline.

Friday evening, when the winners were announced, it was evident that my girls were nowhere near the level of many of the other contestants. Neither girl even finished in the top ten, but we were having so much fun together that losing didn't seem important.

Early Saturday morning, all the bridesmaids gathered in my room, and we had an impromptu bachelorette party with a bit of champagne. Thanks to Ms. Gayle, who stayed an extra day after the pageant to do my hair and makeup, I looked like an ethereal movie star when I left the room later that evening in my mermaid-style dress and thirty-foot train.

The wedding was everything I had hoped it would be, especially the reception, which was a full blown-out party with toasts, laughter, and encore appearances from my girls, who sang the same songs they had sung the night before at the pageant. Afterward, Eddie and I went back to the Bellagio hotel and walked through the casino. As we strolled about, people clapped and cheered for us. I felt like Cinderella at the ball.

That night, before I fell asleep, images from my wedding, the pageants, and the countless days of practicing and planning whirled through my mind. It was the happiest, most wonderful collage of togetherness I ever could have imagined. And I knew that meeting Eddie had made it all possible. It was like all the bad patches of my past had been reassembled to form a beautiful new quilt, and in that merging of old and new, the future looked amazing.

CHAPTER FIFTEEN

"Fame is weird. It appears to be one thing in your head until
you achieve it. You think it's what you want, but if you really knew
what it entailed, would you work so hard to achieve it?"

"Your due date is January 12, 2002," my doctor stated in early spring. That would make our next child almost nine and a half years younger than Demi and nearly fourteen years younger than Dallas. Life as I knew it was about to change in drastic ways. Had I had been able to look into a crystal ball that spring, I would have seen the pace and direction of our lives swinging wildly in new directions, and not just because another baby was on the way.

The girls, as reigning Cinderella winners, continued to make appearances at pageants, and both planned to compete again at internationals. It looked to be an exciting year on the pageant circuit. When July rolled around, I happened to notice an announcement about another open casting call for *Barney & Friends* that was scheduled for the end of the month. Demi, now that she was nearly nine, wanted to audition again.

Just like the last time, we got up early so I could curl every lock of Demi's hair, and for good measure, I clipped on a big ole pageant bow to add a little dazzle. And once again, the audition line was wrapped around the building when we arrived. In all, more than 1,400 boys and girls showed up that day, all hoping for a shot at stardom.

"Uh-oh," I sighed as I got out of the car. The sudden blast of heat made my stomach churn. As we waited in line, the sun grew even more intense. Within minutes, Demi's perfectly styled hair began to droop, and my five months of pregnancy got the best of me. If I didn't find shade quickly, I was going to get sick.

"Excuse me," I said to the mother standing next to us. "I'm not feeling well and was wondering if I could leave my daughter with you so I can go to the car for a bit?"

It was an unusual request, but I was desperate. We had been chatting for a while, and the woman seemed nice. Her daughter, who was Demi's age, had even offered her jacket to Demi so she could sit on it. "Of course," the mother replied. "Take your time."

Over the next few hours, I kept appearing and disappearing as I walked back and forth to my car, where I'd sit for a few minutes in the air-conditioning to soothe my nausea. When both girls finally got called into the audition, I watched as they bounded into the studio. *Please, God*, I prayed, *let Demi do her best so she can be proud of herself.* It only seemed right to put the outcome in God's hands, much like I did with pageants.

Lord, you know our hearts. If we're not ready for this or if it's not good for us, then don't let us get it. To me, it was always about *His* timing, not ours. Oh, I always wanted success NOW! But I also knew if we weren't ready, it could hurt us, and I didn't want that. My family was—and always will be—the most important entity in my life, which is why I continued to utter that same prayer even as the stakes got higher and higher.

When I thanked the woman one last time for helping me out, I didn't expect to see her or her daughter again. But I was certainly wrong about that, as the girl was Selena Gomez and the woman was her mother, Mandy Teefey. I'm sure our meeting that day was destiny, because in the coming years, our paths would cross over and over again.

Typically after an audition, the girls and I soared in anticipation about getting a callback. So much so that for days we didn't dare leave the house, as cell phones were still expensive to use and we relied on our landline. It was all part of what we called "riding the roller coaster"—those rushes of fear, hope, and adrenaline that appeared during and after any audition. No matter how many times the girls walked away from an audition empty-handed, we always believed the next attempt would produce our golden tickets. Each thrilling sequence of ups and downs was just part and parcel of chasing our dreams. But that July, my mind was on the upcoming Cinderella pageant in Las Vegas. When the phone rang, I figured it was Aunt Jan.

"Good news, Mrs. De La Garza," the woman beamed. "We'd like for Demi to attend a special Barney Boot Camp for a few days in early August," the woman said.

"No, I don't think so," I blurted back. "We have plans to go to Vegas in a few days, and we've already paid our entry fees, reserved a hotel, and . . . well, we're really looking forward to going as a family."

The woman cleared her throat. "Okay," she said, "I don't think you understand. We'd reeeeally like to see Demi there."

But I still wasn't persuaded.

"Not everyone from that first audition is being asked to return," she continued. "We'll put everyone through a few days of singing, dancing, and acting, and then we're choosing our new cast." She paused, then added, "I *strongly suggest* you bring your daughter."

"I'll tell you what," I countered. "I'll talk to Demi and let her decide. If she wants to go, we'll make arrangements for her to get there." But the voice in my head wasn't supportive. *We've been down this road before, and nothing ever comes of it.*

Later that night, I called my friend Lisa and asked her to join me as I presented the options to Demi.

"This is your choice," I said to Demi as we all enjoyed some ice cream. "Dad, Dallas, and I are leaving for Vegas in a few days, but you have to decide if you want to go with us or stay behind to go to Barney Boot Camp." I reminded her that there would be another pageant the following summer, but *Barney* auditions only happened every few years. I also told her that Selena would be there but on different days. "It's up to you, whatever you want," I concluded, adding that Lisa and Melody would pitch in to care for her if she didn't want to go with us.

It only took her a few seconds of deliberation. "I'll stay and go to Barney Boot Camp," she said, before finishing her dish of Marble Slab ice cream.

When we left for Vegas, I hoped she wouldn't regret her decision. Then I forgot about her audition because I was so busy with Dallas, who won a few titles that pageant, including International Cameo Girl, a prestigious award for facial beauty. Once the pageant finished, Dallas went home with Kris Smalling, who took her back to Texas to join Demi, while Eddie and I stayed behind to celebrate our first anniversary. Monday morning, Eddie and I were lounging in our room at the Bellagio when my cell phone rang. The number wasn't one I recognized, but I answered anyway.

"Dianna," the man began, "this is Hit Entertainment. We have exciting news—we've chosen Demi to be part of the new *Barney* cast."

"Whaaat?" I screeched into the phone. "Are you serious?" I mouthed the message to Eddie and tried to focus on what the man was saying as I danced around the room. It hardly seemed real because until then, Demi hadn't even booked a commercial.

When I hung up, I shared all the details I could remember. Demi would play the role of Angela and filming would begin in mid-January, right around my due date. Each statement left me grinning more and more wildly. "Guess I need to call Demi," I said, still feeling like I was in a dream.

I called Melody because I knew the girls would be at her house. "I need to speak to Demi," I said calmly. "And I want you to watch her reaction."

"You're telling me she got the part!" Melody gushed. I reminded her to stay calm because I wanted it to be a surprise, though Demi would later tell me that she immediately knew something was going on. Apparently when Melody and her husband walked into the bedroom, they both knelt down and stared at Demi so intensely that she was almost afraid to take the phone from them.

"You're not going to believe this," I said, "but you made the *Barney* show!" Although my excitement had nearly propelled me into doing cartwheels down the hall, Demi sounded nonchalant. "Oh, okay," she said, using her soft, little-kid voice. Even after I told her how proud I was of her, she only had two words for me: "Okay, Mom," which made it seem like getting the role was no big deal.

Her reaction puzzled me until I witnessed a similar reaction a few years later when Madison got the call about making *Desperate Housewives*. In retrospect, I wonder if kids are too young to really process the magnitude of being selected for a role on national television? Of course, Demi's subdued response didn't really matter because I had enough excitement running through my veins for the both of us. *Yes, indeed*, I mused. *Now my baby is gonna be a star!*

A few weeks later, I sent Demi off to fourth grade as Dallas headed to junior high. "Enjoy a normal school day while you can," I told Demi that morning, knowing that by January she'd have to withdraw from public school because of her filming schedule. By evening, we were all gathered around the television watching the events of September 11 and wondering if we'd ever feel normal again.

As the world tried to regain some stability, so did we. Thanks to a tip from my friend Kris Smalling, we were back on the audition circuit by late October. This time it was a well-advertised cattle call for Radio Disney DJs. "They both have great voices," Kris encouraged. "You should let them try." So I did, and this time Dallas, not Demi, got a callback.

While we were at the second audition, I ran into another pageant friend and happened to remark that I was looking for someone to work with my girls so they could improve their skills. "You should try Cathryn Sullivan," she said. "She's one of the top acting coaches in the area." By the next afternoon, I had already penciled in *acting lessons* onto our November calendar. Nothing ever came from the callback, but by being in the right place and asking the right question, we gained a valuable teacher and mentor.

After just two sessions, Cathryn came to me and asked, "These girls are half Latino, correct?" Yes, I nodded. "I need to make a phone call," she abruptly announced. Within seconds, she was on the phone with Jennifer Patredis at Kim Dawson Agency. "I have these two beautiful, sweet, amazing girls here that are half Latino," she raved. "You need to look at them and send the older one to the audition we talked about."

And just like that, we finally had an invitation to the best modeling and talent agency in Texas. When Kris Smalling heard about our appointment, she, too, called the agency and told them to hire my girls. "Their mom is really great, too," she stated, which I'd later learn was an important referral because the agency never wanted to work with pushy stage moms or "know-it-all" parents. I decided right then and there that I would become the easiest, most congenial, and most responsible mother anyone had ever worked with. I had no idea that my lofty goals would slowly unravel my sanity.

The last thirty days of 2001 were a flurry of activity. We walked into the appointment with Jennifer Patredis at Kim Dawson Agency on December 10 with high expectations, and we weren't disappointed. Dee Ann Vernon, head of the print division at the time, took one look at my extended belly and laughed, "I'll take that one, too!"

Wow, I thought, *not even out of the womb and she already has a contract.*

Within two weeks of that meeting, Dallas booked her first commercial. Actually, she booked two commercials, but because they were filming on the same day, she had to choose the one she wanted more. Talk about beginner's luck! Ten more offers followed. Demi wasn't as quick out of the gate, but she, too, eventually landed her share of commercials and print ads. Kim Dawson was all about involving the whole family, so if Dallas auditioned for something and Demi could fit the part, too, then they'd both audition for the same role. Everything went to Dallas for a while, but it was still valuable experience for Demi.

As Christmas approached, Demi started fretting about possibly missing out on the birth of her new baby sister because of *Barney*. "Sorry, honey, but you can't be excused from work for something like that," I told her, not wanting to make any trouble with the director. "It's a job, and you need to take it seriously."

But truthfully, I was disappointed, too. Filming was slated for a weekly rotating schedule that started with one day a week, then two days a week, and ended with five days a week before starting all over. I kept my fingers crossed that I'd go into labor during one of those off weeks when Demi wasn't at the studio every day. One thing was certain—life was rushing at us, and I needed to start thinking about managing the demands of three children, not just two.

A few days after Christmas and two weeks shy of my due date, I went to a doctor's appointment and discovered my blood pressure was rising. "Time to induce you," my doctor concluded. Relieved that I wouldn't have to worry about juggling Demi's work schedule and my delivery any longer, I called Eddie and told him to meet me at the hospital. "We're having a baby today," I exclaimed.

Although we were hoping for a natural delivery, things didn't work out that way. "Something's wrong," I shouted at one point, hours after labor had started. When the doctor discovered that my baby was trying to come out sideways, he shooed everyone out of the room, which actually was a bit of a relief, as there was quite a party going on in there. For this delivery I wasn't just surrounded by Eddie's family; he also had invited my grandmother, people from work, and even the mother of his best friend from high school to come over. Once everyone was gone, the nurses began prepping me for a C-section.

Still reeling from the panic and pandemonium of being whisked into the operating room, I was more than grateful to hear the doctor say, "It's a girl, and she looks perfect." It was December 28,

2001, and we couldn't have asked for a better post-Christmas surprise. After Eddie and the girls left, I held my new daughter in the pleasant stillness and looked her over from head to toes.

"Madison De La Garza," I declared, "you are going to take after your father and become a scholar!"

CHAPTER SIXTEEN

*"After Madison was born, I quit eating to lose weight. I was
dealing with postpartum depression, my need to look and
be perfect, and the schedule of two teens working in the
industry. Lots of things started caving in on me."*

"*L*et's go!" I hollered to Demi, who was still upstairs. "You
can't be late . . . not today or EVER!"

It was January 12, 2002, the day filming started for
Barney & Friends. From then on, our lives began whirling at a
frantic pace. Every morning I was up before dawn because Dallas
needed to be at school by 6:00 a.m. for cheerleading practice. But
I couldn't just throw on a pair of sweats and jump in the car. No,
my self-esteem was so tied to my appearance that I couldn't imagine leaving the house for any reason without first showering,
styling my hair, and applying makeup, a process that took almost
two hours. After I dropped Dallas off, Demi, Madison, and I
would head to the studio in Allen, Texas, which was about an hour
away. Once I handed Demi off to her wrangler, the person who'd
supervise her on set, I'd head back home. By afternoon, I was

driving back to the studio to pick Demi up. It was a grueling routine, especially because Madison was colicky and often had me up until two in the morning.

Two weeks into filming, I was returning from Demi's morning studio drop when I approached a red light about a block away from home. As I put my foot on the brake, my world went dark. When I finally opened my eyes, I discovered that I was drifting through the intersection. I shuddered to think what might have happened had it been rush hour. *How could I have fallen asleep so quickly? What if my baby had been hurt?*

"I can't go on like this," I pleaded to Eddie that night. When he suggested I hire someone to help out since he worked long hours every week, I reached out to my friend Lisa, who was between jobs at the time. Agreeing to cover the night shift—arriving around 8:00 p.m. and leaving by 3:00 a.m.—she quickly became an integral part of our lives. Even months later when Lisa found another job, she still pitched in and helped when she could. Without her, I never would have survived.

Barney, which filmed from January 2002 until July 2003, wasn't the only thing that kept us busy. In addition to supervising Demi's homeschooling and taking care of Madison, I also was shuttling Dallas and Demi to Cathryn Sullivan's acting classes several times a week. On top of that, there were auditions and modeling jobs. All of it seemed exciting, especially the paychecks the girls were earning with regularity. But the costs of chasing our dreams—both the obvious and the subtle ones—were piling up, too.

While doing *Barney*, Demi also landed some voice-over opportunities and starred in a few "industrials" that promoted several local businesses. Because she could sing as well as act, AmeriCredit Corporation even chose her in 2002, as she was turning ten, to host and perform at the company's ten-year-anniversary celebration in Walt Disney World. Because I didn't want to travel with Madison, I hired a chaperone to accompany Demi so she wouldn't have to pass on the opportunity. It was all part of the juggling act that was now my life.

Demi, a little chubby at the time, was also modeling plus-size clothes for J.C. Penney. (Yes, that long-ago dream had finally come true!) I was the proudest mom in Colleyville every time I walked through our local mall and saw posters of my little star hanging from the rafters. She looked so adorable!

But Demi's weight was one of those subtle warning signs that I didn't pay attention to. I simply thought she was going through a stage that would evolve into taller and thinner as she got older. But her eating issues had already begun. Spurred on in part by the unsettledness of being pulled from public school for *Barney* and the sting of no longer being the baby of the family, Demi turned to food, mostly sweets, to ease her anxiety. One day a plateful of cookies might disappear, the next it might be several doughnuts. I never suspected anything. After all, what kid doesn't like sugar? I hadn't yet learned that when mothers have eating issues, their daughters often have issues, too. It was a red flag of distress, but I missed it because I was mired in my own disease. I was also happy to focus on more positive things like helping my kids with their careers.

Dallas kept me busy, too. Right out of the gate, she took off like a racehorse because she had such a commercial look. Voice-overs, commercials, and industrials all came her way. In many ways, it seemed like she was the one destined to become a star. One of her early hires was for Arlington Recycling, where she costarred with our friend Brent Anderson, who had made appearances in *Walker, Texas Ranger* and who'd go on to star in the 2015 TV series *American Crime*. She also did so many commercials for Mattel's Hit Clips, one of the first media players on the market, that she became an "unofficial" spokesperson for the company.

Even Madison, at four months old, jumped into the fray by booking her first modeling job and appearing in a flyer for Dillard's department store. Needless to say, we weren't exactly a conventional family, but by then we weren't interested in being normal. My girls wanted to be successful. They wanted to be discovered. They wanted to be stars. Having been down that road myself, I knew the earlier they got noticed, the more likely it was to happen. Whatever doors I could open for them, I would. Besides, we were having the time of our lives. That is, until bouts of depression suddenly crushed my world.

Why? I wondered. It seemed completely illogical, considering I was happily married and thrilled to be helping my girls. The symptoms—crying spells, dark thoughts, and obsessive fears— were similar to those I had encountered after Demi's birth, but this time they were more intense. With alarming frequency, I found myself holding Madison in my arms as slow-motion movies played in my head, detailing my failings as a mother. In one disturbing sequence, I saw myself carefully bathing my baby in the sink, only to watch her slip through my fingers and crash headfirst onto the floor. With every scary frame flashing through my mind, I grew more distraught. Yet, I couldn't bring myself to tell anyone. Neither Eddie nor Lisa had a clue about the darkness circling around me.

I knew that I was exhausted and hanging by a thread, but admitting that I was struggling with my motherly duties would have meant disturbing that all-important perception that my life was perfect. *Hadn't I already confessed about my failed marriage?* Surely I could handle this problem on my own. Besides, Eddie and I had established a set of rules when we first started living together, and I wanted to uphold my end of the bargain. He was the provider, which meant he worked sixty-plus hours a week at the car dealership and handled our finances. I was in charge of raising the kids and making decisions at home. Leaning on him wasn't my style. I was strong, independent, and fully capable of handling details such as making sure our girls got fed, went to the doctor when they needed to, completed their schoolwork, and arrived at auditions on time and prepared. In my mind, asking Eddie for help would have been a sign that I was falling short on my responsibilities.

Determined to carry on like nothing was wrong, I doggedly tried to fix my life. Instead, old patterns returned, especially my obsession about being thin. My dark moods, I decided, came from all those extra pounds from pregnancy, so I stopped eating, which made breastfeeding nearly impossible. *I can't worry about eating properly*, I told myself. *I'll simply give Madison a bottle.* After that, everything started caving in on me.

"I can't seem to stop crying," I bawled in my doctor's office one afternoon. "I need help!" My doctor was the only person I was willing to confide in because I trusted him to keep my visit confidential. He listened to every word I said, suggesting that, once again, postpartum depression seemed to be the cause of my problems. Then he prescribed some medication. I'm not sure if it was Prozac or Wellbutrin, but it did the trick—at least for three or four months. Once I felt I was back on an even keel, I stopped the meds, telling myself that I was fine. Besides, I was pretty sure those pills were keeping me from losing weight. It was a foolish mistake.

One of the sad and frightening things about dealing with mental-health issues is that making excuses, living in denial, and deferring treatment often become acceptable life strategies. I kept telling myself that I could tough it out. Over time, I carried that logic a little further and convinced myself that if I could just guide my family to stardom, my problems would disappear. The formula in my head looked something like this: stardom=money & recognition=less anxiety & more satisfaction=less depression & more happiness=fairy-tale life. And I wasn't about to let tiredness or sad thoughts stand in our way.

By the time Madison turned two, our lives ran like a cassette that kept being rewound. Each week, we'd schedule practices, classes, filming, photo shoots, auditions, and schoolwork. The following week we'd hit "replay" and do it all again. Whenever the pinpricks of depression needled my mind, I'd focus on the activities of the day and push forward.

My job was getting everyone where they needed to be, and my number-one rule was: BE ON TIME! Sometimes I was so worried about being late that I'd make everyone leave two hours early when only one was necessary. We spent endless trips together in our Ford

Expedition, often logging more than a hundred miles in a day. With a toddler in tow, I knew I had to be prepared. Eventually, I had the routine down to a science.

"Do we have everything?" I'd ask the girls before I left the driveway. "Food? Water? Diapers?" The girls would look around then shout, "All here!" To be sure, I'd ask again. "Really? How about those *Elmo* and *Dora* DVDs?" I was obsessive about being prepared, yet I always seemed to forget something.

"Crap," I shouted more than once as I backed out of the driveway. "We need head shots and résumés!" Even if we didn't, I wanted them, just in case. Leaving things to chance wasn't part of my playbook, so I constantly tried to anticipate every stumbling block or pitfall that we might encounter. Sometimes, though, I drove my girls crazy, especially with all my questions.

"Dallas, did you study your lines?" "How's that science project coming, Demi?" "Where are the auditions tomorrow?" When the girls grew weary, a round of drama always followed.

"Mom, really," Dallas would sigh in exasperation, while Demi rifled off, "I know! I know!" like she was a parrot. When they both started rolling their eyes, I'd lose it. "Do you want me to stop this truck right now?" I would screech. Lord, we were noisy.

Of course, I didn't really mind. It was all part of staying connected with my girls. Amid all that shouting, we also did a lot of talking. If someone was worried about forgetting her lines or messing up, we talked. If someone was excited about an upcoming birthday party or needed a new outfit, we talked about that, too. No topic was off-limits, though we rarely got into anything too deep. More often than not, I'd glean little insights about Dallas's new boyfriend or Demi's latest music idol. Every mile traveled was an opportunity to learn something new.

Madison, still a bit shy, was included, too. "Show me happy," Dallas asked one day, showing her a big smile. When Madison smiled back, we all clapped and cheered. "How about sad?" Demi asked, putting on a big frown. Before long, Madison was making exaggerated faces to please her sisters and becoming quite the little actress in the process. But when Dallas and Demi were busy at a studio or in someone's classroom, I knew I was in charge of entertaining Madison. That's when I decided to turn our truck into a playground.

With three seats in the back of the vehicle, I folded two completely down and folded the third halfway, which made a perfect sliding board. Throw in a potty seat and some Legos and we had everything we needed for an afternoon's worth of fun. As crazy as it sounds, those years spent in the car were some of the best bonding times ever—though I do believe we spent more on gas than some folks do on college tuition.

We doled out time and money during those early years like we had an endless supply. We didn't, of course, but that didn't stop us. I was a mom on a mission, determined to assist my girls in any way I could. With so many gifted teachers in the Dallas-Fort Worth area, I couldn't resist signing them up for more and more classes.

Cathryn Sullivan, a tough, no-nonsense kind of woman who could command attention just by snapping her head of long blond hair, was a godsend when it came to teaching acting skills. My girls loved her and so did I. Since I had three girls and Cathryn had as many boys, we always joked that someday we'd play matchmaker with our offspring in hopes that we could live out our sunset years together, rocking our grandchildren to sleep. It never panned out that way, but we all remain close friends to this day.

One thing is certain—Cathryn made our dreams take flight. As she taught, pushed, and cajoled my girls to become better actresses, more and more opportunities came their way. Today, Cathryn is recognized as one of the top acting coaches in the nation and her impressive list of successful students includes not only my girls, but also stars such as Selena Gomez, Cody Linley, and Madison Pettis.

But Dallas and Demi weren't merely aspiring actresses. I knew they also had musical talent and ambitions, which meant they had to learn to use their vocal cords properly. So, I looked up an old acquaintance from my own performing days, Linda Septien, who was becoming recognized for her highly competitive "master classes" in vocal and instrumental training. "I'll gladly let your girls audition," she told me, "but I can't guarantee I'll accept them."

Of course, even auditioning required a fee. When I told Eddie, he wanted to know more. "Sounds like a budget buster," he said, but agreed we could make it work if we didn't take any vacations or splurge on trips to the movies or expensive restaurants. Thankfully, our household never did have those I-want-a-hundred-dollar-pair-of-shoes arguments because there wasn't enough money for frivolous shopping trips. Everything that came in was going back out, toward the girls' careers.

"Oh, I'd really like to work with them," Linda gushed after she heard my girls audition. "But this is serious work," she added. "They'll need to come for several hours each week." *Of course*, I thought, *I can't imagine what I'd do with a little free time!* Somehow in the midst of everything else we were doing, we started traveling to Addison, Texas, every Saturday morning.

Taking voice lessons is one thing, but Linda's system was something else entirely. She was all about learning every aspect of becoming a great musician, which meant mastering good vocal techniques as well as learning how to play various instruments and understanding the subtleties of songwriting. Tall, blond, and impeccably dressed, Linda was (and still is) one of those can-do ladies who always looked like she stepped off the set of *The Real Housewives of Beverly Hills*. She was also adamant about using social media to bolster one's career, even before it was mainstream to do so. (Facebook and Twitter weren't popular yet.)

"You need to create a website, promo kits, and laminated bios with pictures and CDs attached," she instructed, which is why her studio not only had a stage, recording areas, and rooms for lessons, but also classrooms to learn about posting videos to YouTube and creating web pages. If it sounded like too much work, she suggested you find another studio. Thanks to her, I spent hours learning how to use PowerPoint and mastering the laminating machine. I even watched tutorials on how to burn CDs. Before long, I was busy developing marketing strategies whenever Madison was napping.

It was Linda who helped Demi, as a budding teenager, make her first demo CD, and years into the future she'd also be the one who would fly across the country at a moment's notice if Demi needed her help. Once, Linda rushed in the night before Demi was scheduled to appear on *Good Morning America* because Demi could barely talk, let alone sing. After patiently teaching Demi how to coax her vocal cords to work through the problem, Linda proudly watched offstage as her former student sang her heart out.

I wasn't alone in my efforts to help my girls. Impressed by their ambitions and dedication, Eddie surprised them one night by handing each of them an Ovation guitar. Demi, then eleven, gushed a big "thank you" and promptly disappeared into her bedroom. For the next forty-eight hours, she practiced and practiced until she could play a new song. Dallas, though, didn't have the same passion. In an effort to keep both girls interested, I hired Boo Massey, a friend of Eddie's who lived nearby, to teach them. With his messy hair and worn T-shirts, Boo looked like a typical rocker, and Demi adored him. After her very first lesson, she even ran upstairs and wrote a song. It wouldn't be her last. Thanks to Boo, Dallas learned to play guitar but Demi blossomed into a musician. Years later, my sister Kathy would remark that Demi's first guitar "was like an extension of her arm." She never went anywhere without it—except to dance class.

During that same time, I also hired Karen Jeter, a piano teacher who came to our house. Again, it was Demi who soaked up everything she could learn. And oddly enough, Demi, like me, preferred to memorize and play by ear rather than read sheet music. Her talents, though, were far superior to mine. She only needed to listen to a song once or twice before she could play it back note for note. Karen, too, encouraged Demi to write her own songs, many of which had gut-wrenching lyrics. In fact, the very first song the two of them ever worked on was "Pennies in a Jar," a song about Demi's real father that she played at her first recital. No one could listen to it without welling up with tears. Although the lyrics made me realize that my first husband had left some deep wounds in my daughter's heart, I never asked if she needed to talk about what had happened. Exploring the territory of the past wasn't something I felt comfortable doing for myself, let alone with my daughter. *Better to focus on the future*, I thought. And the future started revealing itself rather quickly, as Demi started skipping sleep to write music. One month after cowriting the song with Karen, she had more than fifty new songs to add to her collection.

This was also the era of Britney Spears, when singers who could dance were all the rage, so I figured a little more training was in order. Kat Garcia, an adorable, petite spitfire of an instructor who lived about an hour away, volunteered to work with both girls, though she'd prove to be a hard taskmaster.

"Thirty minutes on the treadmill," she demanded at the start of every session. "After that, you'll dance for several hours." It was grueling, but all that exercise improved their performances onstage.

For all her help, Kat never asked for a dime. "I believe in your girls, and I want to see them make it big," she told me. All I could do was thank her and hope that we'd both get to see that wish fulfilled. To aid those efforts, Kat often entered the girls in numerous contests and festivals, even pulling together a group of backup dancers to perform with them.

"When you practice," Kat advised, "dress the part and treat it like a real performance." And BINGO! That's when we knew that our girls were *very* different. Dallas would parade into our living room-turned-stage in full pageant-style hair and makeup, dressed to the hilt—mostly in pink outfits plastered with sequins. After she finished belting out tunes such as Whitney Houston's "I Will Always Love You" or Celine Dion's "Power of the Dream," Demi would come marching into the room looking completely goth in her black jeans, black T-shirts, and black eyeliner. The only bit of color she allowed herself was a bit of red lipstick. She even begged me to let her paint her nails black, but I refused. No amount of cajoling ever persuaded Demi to wear a few sparkly sequins. And she never sang the same songs as Dallas unless the two were trying to outdo each other, preferring instead to belt out songs such as Christina Aguilera's "Fighter" and FeFe Dobson's "Take Me Away."

Headstrong and determined, Demi also had a temper. At eight, she tried to master Billy Gilman's "One Voice," a song with really high notes. Though she wanted to sing it as perfectly as he did, it didn't come easily.

"One voice, one simple word . . . Hearts know what to say," she sang from her bedroom, sounding strong and steady until her voice cracked. "Arrrrggghhh!" she screamed. Two beats later, I heard her pounding on the wall. Unwilling to give up, she broke each run into smaller and smaller parts until she could master the notes. When she put it all together, I bowed my head and crossed my fingers, hoping she'd make it to the end. A few years later, when Christina Aguilera dominated the music scene, Demi did the same thing with her songs but with even more intensity. One night she tried and failed so often to perfect a particular song that she broke her bedpost in frustration.

"No cursing," I yelled up the stairs when I sensed her losing control. "You have to wait 'til your eighteen!"

So few people realize what goes into achieving a dream. The classes, the practice sessions, the performances at small festivals and local restaurants, the training, the organizing, the hiring of band members, and the hours we logged in the truck were just a foretaste of the commitments and challenges to come. Not to mention all the money we spent on what our friends and family called "a pipe dream." But no one could have stopped us! We were sure that we were on the right path, though it wasn't without sacrifices.

No one ever thinks about all the birthday parties my girls missed. The vacations they never took. The sleepovers they were denied. Or the times they worked when they didn't feel well. And no one ever saw me packing the car each morning or heard the pep talks I gave my girls when disappointment overwhelmed them. Getting to the top was a struggle, but I never forced them to continue. "You can quit," I said more than once, "but only after you fulfill the commitments you've already made."

Not one of us ever jumped ship. We always found the strength and inspiration to continue. Even when the car business went south and Eddie's salary began to slip, we didn't give up. Instead, we became resourceful. Demi, at ten, recorded a karaoke CD and sold it to the neighbors so she'd have money to go to the Cinderella pageant that summer, while Eddie and I remortgaged the house—not once, but twice. And I wasn't too proud to make a trip to the pawnshop, if needed.

Did it hurt to part with special keepsakes such as my beautiful pair of diamond earrings and the Rolex watch Eddie had given me for Christmas one year? Of course, but I wanted our girls to keep dreaming. Would it have been nice if someone had patted me on the back for my efforts? Sure, but I wasn't looking for praise. I knew deep in my heart that when you put enough work into something, good things follow, and that was all we needed. In the end, it wasn't the things we gave up that mattered. Rather, it was everything we ignored that exacted a heavy price.

Excerpt from "Pennies in a Jar"

By Demi Lovato

Sunshine breakin' through the rain

I know I'm gonna be okay

But sometimes, it feels like this pain

Is never gonna go away.

Gotta tell my heart not to fall apart

When the teardrops start to fall

Somehow I'll get through find a sky of blue

I'll be fine when you don't call

I'm talkin' to the sky—hope he'll tell me why

You didn't say goodbye at all

You didn't say goodbye

Chorus:

I've got pennies in a jar to prove I once had you

I was too small, I don't recall that gift from you.

I was counting my pennies on the floor

As you carried your bags out the door

Guess that's what you had in mind

When you left your little girl behind

You couldn't give your heart

Just pennies in a jar

And every time I look at them I wonder . . . where you are . . .

Pennies . . . to prove . . . I once had you.

CHAPTER SEVENTEEN

"My kids aren't perfect; nobody's kids are. Everything I had tried to sweep under the rug exploded that day when she called me from the bathroom."

A s the spring of 2004 approached, our family took a deep breath and tried to assess where we were on the grand highway to stardom. The general conclusion was that we had made progress but nothing big—except for *Barney*—had really materialized. More and more, it seemed that getting on the Disney Channel might be the best route for our goals, but auditions in our area for that channel were few and far between. We figured we'd keep plugging along until the right part . . . the right script . . . the right something came along. For a while, the only thing that came knocking was trouble.

For starters, my depression returned. I couldn't make it through a single day without dissolving into tears. Desperate for help, I ran back to my doctor. Again, I told no one. He listened, nodding his head as I tried to describe what my life was like. "You know," he said, "you have a toddler to care for and two busy teens. That's a lot to manage. Maybe talking to a psychiatrist would help." When he handed me a list of names to consider, I randomly picked one and set up an appointment.

"I start cleaning the kitchen only to end up in a corner of the room scrubbing a single, tiny tile with a toothbrush, while everything else remains untouched," I explained. "Then I start crying and walk away in frustration."

He looked at me curiously. "I don't think you're depressed," he said. "I think you have ADHD (Attention Deficit Hyperactivity Disorder)." He promptly wrote me a prescription for twenty milligrams of Adderall and told me it would help.

I'd later learn that dosage was a bit high for my height and weight, but I left his office feeling optimistic. The doctor never mentioned possible side effects such as irregular heartbeats, euphoria, or anxiety, and he certainly never warned me that the drug could be addictive.

The next morning, I took the medication and proceeded to buzz about the kitchen getting all the cleaning done in record time. I was ecstatic. *This is great! I finished in less than thirty minutes, and I'm not hungry, either!* For good measure, I proceeded to dust the entire house. Then I got everybody ready for the day, marveling that I didn't feel totally drained. In fact, I had energy to spare.

"Let's go," I commanded, heading to the car. "Dallas needs to be put on tape."

The digital age was still about a decade away, so when the girls auditioned for roles that were being filmed in Los Angeles or somewhere other than Texas, they needed to be "put on tape," a process that involved going to a studio to be filmed and put on a VHS tape. The first part was "slating," which meant standing in front of the camera and stating their name, age, and the agency representing them. After that, whoever was auditioning read her lines for a scene or two while another person read the other parts offscreen and someone else filmed. Cathryn was also on set to give instructions and feedback. It was a long process because the scene was filmed over and over until it seemed perfect. Only the best version stayed on the tape.

It was also a costly process as the fees for everyone's services ran between seventy-five and a hundred dollars. Then I'd have to spend another forty or fifty dollars at the post office to overnight the tape so that it would arrive at the producer's office by ten the next morning—and there was no guarantee that anyone would even watch it once it arrived.

Although Dallas was the one being put on tape that morning, I made Demi ride along while Madison stayed behind with Lisa. For some twenty minutes, I happily hummed a tune as we sailed along. Then everything changed. Without warning, my heart started beating wildly, like it was going to pop right out of my chest. I clutched the steering wheel and tried to take a deep breath. I couldn't. *My God*, I thought, *I'm having a heart attack!* I didn't want to alarm the kids, but I couldn't keep driving, either. "Sorry, girls," I said as calmly as I could. "Need to pull over and get out of the car for a minute." When I jumped out, I started pacing on the shoulder of the road. Over and over, I marched from the front of the car to the back while the steady whoosh of traffic passed by me, just inches away.

What's happening? Am I going to die? Is this because I didn't eat anything? My mind seemed just as erratic as my heartbeats. Scared and anxious, I realized I was reacting to the medicine I had so confidently taken that morning. Some fifteen minutes later, after calming myself down, I climbed back into the car and continued driving to our destination.

As soon as we returned home, I threw out the bottle of pills. "Never again," I vowed. "I will suffer with whatever problems I have before I ever take *that* again."

That spring, when Demi was approaching twelve and Dallas was sixteen, I just knew I didn't want to risk taking Adderall again. Not ever. Not even at a lower dose. For three more years, I wouldn't even go back to the doctor to consider other options. I just decided that my mental health wasn't going to interfere with the happiness or success of my family. *Be strong!* I told myself, as though it was as simple as mind over matter.

As May loomed in front of us, I couldn't wait for the school year to end. Demi's return to public school hadn't gone well, and her sixth-grade classmates seemed hell-bent on making her life—and mine—miserable. Apparently, not everyone was enamored with Demi's talents or success. The name-calling had actually started back in fifth grade, right before the start of *Barney*, and most of it was directed at Demi's weight. Now that she had thinned out, the jeers and sneers took a more sinister turn—and so did Demi's self-image.

"They call me 'fat bitch' and 'slut,'" she told me on many afternoons, the hurt lodged behind her eyes.

I handled the matter the way my parents would have dealt with it. "Take the high road," I told her. "Forgive and forget—we're not tattletales!"

During this same time, Dallas came running into the dining room one afternoon looking alarmed. "Mom," she said, "You need to come see this! Demi is visiting some really weird websites."

"What do you mean?" I asked.

"Well, they're all about anorexia and bulimia," she said, "and her passwords are logged into all the sites."

"Oh, Dallas," I sighed. "She probably got on them by mistake." I walked away, completely ignoring her concerns.

It wasn't the right thing to do, and I'm horrified when I look back and see how lightly I treated the matter. But sometimes we so desperately want to believe the best about our children that we ignore the obvious. And, I was still in denial about my own eating issues. In my mind, I believed that Demi's weight loss was due to a growth spurt—because that's what I wanted to believe. I even gloated that she might get more jobs because she was thinner. Not once did I draw a line between the pounds she had shed and the bullying at school.

Even when Demi was handed a letter from a group of girls listing all the reasons they didn't like her—a list that included criticisms such as "You're a fake celebrity," "You suck," "Nobody likes you," and "You're an ugly bitch"—I still didn't get involved. Worse, I didn't even tell a single teacher what was going on.

"It's terrible and heartbreaking," I told Demi, "but you're supposed to learn something from this. Real life is full of people who act this way, and you have to learn to deal with them.

"Besides," I added, "They're just jealous about all the work you're doing. Remember, you're the one laughing all the way to the bank."

But Demi wasn't laughing. Instead, she was starving herself. She was also preparing to strike back. The next time someone said something nasty to her, she returned the gesture with a few choice words of her own. When she got another letter, she wrote one back, lashing out at all the girls who despised her. But I knew nothing about her retaliations until the school called one afternoon, demanding a conference. When I walked into the meeting, every one of Demi's teachers was there, and no one looked happy. Everyone started yelling at once.

"Demi's writing nasty notes," said one teacher. "And she's using vulgar language," said another. The volley of complaints made me feel like I was standing in front of a firing squad.

"But you don't know what they did to her," I tried to explain as the din grew louder. "Wait!" I said. "I told her not to bother you. . . ."

But my words were meaningless. So, too, were the tears running down my cheeks. There wasn't an ounce of sympathy for Demi or me that day, except from the drama coach and the choir director, both of whom tried to speak on Demi's behalf. The verdict was already in: Demi was a bad girl. And our family was put on notice. When the school year ended, we all breathed a sigh of relief.

As summer vacation came to a close, Dallas decided she wanted to be homeschooled. "It's too hard to juggle classes and auditions," she moaned.

The previous year had been especially tricky because I had allowed Dallas, then a sophomore, to travel to Los Angeles with a chaperone in February so she could attend pilot season. Anyone serious about breaking into the industry knows the value of pilot season—a frantic period of auditions, production, and decision-making about a slew of potential new TV series. Being there is a rite of passage for those trying to break into the industry, but it also requires missing more than a month of school, which meant I had to unenroll Dallas from public school and then re-enroll her when she returned. Neither of us wanted to deal with that hassle again.

Demi, who had decided she wanted to back off of acting and focus on her music, decided to stay in public school. Considering she'd have a whole new group of teachers to work with, I was optimistic that seventh grade would be more fun than the previous year had been. My optimism didn't last long.

Less than two months into the new school year, my cell phone rang as Dallas and I were parked at Sonic, waiting for our breakfast to arrive.

"Mommmaaa," Demi sobbed, "I c-c-a-n't get out of the b-b-bathroom."

Demi's voice shook with terror.

"Where are you?" I cried, knowing I had dropped her off at middle school that morning.

"I locked myself in a dark bathroom," she cried. "But I can hear them going up and down the hall. They're saying they're going to k-k-ick my ass! I have my legs propped against the door so they can't get in."

"Who? What?" I asked.

"Those girls," Demi pleaded. "They're going to hurt me!"

It was those girls again, the very ones who had been tormenting Demi since the previous year. Apparently when Demi had gotten to her locker that morning, the girls had surrounded her, accusing her of stealing another girl's shirt. "Why would I steal a shirt that I can't wear? Besides, I can buy my own shirts," Demi told them. When she brushed past the girls and headed to class, Demi overheard their rumblings for retaliation. "Let's beat the bitch up," one of them suggested. Fearing they'd catch her, Demi ducked into a bathroom that no one ever used.

"Demi, I'm coming to get you," I promised, "but you need to run to the principal's office and wait there. Run as fast as you can!"

Demi was in danger, and I doubted that the school would be on her side. When I ran into the office, I found Demi sitting in a chair, trembling and shaking like she was in shock.

"We're trying to sort this out," the secretary mumbled. When I asked what would happen to the other girls, she nonchalantly shrugged. "We'll look into it."

"Don't bother," I seethed. "We're checking out—right now and for good. We're done!" Then I put my arm around Demi, and we walked out of the office. On the way to the car, Demi pulled me into another bathroom.

"It's the hate wall," she said, pointing at all the graffiti.

Every word was directed at her, much of it echoing the sentiments of the letter the girls had written the year before. My heart broke into a thousand pieces. No one should ever have to endure such humiliation and shame.

"And I know whose handwriting that is," she said, pointing to one line in particular.

Months later, we heard that the wall was covered with a fresh coat of paint, but no one was ever punished, even though I had shared Demi's observations about the handwriting with the principal. Perhaps the administration just wanted a clean slate, but wiping away the scars in my daughter's heart wasn't so easy.

From that day forward, Demi never took another class in a public school. She was bruised from the experience and so was I. Although I felt guilty because I had failed to protect Demi, mostly out of my need to avoid conflict and to appear perfect, I pushed the experience aside and focused on the future. Holding in emotions, stuffing down feelings, and keeping quiet about concerns were the rules I had lived by for so long that I didn't have a clue about how to do things differently. So instead of exploring how to heal and integrate what we had been through, I latched onto the desire to help my kids become successful with even more intensity. Stardom, I decided, would be the golden ticket to acceptance. And if people accepted my kids, they'd accept me, too.

It was flawed reasoning, for sure, but by the time I realized that, we were a family knee-deep in crisis.

CHAPTER EIGHTEEN

"It's not my place to tell people how to believe, but they should believe in something bigger than themselves."

By the start of 2005, I thought our family was running as smoothly as a fine-tuned engine. Every day, I'd make Dallas and Demi sit down to do their homework for a few hours, while Madison sat at her little desk and pretended to do her own schoolwork. A few days a week, Selena, who was also being homeschooled, joined us because Mandy, her mother, was working full-time. All the laughter and commotion that erupted most days made it seem like the trauma of Demi's bullying was behind us.

If Demi wasn't busy trying to learn a new song by Kelly Clarkson (her go-to artist ever since she had won *American Idol*), she and Selena were pretending to mug for the paparazzi as they used their T-Mobile Sidekicks, first brought into the public eye by Paris Hilton and Nicole Richie. Of course, we had those devices before anyone else in Texas did because we *had* to have the latest and greatest thing from LA. We'd pop those suckers open and bang out a text so fast it would make your head spin. While other kids were playing Nintendo, my kids were texting on their Sidekicks. It was all part of our incessant need to imitate the stars.

One afternoon, Demi and Selena even pretended to flee from the paparazzi, which resulted in Selena hijacking Madison's motorized, red Barbie Corvette—and she drove it right through our neighbor's yard! Of course, I was the one who had to explain why his grass had tire marks everywhere. Sometimes keeping my three kids and Selena under control was an impossible task. In the midst of the chaos, Madison often escaped to the family room to watch TV. As I went to check on her one day, she pointed to the screen and said, "I want to do that."

"You want to do what?" I asked, hoping to understand.

My four-year-old pointed at the screen, insisting, "I want to do what those people are doing!"

Really? My eyes brightened at the thought. *Was this the same girl who was so painfully shy just a few years ago that she couldn't even tolerate strangers looking at her?* I guessed that watching her sisters read scripts and audition for commercials was bringing her out of her shell. "Let me call Cathryn to see if there are any classes you can take," I told her. Within days, she started acting classes and then promptly insisted she wanted to try an audition. We talked it over and Jennifer, Madison's agent at Kim Dawson, sent her on a movie audition in Shreveport, Louisiana. We embarked on the three-hour drive with a lot of enthusiasm, but halfway there, Madison started having doubts. By the time we arrived, she was a bundle of nerves.

"I don't think I can do this, Mommy," she said, fighting back tears.

But I didn't like my girls backing out of things at the last moment. "Just do it this one time because we told Miss Jennifer we would," I said. "If you don't like it, you *never ever* have to do it again, I promise." With that, I walked her up to the room where a panel of four casting people awaited her arrival. My little girl took a long, deep breath and stepped inside.

Then I got nervous. All I could picture was Madison crying behind the door. As the minutes dragged on, I was sure I heard her sniffling. When the door burst open, I was mystified to see Madison skipping toward me, grinning from ear to ear. "That was so much fun," she exclaimed. "I want to do this for the rest of my life!"

Right then, all those hopes of my baby becoming a doctor or a rocket scientist vanished. Those scholarly dreams were history. I knew Madison was hooked, just like my other two. And considering she actually got her first callback from that audition, I figured she probably had the talent to break into the business at an early age. Little did I know how accurate my assessment would be!

One morning in the car as we listened to our favorite radio station, 106.1 KISS FM, Kidd Kraddick, a well-known and beloved DJ in the Dallas metroplex, made an announcement. "We're having a Kelly Clarkson sing-alike contest," he said. "We want you to call in and sing 'Since U Been Gone,' but using the lyrics we've written." After listening to a few contestants, we realized the new words changed the song into a jingle promoting the radio station.

On the way to dance class later that week, Demi insisted, "I can

Me as a baby, 1963

My daddy, Perry Hart, and me, 1967

My brother, Joey; my sister Julie (scowling); and me holding my sister Kathy, Christmas 1972

Me singing at a revival in East Texas, accompanied by my dad on guitar (right), 1973

Me with my little sisters, Kathy and Julie, and my brother, Joey, Easter 1973

Our promo picture for gospel-music group The Harts, 1977

My senior picture,
Irving High School, 1980

Me (left) with the cast of The Crazy
Horse Saloon show at Six Flags over Texas,
my first professional singing job, 1980

Me getting ready to go onstage
at The Grapevine Opry,
Grapevine, Texas, 1983

Dallas dressed for her first
pageant swimsuit competition, 1988

Patrick and newborn Demi, 1992

Demi and Dallas at Grandma's house, 1993

Dallas, me, and Demi backstage
after my performance at Johnnie
High's Country Music Revue in
Arlington, Texas, 1997

Me and Demi at the Texas State
Cinderella Pageant dinner
in Houston, Texas, 2001

Dallas (left) being crowned
Texas State Cinderella Teen
in Houston, Texas, 2002

Me and Eddie at our wedding,
with Dallas and Demi, in
Las Vegas, Nevada, 2000

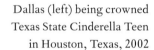

Dallas, me (three days before Madison was born), and Demi, Christmas 2001

Me and newborn baby Madison, 2002

Demi, Madison, and Dallas, 2002

Madison on the phone, 2004

Dallas and me in
San Antonio, Texas, 2004

Demi and Dallas at a Kelly Clarkson
concert in San Antonio, Texas, 2004

Demi in the studio, recording her first demo, 2005

The note Demi left me as she went into treatment, October 2010

I'm gonna miss you every day of the minute at night. I love you, you're the Best mother I could ever ask for.

❤ Dem

Family picture of Demi, Dallas, me, Eddie, and Madison, 2012

do that song, Momma. I know I can!" After class, I shared the details about the contest with Kat and she was all for it. "Hey," she exclaimed, "why don't you just go up to the station at six a.m. and make them put you on the show?"

"Oh, God, no," I said in horror. "They'll get mad at us and probably ignore us."

"No, they won't," Kat insisted. "And, I have an idea—meet me there, and I promise, I'll get her in. But, grab some bright-pink poster board and make a sign that says: I CAN SING LIKE KELLY CLARKSON!"

My blood ran cold. I'm not sure if it was the thought of being embarrassed or having to get two teenagers and a toddler up by 5:00 a.m.! Regardless, I stopped for poster board and markers on our way home, and shortly before midnight, we all fell asleep, exhausted. The next morning, I still thought barging onto the show sounded like bad manners, but I shoved coffee in the older girls' faces and off we went. If Kat didn't show up, I decided I wouldn't go through with it. But just as she promised, Kat pulled into the garage right behind us.

"Follow me," she ordered. We walked into a courtyard and stood by a large bay window where Kidd and his cohosts, Kellie Rasberry and Big Al, sat inside with headphones on, speaking into microphones.

"Demi, over here," Kat said. "Hold up your sign where Kidd can see it."

Demi, dressed in a plaid skirt and maroon blazer, along with a pair of knee socks and black platform shoes, waved her very pink sign in front of the window as Kat, Dallas, Madison, and I stood behind her. We waited . . . and waited.

Then it happened. The loudspeaker in the courtyard sprang to life. "What do we have here?" Kidd exclaimed. "Seems like there's someone who wants to give the Kelly Clarkson jingle a try." After he asked Demi a few questions, the two of them chatted like old buddies.

"You are so cute," cried Kellie, who loved Demi's outfit and matching hat. "I certainly wasn't that fashionable at twelve!"

"Well," Demi replied rather shyly, "my stylist helped me."

"Your stylist?" Kellie gasped. "Who are you?"

Of course, she didn't have a stylist. Kat had merely suggested she wear the outfit, but everyone got a chuckle out of her remark. "Well," said Kidd, "let's hear the jingle." But Demi had another interesting comment to make first. "Ah, Kidd," she began, "I know you!"

Kellie, who couldn't resist mimicking Demi, looked at Kidd and teased, "Oooh, are you my daddy?"

The room erupted in laughter, but the joke was lost on Demi, who sweetly explained that she had met Kidd two years before when he was a judge at one of Linda Septien's talent contests. Demi was sure he'd remember her because she was the only contestant whose microphone hadn't worked, though it hadn't flustered her at all. Kidd had been so impressed with her poise and talent that he'd written on her scoring card: *Someone to watch out for because she's going places!*

Yet Kidd seemed to have forgotten. "Ah," he replied nervously, "did I like you?"

"Yes," Demi giggled. "You did."

Wasting no time, Kidd asked, "You ready to sing?"

The moment Demi opened her mouth, the booth went quiet. Eyebrows went up and heads shook in disbelief. Everyone was grinning. After she hit those really high notes in the chorus, the room erupted in excitement. Demi's back was to me, but I was sure she was smiling.

"Whoa! That was amazing," said Kidd. When Kellie agreed, Kidd suddenly announced, "Contest is over! No need to continue it any further." That's when Demi finally turned around. Her smile couldn't have gotten any bigger.

Minutes later, my friend Lorna, who just happened to turn on the radio as she was leaving for work, called and gasped, "I just heard Demi on the radio." Before I could respond, she shouted, "On the radio! She sounded amazing!"

I couldn't have agreed more.

We never heard about any prize, but that whole exchange between Kidd and Demi was played over and over again through the years, and so was Demi's version of the song. People just couldn't get enough of it. I guess she owned the show in more ways than one!

Kidd would go on to interview Demi a few more times during her career, and they'd always laugh about that day when a little girl held up a pink poster outside the station window. No one was more proud of the "hometown girl who'd made it big" than Kidd. Sadly, he passed away suddenly while participating in his own charity event for Kidd's Kids, a nonprofit that sponsored trips for chronically and terminally ill children. Our family, like the entire Dallas area, still misses his generous and kind spirit. To this day, the Kidd Kraddick Morning Show still bears his name, which only seems fitting.

By spring, our schedule of classes, auditions, and work commitments was moving along at a brisk pace. Madison, still taking acting classes, wasn't seeing a lot of action, but the older girls were. Had any of them decided they wanted to play baseball or soccer that summer, I don't know how we would have fit it in! One Saturday morning, we loaded up the truck and headed for Austin, three hours away, for an unspecified network audition, although we suspected it was for Disney because the sides (the specific lines from the script that had been sent to us) were from an old Disney Channel movie about a group of girl soccer players.

We took off on Interstate 35 East, hoping to make it in time. Dallas was riding shotgun, and Demi was sitting behind me in the backseat. Madison, strapped into her car seat, was in the middle, and Selena, who was also auditioning, was behind Dallas. We tried to make the best of the long drive, even though I was nervous we'd be late. There was always that lurking fear that we might hit a traffic jam and miss the audition.

As the radio blared, we sang, told jokes, and laughed our way closer to Austin. About halfway there, Dallas insisted we stop at McDonald's because she wanted a strawberry milkshake. "You better not spill it on anything," I warned. "I don't have time to clean up any messes."

With everyone munching on food and Dallas slurping her shake, I flew down the highway. Glancing at Dallas, I saw that she was rolling down her window. "What are you doing?" I asked. When she held up her milkshake and started tipping the remaining contents out the window, I screamed.

"Dooonnn't . . ." was all I could say before the pink liquid from her cup went flying out the window, only to sail right back inside and splatter across Dallas's face. The trio behind me fared even worse. Big, baby-pink polka dots sprung from their hair and clung to their cheeks. Poor Selena looked the worst, her hair and clothes drenched in the gooey mess.

"Look what you did," I screamed. *Oh my God!* I thought. *Mandy is going to kill me! What if Selena can't audition?* No one dared to speak until Selena started laughing. When the others joined in, I demanded that everyone calm down. "Look for a gas station, now!" I ordered. When Dallas pointed to one up the road, I raced toward it.

One look at the building, and my heart sank. I was hoping for a nice convenience store or a fancy truck stop, but this place was as old as the hills. Every inch reeked of stale motor oil and cigarettes. "This is no time to be particular," I announced. "Everyone head to the bathroom." I dunked Selena under one faucet and Dallas under another, trying to rinse out their hair. Then I shoved them both under the automatic hand dryer while I worked on Demi's hair. There was no time to worry about Madison, who only got a swipe of wet paper towel across her face. "Now, go!" I yelled when Demi's hair was dry, frantically pointing to the truck.

When we pulled into the audition parking lot with only a few minutes to spare, my hands were shaking. *Dear God*, I silently prayed, *thank you for getting us here on time. Now let them do their best. Each and every one of them!* The three girls ran inside as I stayed outside with Madison.

That very day, despite the pink catastrophe, Disney discovered their new star. But it wasn't Demi they wanted; it was Selena, who booked a pilot for a spin-off of *Lizzie McGuire*, titled *Stevie Sanchez*.

That pilot would wind up going against *Hannah Montana*, starring Miley Cyrus, so we all know who won out on that deal! But Selena's moment quickly followed when she was picked to be the lead in *Wizards of Waverly Place*.

Although Selena and Demi had dreamed about getting discovered at the same time—you know, getting to say, "Hi, I'm Demi Lovato!" and "Hi, I'm Selena Gomez!" as they waved their wands and announced, "And you're watching Disney Channel"—it didn't turn out that way. Demi would have to wait a bit longer.

As summer approached, we began to plan for my sister Kathy's arrival. Every July, she and her husband, Jason, would come and stay at our house so they could attend the Believers' Convention in Fort Worth, a weeklong gathering that featured well-known evangelists such as Kenneth Copeland, Creflo Dollar, and Jesse Duplantis, as well as top-notch musical artists. "You know the Lord will bless you for letting us stay here," she always said, and sure enough, after they left Eddie always seemed to get an unexpected bonus or the girls would book a big commercial. It never failed.

The convention also featured a children's ministry known as Superkid Academy—a service just for kids twelve and younger. That particular summer Kathy really wanted Demi to go because once Demi turned thirteen—which would happen in August—she'd no longer be eligible to attend that portion of the event.

But Demi was hesitant. "I'll be right next door with the grown-ups," Kathy insisted. "And I promise you'll have fun." Still dealing with the trauma of having been bullied, as well as some social-anxiety issues, Demi wavered. "Are you sure I don't have to sit next to girls?" she asked, her voice trembling. Kathy assured her she could sit wherever she wanted to. "Tell you what," Demi bargained. "If you come to my church with me on Wednesday evening, then I'll go with you on Thursday morning—but only if you promise I can sit next to a boy!"

On Thursday morning, Demi tentatively followed her aunt toward the auditorium that was filled with more than three hundred kids. Before they parted, Kathy took Demi's hands and looked into her dark eyes. "I'm going to pray that something special happens in there," she said.

Two hours later, Kathy met Demi at the same door where she had left her and knew from the look on Demi's face that something had indeed happened. "So, how'd it go?" she asked. Demi was superexcited and could barely stand still.

"I got a message in there," she gushed. "You've got to tell me what this means! Right now, I need to know!" Kathy suggested they go to lunch so she could hear all the details. Apparently, the service had started out like any other youth service Demi had been to. There was music as well as praise and worship, pretty typical stuff. Then a lady took the stage and began talking about people in the Bible who had been called to their appointments from God at an early age. She talked about boys such as David and Saul. She also mentioned Jesus, who was only twelve when he taught in the temple. Each of them, she emphasized, saw their appointments as an honor. Women were mentioned, too—such as Mary, who was just a teenager when she became the mother of Jesus, and Esther, a young bride who risked her life by going before the king to speak in favor of saving the Jews from extermination. "That took courage and bravery," the woman said. Then things got really interesting.

The speaker stopped talking and started looking at the crowd of young people, scanning from one side of the audience to the other. Then she stared and pointed at Demi. "YOU," she stated with authority, pausing until Demi looked back at her, "have been chosen by God at an early age for your appointment."

Frozen by her words, Demi held her breath, waiting to hear what she would say next. "What you're doing *right now*," she added, "is what He has appointed for your life!"

I'm working on my music, Demi thought. *That must be what God wants me to do!* The woman started to walk away but suddenly spun around, looking right at Demi one more time. "One day," she boldly proclaimed, "you will reach millions of people and make a real difference in their lives." She paused, her eyes still locked on Demi. When she finally spoke, her words pierced the air. "ARE YOU READY?" she demanded. Stunned by the woman's boldness, Demi nodded her head and answered, "Yes."

By the time Demi finished talking, Kathy was covered in goose bumps. "Write everything down," she said to Demi, handing her a piece of paper. "It was a prophecy, and God will bring it to pass." Demi listened, and to this day, that piece of paper lies in a box of keepsakes that's buried somewhere in our Texas home.

All my life I had heard prophesies in church, so when Demi retold her story to me, I knew beyond a shadow of a doubt that what that woman said came straight from God. I accepted the message as confirmation that we were on the right path, doing what we were called to do. Strangely, I didn't feel euphoric. Not once did I jump up and down in celebration. Nor did I hear that familiar chant that my baby was going be a star. Instead, a calm steadiness fell on me that assured me everything would come to pass just as God had promised. Even though I didn't know how or when, I knew that God would put everything into motion. I also sensed that there was a bigger purpose at work than I could understand.

Two long years would pass before we began to see the fulfillment of that prophecy, but whenever I started to lose hope, I'd get another reminder that God was in control of Demi's career, not me.

CHAPTER NINETEEN

"I always left it up to God. To me, it was about His timing, not ours."

*M*uch of what we learned about the entertainment industry was by trial and error, which is another way of saying that sometimes we wasted our time and money. In February 2006, when Dallas was eighteen, Demi heading toward thirteen, and Madison a newly turned five-year-old, I decided we'd all go out to Los Angeles for pilot season. Eddie, though, would stay behind to work. Although Dallas had tried her luck at a previous pilot season, we had since learned that having representation was key for getting sent to auditions. That little detail fell into place thanks to Cathryn, who had organized a showcase during the fall at her studio in Texas, where Mitchell Gossett, a well-known LA agent with CESD Talent Agency, got to see my girls in action.

Cathryn encouraged all the participants to find a monologue of their choosing. Demi, young as she was, settled on portraying Lisa Rowe, a sociopath committed to a mental institution in the riveting drama *Girl, Interrupted*, while Dallas chose to play the mentally challenged Carla Tate in the romantic comedy *The Other Sister*. Gossett loved them both. "Wow, both of you girls have improved so much from the last time I saw you," he raved. When he asked if they had representation for pilot season, both shook their heads. "Well, you do now," Gossett replied.

I was standing nearby and heard the whole conversation. A rush of pride swept over me that was quickly replaced with dread. While many scurried out to LA for pilot season, I liked the fact that my girls stayed behind and got lots of extra work while everyone else was gone. But I assumed that Gossett's endorsement meant he expected to see them out on the West Coast that February. My mind filled with questions. *Where would we find the money? Where would we stay? How would I break the news to Eddie?* After I politely thanked Mitchell for the amazing opportunity he had extended toward my girls by offering to represent them, I also prayed. *Lord, if we're ready for this, please provide a way!*

Pilot season is an eight-week investment, which at that time ran about $25,000 for both girls. Today, the costs would be even higher. Coaching, which can eat up half the budget if you have a lot of auditions, is considered a necessity by most agencies. In addition, there are the expenses of lodging, food, gas, head shots, and other miscellaneous things. Finding that kind of money seemed impossible, but when I asked Eddie about going, he didn't even seem surprised. "We'll figure it out," he said. "We always do, don't we?" And we did, thanks to a hefty tax return and Dallas, who chipped in with a nice windfall from a voice-over job. When Betsy McHale, a fellow Texan and mother of Kevin McHale (an aspiring actor at the time who'd go on to star as Artie Abrams in the FOX TV series *Glee*) offered to rent us two rooms at her Santa Clarita home, I thought the pieces of our future were snapping together as God intended. The girls' new status with CESD seemed promising.

But my expectations didn't exactly go as planned. For starters, Santa Clarita was a thirty-minute drive from most of the studios. Whenever we managed to get an audition notice, I had to negotiate my way through LA's notorious freeways and its horrendous rush-hour traffic, which left me as jumpy as hot grease in a skillet. Then I learned that to be hired for any of those auditions, my girls needed California work permits. It was something I hadn't thought about, and to get the process started, I needed to retrieve their birth certificates, which, of course, were back in Texas.

After making numerous phone calls, filling out forms ad nauseam, and paying a hefty fee to expedite the process, I finally received their birth certificates about a week later. Elated, I dragged the kids and the certificates into the permit office in Van Nuys, only to have the woman behind the counter glare at me in frustration. "I'm sorry," she sighed, peering at me over the top of the reading glasses perched on her nose. "You also need to provide proof that your children are taking classes from an accredited school."

When I explained that I was homeschooling them, she insisted, "That doesn't matter. I still need a seal of approval." But Texas, at the time, allowed me to teach them at home without a seal of approval! I left Van Nuys in tears. Eventually, despair set in. *What are we doing here? Why are we even trying? Even if my girls get some-thing, they won't be able to work!* When Betsy suggested I speak to someone like Trisha Noble at www.childreninfilm.com, the gates of heaven finally opened.

"Don't worry about that," Trish laughed when I explained my dilemma. "We have a service that can do that for you." Within the week, we had our permits. It was an important lesson about the value of having an advocate to work with in an industry with a lot of confusing rules and regulations. As I wrote the check for the company's services, I vowed I'd never let those permits expire. I also vowed to stay in touch with Trish, whose friendship and advice I still cherish today.

Of course, by the time we got those permits figured out, our window of opportunity had dwindled considerably. Add to that my lack of experience driving on California's freeways as well as my penchant for getting lost (these were the days before GPS), and it all added up to one futile and expensive trip. Later, I'd also learn that although my girls had representation, they were too new on the scene to be invited to many auditions. Even if their work per-mits had been approved sooner, they probably wouldn't have been any more successful. "Oh, well," I told the girls, "at least we got to see Disneyland for the first time in our lives."

Ever since the Believers' Convention, my sister Kathy and I had become close—and not just emotionally. It was like we shared some kind of spiritual-mental telepathy. One night, I might pray pri-vately about a situation and the next day my sister would call delivering a message about what I should do. "I think the Lord needs me to tell you something," she'd say and sure enough, her message was just what I needed to hear. It was uncanny.

Shortly after our return from LA when I was fervently praying about my girls' careers, Kathy suddenly called and delivered a message that made my spine tingle. "Something big is about to happen with Demi's career," she said. "But it's not like ripples on the sea—it's more like a tidal wave!" At the same time, I had been hearing the Lord's voice telling me to "get my house in order." Too afraid to ignore the messages, I knew what I had to do.

The very next day, I began a yearlong process of sorting, organizing, and cataloging every item in our house. No drawer went unopened, no closet untouched. I did more than file important papers and take bags of old clothes to Goodwill. Everything from the smallest hair clip to the largest piece of artwork was scrutinized for its usefulness, placed in an appropriate location, and itemized on a list. In the end, you could have asked me, "Where's that green pencil with the frog on the end of it that we got at last year's pageant?" And I would have told you, "It's in the right-hand drawer on the bottom set of cabinets under the island in the kitchen."

It was all preparation for what was to come, though I didn't know exactly what that would be.

Although my spiritual connections were growing deeper by the day, my mental health issues didn't disappear. I still wasn't eating much and bouts of anxiety and depression still hovered above my busy, exciting life. No one knew about my struggles, though, as I tried my best to stay happy and focused on every new opportunity that came our way. And for Dallas, the opportunities weren't just in Texas.

After pilot season that year, Dallas decided to stay behind and continue looking for work. Now eighteen, she wanted to spread her wings and fly on her own, so I let her. Eddie even sent a car out to her on a transport so she'd be able to get around the city. But when she called home on Mother's Day, I knew something was wrong.

"I just can't seem to make it work," she moaned over the phone, "but what bothers me even more is that every time I talk to Madison, she seems older and more mature. I feel like I'm missing out on seeing her grow up."

I immediately flew out to LA and helped her pack her things. Together, we planned to make the long drive back to Texas in her car, stuffed with all her belongings. Then, days before our scheduled departure, she suddenly landed a role on a new pilot called *The Amazing O'Malleys*, which eventually would be renamed the *Wizards of Waverly Place*.

After filming ended, Dallas and I once again prepared to make the journey back to Colleyville, just as Demi was preparing to audition for a guest role on *Prison Break*. Since I wasn't around, Eddie agreed to take off work so he could go with her, even though he had never taken the girls to an audition in his life. By the time the two of them were seated in the waiting room, Eddie's excitement was evident by the sheer volume of texts he kept sending me. It became my personal play-by-play account of Demi's experience.

"Okay, Jennifer Stone just got here," he texted. Then, "Uh-oh, Selena's here, too." He even started timing the interviews. "Jennifer

187

was in there for five minutes and so was Selena." When it was Demi's turn, he was utterly beside himself. Every single minute I got an updated text with the same message: "She still hasn't come out yet!!!!" Some fifteen minutes later, Eddie was still sending me the same message.

It was hysterical. My calm, intellectual businessman was more nervous than any mom I had ever encountered. And I couldn't resist upping the ante by throwing ridiculous questions his way. "What's Selena wearing?" "Is Jennifer's mom there?" "Who else is auditioning for the role?" All the back-and-forth banter made me realize how much I missed being part of the action. I suddenly couldn't wait to get home and hear about all the details in person, so Dallas and I decided to drive straight through, taking turns at the wheel. Shortly after we pulled into our driveway some twenty-six hours later, we learned that Demi had landed the role of Danielle Curtin for a future episode of *Prison Break*, titled "First Down." I couldn't help but wonder if it was the first glimmer of that tidal wave my sister had talked about.

Unfortunately, Dallas's shimmering opportunity didn't materialize. About six months after we got back to Texas, we learned that her role on the show got cut from the script. It was just another example of the highs and lows of an industry that can change in a heartbeat. Nothing is ever guaranteed until you sign that all-important contract! As always, I kept hoping that both of my girls would get to sign on that dotted line in the near future.

Filming for *Prison Break* began in July, though we wouldn't get to see Demi on television until sometime in September. In late August, after Demi turned fourteen, the Disney Channel announced that they were having a nationwide search for new talent. Both Dallas and Demi wanted to go. Shortly after that audition, Demi got another audition notice, but this time it wasn't network specific. We thought it was either Disney or Nickelodeon, but we didn't know for sure and neither did Cathryn. But we did know that it was an interstitial, which is a two-to-five-minute vignette that runs in between scheduled programming. This one was a comedy titled *As the Bell Rings*, and it would be shot entirely through the view of a huge bay window in a school hallway.

Cathryn, who had a few other students going to the same audition, set up a practice session to get everyone ready. When Demi showed up unprepared, Cathryn was furious. "You can't work with the other two boys if you don't know your lines," she grumbled. "So why are you unprepared?"

"Because," replied Demi, looking at her feet, "I'm not going to get this anyway—I'm just not funny."

Cathryn was stunned. "Not funny?" she bellowed. "What makes you think that?"

Demi went on to explain that she had never booked anything comedic. "I've only gotten commercials and *Prison Break*," she said. "I'm better at drama."

Cathryn looked at Demi and shook her head. "You can be anything you want to be, if you're willing to put in the effort," she said. "I've been coaching you for years, and you've learned to do every kind of role—comedy, drama, and even crazy—but if you're going to defeat yourself before you even start working on the part, then don't show up and waste my time!

"You can book this," she added, "I know you can—but you

won't if you show up unprepared and touting the wrong frame of mind. It's time for *you* to start believing that you can do it. Now go home and learn your lines! And if you don't tell your mother what happened here today, then I will."

Demi came home and told me everything, even the part that she needed to practice her lines three times a day until the next work session. I loved how Cathryn believed in her actors, and as a parent, I appreciated the way she pushed my girls to their limits and demanded that they do their best. When Demi showed up for the next work session, she impressed Cathryn with her comedic timing. "I'm proud of you." Cathryn beamed. "I knew you could do it." When Demi got in the car, her triumphant smile told me everything I needed to know.

The next day, Demi and I headed to Austin for the big audition. By then, we knew it was for Disney, which made us both excited and nervous. "Faith, not fear," Demi told me, repeating the line my sister Kathy had given her the night before.

"That's right," I told her. "And Aunt Kathy will be praying for you the entire time." At 2:00 p.m., we walked into the modest hotel listed on our page of instructions. Then we were directed to our own hotel room, where we filled out some paperwork. Once everyone who was auditioning was checked in, we all gathered in a large meeting space and waited for the process to begin. As the first few names were called, I watched each child as they were ushered to another room down the hall. They all looked confident and sure of themselves. *Oh, yes*, I mused, *let the games begin!*

Small groups of kids kept disappearing while we sat and waited. Two hours later, we were still waiting to be called. Demi's mantra of "faith, not fear" had disappeared as worry lines sprouted on her forehead. Doubt and discouragement were closing in. Even my faith was waning, but I refused to show it. *Why were they calling everyone except Demi?*

"They don't like me," Demi whispered.

"Now, you don't know that," I said. "Remember, faith, not fear."

We waited a few more minutes, and Demi tugged on my arm. "Mom," she gasped, "I'm sweating."

"It's okay," I told her. "You want some water?"

"No, Mom, I mean I'm *really* sweating," she said, lifting her arms.

My eyes went wide as I stared at two giant puddles of wetness seeping from her armpits to her waist. "Oh, dear," I said, trying not to sound alarmed. "Well, let's take care of that right quick. Come with me—I have an idea."

We ran down the hall back to our room and ducked inside. "Take off your shirt," I shouted, grabbing an iron and ironing board out of the closet. Sixty seconds later, I plunked that iron down on her yellow shirt until it sizzled. Demi stared, mesmerized by the action. When the shirt looked dry, I threw it back on Demi and we ran down the hallway, laughing. Just as we reentered the meeting room, we heard, "We'd like to see Demi and Tony next."

When she returned, Demi was all smiles. *Whew, at least she's happy with her performance!* An hour later, someone announced six names, including Demi's, and said, "Congratulations! You're the new cast for Disney's *As the Bell Rings*!" After much clapping and cheering, we went back to our room, but there wasn't much sleeping that night. The kids, including Seth Ginsberg from Cathryn's studio and Tony Oller, now a successful Columbia recording artist, all wanted to get to know their castmates. And we parents wanted to get to know each other as well. After all, we all had something in common now—recognition from Disney! It was a dream come true, and everyone wanted to savor the moment. It would be Demi's first flicker of network success. Selena, though, was quickly becoming a star.

CHAPTER TWENTY

"I was filled with a nervous excitement—I just knew we were going to get the call and off we'd go. But it didn't happen."

I was talking to Mandy in mid-January when I mentioned that our family wanted to give pilot season another try. Mitchell Gossett had been working with Jennifer Patredis at Kim Dawson Agency all year to send my girls on auditions, so we felt we'd have better luck this time around. I was sure 2007 would be a more successful year, but we still had to figure out logistics such as where we'd stay and how we'd pay for everything.

"Why don't you stay with us?" Mandy offered. "Selena is filming the first season of *Wizards of Waverly Place* in February, and we're renting an apartment in downtown Los Angeles." Stunned, I hesitated to say anything. "Come on, it'll be fun," she added.

We were all such good friends that it actually did sound like fun, so I agreed. I told her we'd leave a few days after she and Selena did. "We'll meet up with you at the loft," I promised. When Dallas booked the highest-paying voice-over job she'd ever gotten with

LeapFrog, we suddenly had the other half of our concerns figured out. *Thanks, God, looks like you want us to go!* But I knew there were a few other matters I needed to take care of, too.

"I'm still fighting depression," I confessed in confidence one more time to my doctor, "and now I'm also having anxiety attacks." When he asked about symptoms, I told him they were very physical. "I can't breathe, my palms get sweaty, and the back of my neck feels like it's on fire," I said, adding, "If I'm driving when it happens, I usually have to stop the car and get out. At home, I go to the garage and keep walking in circles until I feel better."

I left with two prescriptions: one for Prozac and another for Xanax. "Take the Prozac daily," he said, "but only use the Xanax when you feel like an attack is coming on."

The Prozac worked so well that I put the bottle of Xanax in my purse, hoping I'd never have to use it. The pills would be my secret. *No need to worry anyone over my shortcomings*, I reasoned. I wanted people to assume that I had everything under control.

Another matter that needed attention was renting a small U-Haul trailer to pull behind the Expedition. I was planning on taking only a few suitcases and some boxes of supplies for our six-week journey, but Demi insisted that she couldn't leave home without her full-size Yamaha keyboard. "I need it to keep writing," she told me. I also knew that if she got the chance to play for some big record-label executive, she'd do it. *You always need to be prepared, right?* So even though I'd never attached anything to the back of the truck, not even a bike rack, I was determined to help Demi transport that piano. When I called the local U-Haul dealership, they suggested the smallest trailer they carried.

"Well, hellooo," a young man greeted when I arrived. "Looks like it's your lucky day." I looked at him and shrugged my shoulders. "We didn't have the trailer you wanted," he continued, "so we're giving you the *huge* one at no extra charge!"

I stared at him numbly, forcing myself to smile. "Isn't it great?" he asked. But all I could think about was the panic rising inside me. *How could I possibly drive from Texas to California with* that *hitched to the back of the truck? How would I manage the freeways?* "Ah, yeah," I mumbled, "it'll be fine." Ever the proper southern lady, I wasn't going to argue with his generous offer.

When I showed the girls our trailer, I told them we might as well pack a few more items to take along or else our meager possessions were going to bounce around like BBs in a matchbox! I piled on extras of everything—Madison's toys, clothes, air mattresses, blankets, and a few more boxes of snacks and staples, carefully wedging everything around our original suitcases and the all-important Yamaha keyboard. When Eddie got home, he took one look at the driveway and shouted, "What's that?" He, too, was worried about how I'd handle the load, but when he calmed down, he assured me I'd do fine. "But *do not* speed under any circumstances," he insisted.

The next morning, we crawled out of the driveway, hoping to get halfway. Instead, the trip would take three days. Along the way, I sang "Route 66," an old Nat King Cole song made popular again by Asleep at the Wheel. "If you ever plan to motor west," I belted out, swaying back and forth like I was on a dance floor. "Get your kicks on Route 66." The Prozac was working its magic!

Sometimes the girls would humor me and hum along; some days they merely rolled their eyes. I kept on singing, partly to help me remember the cities we'd be looking for along the way. "Amarillo . . . Gallup, New Mexico, Flagstaff, Arizona, Winona, Kingman," I sang, ticking off each one as we passed by. By the time we finally reached the city of Barstow, California—our last overnight stay—I got a call from Mandy. "Oh, Dianna! I just pulled up to our loft, and I've made a terrible mistake," she sobbed. "It looked nice online but—there's a homeless man in front of our building pooping on the sidewalk!"

I glanced in the rearview mirror, noticing that the girls' eyes were wide with disbelief. "I'm sure it's fine," I laughed. "No matter what, we'll make the best of it—we just won't walk around after dark!" *How bad could it be?* I thought. *After all, we're talking about a city full of dreams, ambitions, and adventure.*

The next day, after driving through rain, snow, and fog, as well as LA's crazy freeways, I pulled up to the loft and thought I was the one who would burst into tears. The sight was shocking. Rows of cardboard shelters lined the sidewalks, and trash dotted the landscape like unappealing artwork. Mandy was right; we'd be living on the edge of civility, right where renovated downtown met bum condo city. We pinched our noses at the stench of urine and tried not to stare at the dazed individuals who were talking to themselves. But I couldn't stop wondering how many of those destitute people had come to LA in search of becoming stars just like us. *What had gone wrong?*

After Mandy came down, she pointed out where to park the trailer and invited us up to see our new home. That's when it sank in—a loft apartment meant *no bedrooms*! The six of us, thankfully all girls, would be sharing one giant room. The only door in the whole space was to the bathroom. My heart lurched a bit when I realized we'd have no privacy and no place of escape, especially since taking a walk around the block didn't seem like a good idea in the dark or the daytime. But none of that really mattered because in the end, the six of us would go on to share some of the happiest and most exciting weeks of our lives.

It took numerous trips back to the truck to unload our stuff. Thank God the elevator worked, because I'm not sure we could have managed to carry that keyboard up the flight of stairs. Once we blew up the air mattresses, we all claimed our spaces. By evening, I knew everything was going to be just fine. That first night, like the rest that followed, was like a giant slumber party. We danced, sang, told stories, cracked jokes, and laughed more than we had in years. Every evening there was something to talk about, because just as Selena started her filming schedule, my girls got busy with auditions.

One day on our way back from an audition in the heart of Hollywood, Demi and I were driving down the 101, near the Vine Street exit, when we passed the iconic thirteen-story tower that's home to Capitol Records. We both stopped talking and took in the sight. Although the structure was meant to resemble a stack of records, I thought the arched rooflines made it look more like a spaceship ready to take flight. One thing was certain: Ever since 1959, more than a few great artists had recorded there—people such as Frank Sinatra, the Beach Boys, and even Judy Garland. And that history didn't go unnoticed.

"Mom," Demi said, staring out the window, "do you think I'll ever get my break?" The uncertainty in her voice seared my heart.

She took a deep breath and sighed, "All I really want to do is sing. I don't care if I ever get to act—I just want to sing."

When I glanced over, I could see the pain on Demi's face as tears sprang from her eyes. A rush of compassion welled up inside me. I recognized the desire and longing in her voice and I understood her passion. All of it was an echo rising from the past of my own childhood. I also knew that her confidence was wavering. "You'll get there, Demi," I said. "I know you will."

The best part of that trip was using our down time to visit Selena on set at Hollywood Center Studios, just off Santa Monica Boulevard on North Las Palmas Avenue. It was our first chance to see what really goes on behind the scenes of a Disney production, and it was magical, especially since we were treated like family and got to hang out backstage. Most days you could find us in Selena's dressing room where we snapped selfies, listened to music, and talked for hours on end. Madison and I—the self-appointed snack-bearers—made copious trips to craft services, where we'd load up on food and drinks for everyone.

But our favorite part of every day was anticipating who might stop by and chat with us. Often it was Jennifer Stone and her mom, Christy, or David Henrie and his mom, Linda. It was both comforting and exciting to talk with other families in the industry. I suppose they made us feel more connected to the world we so desperately wanted to be a part of.

The atmosphere on the first night of live filming for *Wizards* was electric. We, like everyone else, were excited beyond belief, especially since our seats in the studio audience were just a few feet from the stage. "Look," I whispered to Demi, pointing to big-name Disney executives as they darted about the set. Lights flashed and last-minute directions hurled through the air. With only seconds to spare, the hive of activity grew more intense as swarms of people scurried on and off the stage, taking care of everything from switching out props to touching up makeup. When the director yelled, "Action!" the crescendo of activity stilled and a rush of adrenaline spilled over us, telling us we were in the right place, at the right time, to witness something special. And just like that, Selena, looking confident and beautiful, stepped into the spotlight.

When I glanced at Demi, I knew she was proud of her friend, but I also knew she was a bit wistful. After all, she had hoped for so long to be doing the same thing. Although acting was no longer her first priority, Demi understood how a television show with Disney Channel could be a stepping-stone to the music career she longed for. Shows such as *Hannah Montana* and *High School Musical* had been more than entertainment for us; they had inspired us to pursue a similar path. For Selena, it was unfolding right before our eyes.

Mandy, who could have been on the floor with her daughter, chose instead to sit with us in the audience. It was Mandy's way of reminding me that as a mom, you didn't have to be in the middle of everything to feel important. In between scenes, two comedians would come out in front of the audience, trying to keep everyone engaged. They told jokes, played games, and encouraged the crowd to make a lot of noise. These "green light" moments were full of raucous clapping and cheering, which kept us awake as the evening progressed. After several hours, someone even handed out pizza and candy to everyone. But the moment filming commenced, no one was allowed to make a sound, except for applause and laughter.

"Time for an *American Idol* singing contest," the comedians announced during one break. My eyes lit up and so did Demi's. No family in America had watched more episodes of that show than us, but when I looked at Demi to see if she would raise her hand, Demi's face told me she wouldn't. "I can't, Momma," she said. "This is Selena's big night, you know?" I reluctantly agreed, telling her that maybe they'd do it again another night. Mandy, though, had a different opinion.

"Demi, get up and sing," she urged. "Selena would love it!" Two seconds later, someone saw Demi's hand waving in the air and called her to the front.

"What's your name?" the comedian asked. Demi proudly answered and announced, "I'd like to sing 'Ain't No Other Man' by Christina Aguilera."

I held my breath because I knew what was coming. Demi had sung this song every day, every morning, and every night for the past few months.

"Heeyyy," Demi started, "I could feel it from the start . . . couldn't stand to be apart." Sheer joy spread across her face as the volume of her voice bounced across the stage.

One by one, heads started turning. Mouths hung open. And Selena started jumping up and down as she tugged on the sleeve of creator Todd Greenwald. I could read her lips as plain as day. "That's my best friend! That's my best friend!" she cried. The entire cast and crew, who were supposed to be on a break, including those Disney executives, remained anchored to the floor.

"Ain't no other man, it's true—ain't no other man but you!" she finished triumphantly. As her last note faded, the entire place burst into cheers and applause. Demi was beaming and so was Selena. "Well, that's gonna be hard to beat!" the comedian declared. We all laughed, not caring if she had won. Maybe she wouldn't hear anything right away, but I felt certain something would come of it. *When the time is right*, I reminded God, *let us know!*

We wouldn't have to wait long.

A few weeks after returning from pilot season, a series of events suggested that Demi's future path was starting to materialize. The first was a phone call from Dallas. She was sobbing so hard, I could barely understand her. At the time, Dallas was working at Buckle, a clothing store in our local mall, and my first thought was that she had been fired. "Mom," she bawled, "I was driving to work and listening to my playlist when one of Demi's recordings came on." Again, she started wailing. Eventually, she'd tell me that Demi was singing "I Can Only Imagine," a song released years earlier by MercyMe, a Christian rock band. The recording was one that Demi had made for one of Linda's showcases.

"I usually just skip over Demi's songs because I hear her singing all the time at home," Dallas explained, trying to regain her composure. "But I didn't this time, and as I listened, I suddenly had this vision." Again she quivered, fighting to catch her breath. "It was so real, so profound," she said. "Clear as day, I saw Eddie and

Demi seated at a table, and Demi was signing a record deal . . . Mom, this is really going to happen!"

Another sign from God? I wanted to believe so, but I wouldn't let myself get caught up in the moment. Not yet. Not even after Dallas shared that when the vision happened she was in a mass of traffic and when it ended she was in the parking lot at work with no recollection of having driven there. Dallas felt so strongly about what she had witnessed that she told me afterward if Demi didn't become a star, her faith would be shattered. "It was such a God moment," she insisted. "It had to be true."

About two weeks later, Demi was sent a script for *J.O.N.A.S.*, an acronym for *Junior Operatives Networking As Spies*, which was to be a new TV series for Disney, starring the Jonas Brothers. Stella, the character Demi was auditioning for, was a flirty teen ignorant of the Jonases' double lives and who secretly dated each of the brothers, then reported the details in her magazine column.

"These guys are really cute and talented," Demi confided to me, "and they're going to go far!" She had seen their music video "Year 3000," and she was super excited about the possibility of working with them. Dallas agreed to coach Demi and put her on tape. When Disney saw the tape, they called and said they wanted Demi to do a screen test. I was certain that Demi's breakthrough moment had finally arrived.

We waited and waited to hear directions about our trip to Los Angeles, only to hear the final instructions a little more than an hour before we had to leave for the airport. That's also when I learned that Disney had only purchased tickets for Demi and me, even though Madison needed to come with us. "Guess we'll be buying an extra ticket at the counter," I told Demi. But when we got to the airport, the line to the counter trailed out the door. Five minutes later, we were still standing in the same spot. The cloud of anxiousness hovering above me burst, drenching me with terrifying thoughts. I knew that if Demi missed this opportunity to get to Los Angeles, it would haunt her (and me) forever.

As the minutes ticked by and our scheduled departure drew closer, I couldn't take the stress any longer. Reaching into my purse, I pulled out that bottle of Xanax and popped one of the pills into my mouth. A few minutes later, when I finally reached the counter and purchased Madison's ticket, an airline official magically appeared and told us to follow him. Each step we took was faster than the last. Demi eventually started running, but I couldn't. Every footstep made me dizzy. When we got whisked to the front of the security line, my legs were so wobbly, I could barely stand. I held on to Demi and tried to ask her to watch Madison, but my words were slurred and garbled.

The last thing I remember hearing was Demi's voice. "My mother's not drunk," she insisted. "She took some new medicine, and I think that's what's wrong." To this day I don't remember passing through security or getting on the plane, nor do I remember climbing into a row of empty seats at the back of the plane while Demi and Madison took their seats toward the front. My deep sleep lasted until we landed in LA.

When I woke up, I was fine. After we got settled at Selena's loft, I checked in with my doctor, and he suggested that next time I only take half the dose. Thankfully, I wouldn't need it for a while.

The audition on the twenty-first floor of the Walt Disney

Company in Burbank was a blur. The morning after, as Demi and I sat waiting for the phone to ring in Mandy's loft, the experience still seemed surreal. Screen testing was as far as it goes in the audition process, and Demi had exceeded everyone's expectations, so we both felt optimistic. But that didn't make the waiting any easier. Sometimes we stared at the phone, sometimes at each other. But we didn't talk. We didn't eat. We barely breathed. Every thought got sucked into the vortex of what was about to happen. Our inertia bristled with the certainty that finally . . . after all this time . . . Disney was going to make Demi a star!

When the phone rang, I answered, grinning from ear to ear.

"Dianna," said Margo, the agent from CESD, "she didn't get the part."

I pulled the phone away from my ear and looked at it. *No way!* I thought. *She's just pulling my leg! I know she got the part!* So I smiled even broader. In fact, I was so sure that she was kidding, I told her, "No, no, no, Margo! Just tell me now. She got the part, right?"

But she hadn't. "I'm so, so sorry," Margo offered. "I really thought we had a good chance on this one." Our disappointment was raw and intense. It felt like someone had kicked me in the gut. For Demi, it was more like a knockout punch. She was standing next to me and seemed to know it was bad news from the start. I confirmed her fears when I shook my head no, and she promptly disappeared. Later, I found her in the gym upstairs, running on the treadmill and refusing to talk. But the disappointment in her eyes said it all.

Not thirty minutes later, Margo called me back. "Judy Taylor at Disney Channel wants to know, can you stay in town for a few more days?" she asked. "They have a couple of other projects they want Demi to read for."

After we agreed to stay, Margo promised to fax over some sides for Demi to study. Those sides, we'd learn, were for another Disney Channel Original Movie called *Camp Rock*. The script, written specifically for a young teenage girl who could sing *and* act, revolved around a camp for musically gifted teens where Mitchie, the main character, dreams of becoming a rock star. We'd learn the Jonas Brothers would also be in the movie. The other set of sides was for a television series titled *Sonny with a Chance*, a sitcom that followed the experiences of teenager Sonny Monroe, who becomes the newest cast member of her favorite live comedy TV show.

Demi read the sides for *Sonny* with Dallas, who decided a few cans of stew were needed. The scene involved a country girl who ducked her head into a pile of pig slop and then popped up exclaiming, "Umm! That's good!" The slimy, dark stew would add a bit of dramatic flair, and according to Dallas, would prove that Demi was willing to go all in, 100 percent, to get the role.

Off we went back to the Walt Disney Company in Burbank to read for both the movie and the TV series, and we took our cans of stew with us. Demi read for *Camp Rock* first; then she sang for the musical director. She nailed it, or at least it appeared that way as the musical director quickly whisked Demi off to meet a few more people. We thought it was a good sign, but we certainly knew that nothing was guaranteed. Besides, Demi still had to go through the actual audition in a few days.

After reading for *Camp Rock*, Demi switched gears and started reading for *Sonny with a Chance*. When it was time for the pig-slop scene, she politely asked to be excused. Upon her return, the group beamed, "Oh, you have props!"

"Yeah," she smiled, placing the bowl of stew in front of her. It made everyone curious. When she got to the right part, she dunked her face into the bowl and popped back up covered in brown slime. To everyone's delight, she had taken another tidbit of advice from Dallas and wedged a piece of meat in the gap between her front teeth. The room erupted in laughter. We hoped it was enough for her to get the part, but we also knew that Disney had weeks to make their decision.

Before we left Los Angeles, CESD also scheduled an audition for *Just Jordan* on Nickelodeon. Afterward, as darkness was descending on the city, we jumped in the car and realized that we hadn't eaten all day. "Let's stop at the first convenience store we see," I suggested. A block later, we hopped out of the car and made a mad dash toward the store, hoping to use the restroom and grab some food. Just as we were about to walk through the front door, Demi stooped over and picked something up off the ground.

"What is it?" I asked, as she held up a business card.

"Momma!" she cried, sounding breathless. "It says: ARE YOU READY?"

We both stopped and looked at each other. Neither of us uttered a sound, but we knew those words like they had been tattooed on our foreheads. *Are we getting closer?* I asked God. Demi tucked that card into her purse, and we walked inside, savoring the hope stirring inside of us.

———

Three days after we returned to Texas, I was puttering around in the kitchen while Demi was still sleeping upstairs. When the phone rang, I assumed it was my sister wanting to catch up on how our trip had gone. But it was a conference call from Mitchell and Margo. "Hold on," I said. "Let me get Demi, and I'll put you on speaker."

Demi, still a bit groggy, took a seat at the kitchen counter and clasped her hands tightly, as though she were praying. "Well," Margo started, "we have some news for you."

Demi, so nervous, could only whisper, "What?"

Together, Mitchell and Margo gleefully announced, "You're our new Mitchie for *Camp Rock*!"

There was no piercing wallop of joy, no scream of excitement. Demi went from zero to sixty in a heartbeat, and her only reaction was to burst into tears. But her face was radiant. And I was thrilled because my daughter was happy. Without a fear or worry about how it all would play out, we rode that wave of excitement for as long as we could. We knew that our big moment had finally arrived, because *Camp Rock* was expected to be the next *High School Musical*. Finally, after all the disappointments and all the sacrifices, Demi was on her way.

CHAPTER TWENTY-ONE

"Did we make mistakes along the way?
Yes, and they were ours to make and learn from."

The year 2007 continued to surprise us. Later that spring, Demi also got called back to LA to screen test for *Sonny with a Chance*. When we met with a small group of producers and writers for the show, Demi was awestruck by the posters hanging in their West Hollywood office.

"Look," she gasped, "There's *Big Momma's House* and *Blue Crush!*"

At that meeting, Sharla Sumpter Bridgett and Brian Robbins, founders of Varsity Pictures, wanted to know what kind of vision Demi had for her future. Not yet fifteen, my wide-eyed daughter didn't hesitate to answer. "Well," she giggled, "I want to have my own TV show and be a star like Miley and Selena." Her innocence and down-to-earth personality charmed them both.

Soon after she finished filming more episodes for *As the Bell*

Rings, Demi was offered the starring role as Sonny Monroe in *Sonny with a Chance*, which would air in August. By late September, she needed to be in Canada for the filming of *Camp Rock*. It seemed that once we signed with Disney, our lives were "Go! Go! Go!" The frantic pace made my anxiety issues return with renewed intensity. One saving grace was that we had a good lawyer who could help us sort through all the contracts we needed to sign.

The entertainment industry is riddled with people who are willing to take advantage of anyone who has earning potential. Blind trust isn't a good idea. We didn't know that; we simply got lucky. Thanks to a friend, we had gotten introduced to Jamie Young, with Ziffren Brittenham LLP, a law firm specializing in entertainment, long before Demi was ever offered a contract. Normally, you can't just walk in and get an attorney of that caliber without already having an established career, but Jamie decided to roll the dice and take a chance on us. She later told us, "I didn't sign you because of Demi's talent per se, but because I really liked the two of you." Her counsel and advice would save us thousands of dollars, not to mention the numerous headaches and anxiety attacks she prevented by helping me to understand legal jargon.

But even with Jamie's help, my nerves were spiraling out of control. Now that the stakes were higher, my fears about Demi getting fired or making a mistake intensified. Nowhere was that more evident than when Demi, Madison, and I flew to Canada in the fall for the filming of *Camp Rock*. Eddie stayed behind to work at the Ford dealership, and Dallas was out in LA, once again trying to launch her acting career.

The first few weeks in Canada were pure luxury, as we stayed at The Grand Hotel in downtown Toronto. Every window, marble tile, and brass fixture gleamed and sparkled like jewels. Although I wanted to absorb all that calm beauty, I couldn't. When I was on set, my nerves were even worse.

Two scenes early on were shot at a nearby multilevel house. Each morning, I fretted about showing up late. "Get up! Get up!" I hollered to Madison and Demi. "We need to go! Now! Keep moving!" The giant ticking clock inside my brain kept reminding me that tardiness was grounds for being fired. I became obsessive about the smallest of details: When to go to bed? What to wear? How to interact with people? And my mind was constantly awhirl with strange fears about people talking badly about Demi and about making mistakes that would be grounds for dismissal.

Things got off to a rocky start on day one when all the moms were sitting outside on the lawn of the big house as they filmed the music video inside for the end of the film. It was typical Hollywood, as scenes are rarely filmed in chronological order. The heat that day was unbearable—and so were the bees.

We're not talking about a few stragglers, either. Dozens and dozens of bees swarmed around us, sometimes dive-bombing into our faces and at times bouncing off our legs and arms. It was terrifying. When people started getting stung, real panic set in, because I've been afraid of bees my whole life. (I actually keep a can of bee and wasp spray in every room of our Texas home—the kind that can shoot twenty feet in the air so you don't have to get close to kill them.) Staying still, like everyone suggested, just wasn't possible. I desperately wanted to make a good impression that day, but I kept jumping up and running away. It felt like I was standing inside the gates of hell without an escape route.

Nothing about that first day resembled the picture in my head of how I thought the experience would unfold. There were no glamorous photo ops, no bursting-with-pride moments. Only sheer torture. I wondered what I had gotten myself into. *Was this what we had worked so hard to attain?*

That night as I relived the horror, my hands and body still twitching, I picked up my bottle of Xanax and gulped down another dose. That tiny bottle of solace was quickly becoming indispensable, especially since the next day offered its own setbacks.

This time, I was on set inside the house with Demi as they prepared to film a scene in the kitchen. It was the part in the movie where Demi, as Mitchie Torres, begs her mom, Connie (played by María Canals Barrera), to go to Camp Rock for the summer. It was a very exciting moment, and I happily struck up a conversation with the hair-and-makeup people as we all stood off to the side waiting for the action to begin. The more I absorbed the reality of the moment—the fact that I was witnessing my daughter making a film, a dream that had seemed so unattainable at times—the more talkative I got.

"Roll set," the director yelled, which stopped me in my tracks. I knew from all the commercials my girls had made that once the camera starts rolling, silence was expected. No one ever, *ever*, interrupts filming because it's considered very bad etiquette. Almost instantly, I realized that Madison was no longer by my side.

"Where's Madison?" I mouthed to everyone around me. Heads turned as everyone started searching. We didn't have to look long. At the sound of the director's voice, my blood ran cold.

"Well, hello, Madison," he exclaimed. My five-year-old, all eyes and big smile, was delighted to be on camera as she unexpectedly stepped into frame. Although everyone was laughing, I was mortified.

Oh, my God, this is it! They're going to fire Demi over my mistake!

That night I tossed and turned, replaying the whole day in my head. *How could I have been so inattentive?* Once again, I reached for another Xanax, telling myself that I'd put my bottle of pills away once things calmed down.

Filming eventually moved to Kilcoo Camp in Minden, Ontario. Our accommodations, a small group of cabins surrounded by a delightful paddleboat pond and a pristine golf course, were at Delta Pinestone Resort, about fifteen minutes down the road. It turned out to be a wonderful change of scenery, but it didn't start out that way. This time it was the check-in experience that left me rattled.

Usually, I handed the front desk my debit card, and they swiped it to cover a small amount of incidentals, as Disney paid for everything else.

"That's $3,500," the woman said as she handed back my card.

"What?" I protested. "That can't be right!" When I explained that I wasn't paying for the room, she apologized and said, "I'll make sure you get a credit in a few days."

"No," I insisted, "you need to put that credit through right now," all the while imagining that our mortgage payment and a slew of other checks were about to bounce. There wasn't that much extra cash in our account.

"Sorry," she said again, "but it takes a few days to sort these things out."

Suddenly the room started to spin around me. While my neck got hot, my hands grew sweaty. I knew I needed to reach Eddie to warn him, but we were so isolated that I wasn't sure my phone would work. That realization made my throat tighten so severely, I felt like I was choking. *I have no choice*, I decided, running to our cabin to gulp another pill.

From that moment forward, Xanax became my coping strategy for every terrifying thought and every difficult circumstance that we encountered. And trying to look perfect, act perfect, and be perfect all the time made every day stressful. There was no room for error in my mind—we couldn't be late, couldn't make mistakes, couldn't get into trouble. We were working for Disney, after all, and we had a responsibility to uphold the company's image. It was just the fuel my brain needed to spiral out of control.

What I failed to notice was that Demi's mental state was just as fragile as mine. Signs, such as her forty-eight-hour binges of not sleeping to write songs and her fluctuating moods, went unaddressed because I brushed them off as normal teenage behavior. I missed so many chances to help her. But I needed help, too.

Years later, after Demi came out of treatment, I was cleaning our Texas home and found an old book. When I opened the cover to see if it was important, I realized it was Demi's diary from that very time when she had filmed *Camp Rock*. The page I opened to told me that my daughter's struggles were far greater than I knew. Each and every sentence confirmed that she battled many of the same issues that I did. She struggled with anxiety, just like me. She had eating issues, just like me. And she worried about people's opinions, just like me. One sentence in particular crushed my heart:

"Nobody loves a fat rock star. Guess I'll have to starve myself so people will like me."

Thankfully, there were lots of sweet moments at Kilcoo Camp to offset the nerve-wracking ones, especially when Eddie and Dallas came to join us for a few weeks. It felt wonderful to have my family together again, even though Dallas, who had been in a car accident right before her arrival, was constantly complaining about her arm hurting. "I'm sure it's just sore," I reassured her. "You probably just need to let it heal." I suggested we take Madison and Frankie (the Jonases' youngest son) on a hike the next time I wasn't needed on set.

On every hike, we got to witness a budding friendship between the two kids. As we explored trails and climbed boulders, Dallas and I also got to see their imaginations go wild. Some days, the pair even pretended to act in their own movies. One afternoon while collecting rocks, the two decided they should sell them back at the camp. But before they set up shop, Frankie directed Madison to "wash the rocks in the creek." Once their display was ready, people started lining up to buy their wares. Madison, though, quickly grew bored. A few afternoons later when someone asked if they were still selling rocks, Frankie hung his head and sighed, "No, we aren't because Madison doesn't care about the business anymore." Madison, in turn, pouted her lips and whined, "All he does is work, work, work while I stay here and clean the rocks!" Dallas and I looked at each other and burst out laughing. They might have been the two youngest people around, but they acted like an old married couple.

Those delightful moments never seemed to last very long. While on set with Madison a day or so later, I couldn't find Dallas. When I asked if anyone had seen her, the medic chimed in, "I sent her to the hospital."

"What?" I cried. "We're in a foreign country, in the middle of nowhere, and she doesn't even have an insurance card with her!" Apparently, Dallas's arm was still bothering her, and when she had asked the medic to take a look, he quickly assessed that it was broken. I was mortified, not to mention that I was also sure she would disappear into a health-care system that would result in thousands of dollars of bills and subpar care. In the end, Dallas healed just fine, but I berated myself for days, which made it that much easier to justify taking more Xanax.

Once filming wrapped up at the end of October, we headed back to Los Angeles, where Disney put us in the Sheraton Universal, right next to Universal Studios, until we could tie up loose ends with *Camp Rock*. All the kids were excited about celebrating Halloween together.

"Why don't you come over to our place and celebrate with us?" Denise Jonas suggested. "We can hang out."

At the time, the Jonas family was renting a home in Toluca Lake, a neighborhood that sits next to Universal Studios. Every street seemed to have at least one resident movie star. I was in awe that Miley Cyrus lived down the street and Marc Cherry, the creator of *Desperate Housewives*, lived across the street. *Could there be a more idyllic place to live?* And, the entire neighborhood was a popular spot for trick-or-treating. I mean REALLY popular. Hundreds of kids from all over LA came to the door that night.

We didn't see much of the older kids, who scooted off to do their own candy collecting decked out as the cast from *High School Musical*. Demi went as Gabriella, while Joe was Troy. Meaghan Martin joined them, representing Sharpay Evans, and Anna Maria Perez de Taglé donned a short, blond wig and dressed as Sharpay's brother, Ryan.

The whole night had a mystical quality about it, especially later when groups of girls camped outside and started singing the boys' latest hits. I couldn't help but think that the Jonases were the luckiest people alive to be living in such an amazing neighborhood. Demi, at that point, wasn't so recognizable, and there was no guarantee that she'd ever get as big as the Jonas Brothers. But that weekend, I had a glimpse of what Disney superstardom might entail, and it was amazing.

We went back to visit the boys a few more times that week, and each time I got a little more envious. One afternoon as I strolled around the block, I stopped at a corner property that caught my eye. Every detail about the Mediterranean-style home—the palm trees by the front door, the peach-colored stucco, the fountain that sounded like falling rain—made me wistful. Three stories tall, it was magnificent. *How crazy would it be to live in a place like that?* I mused. But I doubted we'd ever have the money to afford something so grand. *Besides*, I told myself, *I don't want to live in Los Angeles—my home is in Texas!*

Though I had to admit that having fans show up at your front door sounded pretty exciting.

CHAPTER TWENTY-TWO

"I stood there, holding Madison's hand and fighting
back tears, as I watched them walk away. I wasn't
even sure how I was supposed to get to the airport."

Why were we doing what we were doing? That was the question I had asked myself over and over again through the years. My answer had always been about the future. "I'm helping my kids reach their dreams," I'd say. Or, "I'm giving my kids the opportunity to do what they want to do." But as 2008 loomed in front of us, the future was suddenly very present. Stardom, for Demi, was within reach. It made me remember something I had joked about years earlier. "When you're all famous," I had laughed with my girls, "we'll be like *The Beverly Hillbillies* and move into a big ole Hollywood mansion and become millionaires!"

Of course, fame and fortune weren't the main reasons we had worked so hard. Love and passion were huge factors in the equation, too. But anyone who denies that the financial rewards of success aren't part of the allure of stardom is probably not being honest. Especially because so much time, money, and effort need to be invested along the way. Yet, it was the rush of pride and joy that came after Demi filmed *Camp Rock* that nearly swallowed me whole. It was more powerful than I expected. And the way my daughter handled all of her new responsibilities made me beam even brighter. Life was good, exciting, and wonderful.

As we eagerly anticipated the release of the movie trailer, set to air on Disney Channel at the end of January, a giant wave of satisfaction washed over me. It was as if all those years of believing in my kids' talents were finally being validated, and it was intoxicating. I had nibbled at the feeling before, such as when Dallas booked her first commercial and when Demi booked a guest role on *Prison Break*. But Demi starring in a movie was a whole new level of euphoria. It consumed me at first, making me feel so good, so special, so proud. I'd soon learn that not every aspect of stardom felt so wonderful.

Despite my hopes that success would usher in a carefree existence, every high moment on our radar screen seemed to be followed by a low one. Just as we started counting down the days until we'd see the *Camp Rock* trailers, Eddie got laid off at Five Star Ford in North Richland Hills. He'd been there for ten years. It didn't seem fair, but since he was suddenly free, Eddie decided to travel with Demi, Madison, and me back to Los Angeles for a few days of meetings in early February.

Mandy and Selena, who were now renting a home in Studio

City, graciously offered to let us stay at their place while they were out of town, which made Madison giddy with excitement because she'd get to play with Mandy's four large dogs that she adored. For her, it would be a vacation. For the rest of us, it would be more work than pleasure as we tried to work out the details of Demi's future.

One of those details involved management. Eddie and I had done an amazing job of getting Demi to this point, but now it was time for someone else with better contacts and connections in the entertainment industry to propel our daughter's career forward. Just fielding phone calls about press interviews, photo shoots, and tour dates, as well as trying to locate the right scripts for future movie projects and television shows, would have kept us tied up all day long. We knew it was time to turn over the reins to someone who could handle all the details. "Interview at least three companies before you make a decision," our attorney advised.

Eddie took the lead and met with a few music producers, then scheduled meetings with management firms. "Now that I'm no longer working at Five Star Ford," Eddie had suggested before we left Texas, "I can help manage Demi. After all, I have the management experience; I just don't have the contacts."

The idea resonated with both of us, especially considering that Eddie wouldn't come to the table empty-handed since he had a master's degree in finance. It also meant at least one of us would be with Demi as her schedule expanded, and that was important to me. As a parent, Eddie could help protect our daughter from working too much and succumbing to teenage pressures on the road, while giving me time to focus on Dallas's and Madison's needs at home. I'd continue to help Demi when I could, offering to be with her when she was doing television and movie projects. But I figured Eddie could handle the music end of things. And, if Eddie was part of management, we'd also be able to draw a salary to help pay the bills—something that seemed only fair since we essentially had been managing our kids and paying all their business-related expenses for more than a decade. "Why should someone else reap all the benefits from our work over the years?" we asked ourselves. Our plan, though, wasn't heartily endorsed.

"I want to be part of the team," Eddie said as we sat at the table for our first meeting.

"Of course," the man replied, "parents are *always* part of the team, and we appreciate their feedback."

"No, you don't understand," Eddie insisted. "I mean I want to be part of *your* management team and co-manage my daughter with you."

His answer was swift and firm. "Well, that's not going to happen," he scoffed. So we left and tried again, only to hear similar sentiments. Letting parents get so involved wasn't common practice.

On February 12, we went to dinner with Phil McIntyre, then twenty-five, who owned Philymack Inc., and Kevin Jonas Sr., who ran The Jonas Group. Together, they both co-managed the Jonas Brothers, along with Wright Entertainment Group. We had met the pair on the set of *Camp Rock*, where they both had expressed interest in managing Demi and putting her on tour with the boys. They also seemed open to the idea of parents being involved. Eddie was especially drawn to Phil, who, as he put it, "was full of piss and vinegar." The young manager's energy and vision were appealing.

As we ate dinner that night, it became clear that someone finally understood our desires and concerns. Phil and Kevin Sr. both had an appreciation for teamwork, and before the evening was over, we came to an agreement that involved Demi going on tour with the boys that summer and Eddie helping to co-manage her career. It was an answer to our prayers.

The next day, sitting at Mandy's kitchen table, we signed the papers for Demi's record deal with Hollywood Records, which had been a result of her meeting with Bob Cavallo, chairman of Disney Music Group at the time, in his impressive office. After Demi played her original songs for him on her Ovation guitar, he was sold. Before we left, he told Demi, "I'm going to give you the same hug that I gave Hilary Duff and Miley Cyrus when they left this office." It was a day that wildly exceeded our expectations.

We tried to imagine what we were getting ourselves into, but none of us really knew. There wasn't much time to think about it, either. On Valentine's Day, which also was Eddie's birthday, we met Phil and Kevin Sr. at Demi's photo shoot, scheduled with one of the teen magazines.

It was all smiles and handshakes until Phil uttered a few instructions. "The tour bus is swinging by after Demi is finished—we'd like her to come on board and join us for a while," he said. "She needs to feel what it's like to be part of the group, and it'll give her time to start writing new songs."

Of course, we had talked about Demi going on tour, and I knew it would take place someday, but I had no idea that it would happen so soon. Every maternal fiber within me suddenly felt stretched to the breaking point.

"Now?" I choked. "Today?" As everyone around me nodded, my hands started to tremble. I watched Demi climb on board, pushing back every fear and tear clawing at my composure. The instant those bus doors closed, my world changed forever—and so did Demi's. *My baby girl is gone*, I moaned. *She's only fifteen—and she took Eddie with her.*

Suddenly everything was upside down. For years, it had been me running off to LA, telling Eddie that we'd see him in a few weeks. Now my husband was leaving and Demi was by his side, not mine. Don't get me wrong, there was plenty of joy and excitement, but my heart felt torn and bruised. I no longer had my finger on the pulse of my daughter's life, and it felt odd. And wrong. Everything was off-kilter, and I struggled to feel safe.

That's when I realized I hadn't really thought this part of the journey through. *Saying good-bye wasn't supposed to happen until she went off to college*, I railed. *I don't even know how Madison and I are supposed to get to the airport from here!*

I cried all the way home to Texas.

Back in Colleyville, I clung to the safety of routines. Dallas was still auditioning and taking lessons from Cathryn and so was Madison. And I focused on reuniting with Demi in March, just a few weeks away, when we'd both head to Puerto Rico for the filming of *Princess Protection Program*, another Disney Channel Original Movie starring both Demi and Selena. The movie was projected to be a success, and a year later when it was released, it was, even winning a Teen Choice Award. But that spring, all I cared about was reconnecting with my daughter.

Shortly before I left for Puerto Rico, Eddie called and filled me in on Demi's schedule. "They're thinking Demi should do a small solo tour in June," he said, "and then join the Jonas Brothers on their Burnin' Up Tour in July." The more we talked, the more I began to realize my daughter needed more than Eddie's guidance in the days ahead. She'd need some female companionship, too. Eddie would be great at assisting with tour dates and recording contracts, and I was sure he'd even give Demi a boost of confidence when she needed it. But who was going to help my daughter change outfits in a hurry? Who was going to help when her mascara got smudged? Who was going to hug her and not let go when things got rocky?

I knew those things were important, too. So I called Lisa and offered her a full-time job. "You'll be part chaperone, part assistant, part companion, and part substitute mother," I told her. "But you've known her since birth, so who could possibly be more qualified than you?" It was a lot to ask, but Lisa agreed to step into the role, even though it meant she'd have to quit her job and give away her two cats. She promised to start in June, when Demi went on tour.

I raced off to Puerto Rico feeling like the future seemed a little more secure. Madison came, too, and Eddie met us on set. Our little family reunion, minus Dallas, lasted several weeks. During that time, I also spent a lot of time with Mandy. Sometimes we stood side by side on set, and some days we lounged by the pool exchanging girl talk. We also watched our daughters become as close as sisters, and at times, just as ornery. One afternoon, Demi and Selena started fighting so fiercely that Mandy ordered them to retreat to their trailer, hoping they could settle their argument in private. Instead, the volume of their dispute only escalated. "HELP!" she texted me, "I don't know how to stop the screaming and yelling."

"Leave them alone," I assured her. "I've seen this a million times with Dallas and Demi. Let them work it out. If we try to intervene, it'll just get worse."

Sure enough, they got past it and came out of that trailer hugging and laughing.

About midway through filming, Demi needed to fly to New York City for the weekend because Disney was hosting an executive meeting where they wanted to introduce Demi to everyone on the team. As part of the event, she would sing "This Is Me" from *Camp Rock* to some of the most influential people in the corporation.

Because it was a late-night event that revolved around a lot of socializing, Lisa agreed to fly to Puerto Rico to watch Madison so Eddie and I could fully enjoy the weekend. Judy Taylor planned to accompany us on our flight, while Gary Marsh, who, at the time, was president of entertainment at Disney Channels Worldwide, told us he'd meet us in New York. The thought that I'd be sitting for several hours next to Judy—the woman in charge of talent for Disney—made me queasy. *What would we talk about?* As it turned out, that trip together would cement our friendship for years to come.

Our small posse of four descended on the island airport early in the morning, armed with jittery excitement. We all sensed the importance of the New York event, and everyone had forgone casualwear for dressier attire. Judy and I were both wearing dress boots with high heels, and all of us pulled small suitcases. As we milled about waiting to board the plane, someone suddenly announced that the departure gate had changed. Off we went, running to another wing of the terminal. *Clip-clop! Clip-clop!* Judy and I sounded like a team of mules chugging toward a barn. "Oh, well," I laughed. "A girl's gotta do what a girl's gotta do!"

Just as we arrived at the new boarding area, another announcement told us to head to another gate. Off we went again, this time even faster. Departure was now imminent, and if we missed our flight, we'd never make it to New York in time for the evening's event. Everyone understood the urgency and decided a full-out sprint was in order. Eddie took the lead, shouting, "This way!" Demi, shaking her head in disbelief, ran beside me, while Judy and I *clip-clop*ped across the linoleum floor like high-stepping Arabian horses. The sound of our boots was deafening, making everyone on the sidelines a bit curious. When yet a third change was announced, we made a U-turn and headed back toward a hallway we had already passed. That's when Judy suddenly looked like she was training for a marathon. She swooshed past all of us in a heartbeat. As I struggled to keep up, my footsteps thudded even louder. The whole scenario was surreal. Then it hit me: *This lady in front of me is mega-important to Disney, but right now we're just two ladies in heels trying to make our flight and looking ridiculous.* That insight finally relaxed my anxiety.

As we fastened our seat belts on our connecting flight, the stewardess came on the loudspeaker to give instructions. The trouble was no one could understand a word she was saying. Her accent made every syllable sound like gibberish.

That was it. Judy and I took one look at each other and busted up laughing. And we couldn't stop. The entire morning had been too weird and too stressful, and we simply lost control. Our shoulders shook. Our lungs heaved. And our stifled hilarity sounded like sobs. By the time the plane took off, my cheeks hurt from laughing so hard.

That trip was something Judy and I would talk about for years, and it was just the comic relief I needed to calm my nerves. Maybe it was what Demi needed, too, because that night when she sang in front of all those high-powered executives, she brought the house down. It was the perfect ending to a most unusual day. But I vowed I'd never wear heels in an airport again. And I haven't.

Once filming ended in Puerto Rico, I returned to Texas, packed a few bags, and raced off to Florida with Madison, where we met Eddie and Demi for the Disney Games, a fund-raiser for several children's charities, including UNICEF and Make-A-Wish Foundation, that featured various team competitions at the Walt Disney World Resort. The Jonas Brothers were there, too. Although Demi's schedule was quickly becoming a whirlwind, that particular trip was like a weeklong party, and the festive atmosphere did us all good. Disney put us up in a hotel in Animal Kingdom, and we even had time for typical family activities, such as riding rides and watching fireworks. The most thrilling thing for me was finally getting to see Demi perform in front of a large audience. There was only one sour note the entire week, and it happened at dinner one night.

We were waiting for our food to arrive when my phone rang. "Probably Dallas," I said. But it wasn't; it was her boyfriend.

"I don't know what to do," he bellowed. "Dallas took off to get cocaine from her dealer, and she's not answering her phone!"

The news stunned me. *My daughter? Was he serious?* "Please," I begged, "go stop her. We're too far away to do anything."

All night I thought about Dallas, trying to remember if I had seen any signs of drug use. I hadn't. The only thing that was out of the ordinary was that she had dropped a bunch of weight rather quickly. I didn't think it was related to cocaine use. Then again, what mother really wants to believe her daughter is into drugs? Sure, there were lots of nights when Dallas stayed out late, but she was twenty and could come and go as she pleased. I couldn't recall ever smelling alcohol on her breath or seeing her eyes look glassy.

Maybe it was my desire to avoid conflict or maybe it was what most parents do when they see dangerous signs of behavior in their kids, but I was all too willing to rationalize that my daughter was fine. Besides, in my mind we needed to be the perfect family or Disney wouldn't continue to work with Demi. No, I decided, I couldn't really pinpoint anything specific about drug use, so I wasn't going to accuse my daughter of something that potentially wasn't true. And even if she was using, I figured it wasn't anything more than a phase she was going through. When I got home, I sat down with Dallas and told her that I didn't think she was using drugs but if she was, she needed to stop. "I'm not using drugs," she scoffed, telling me exactly what I wanted to hear.

That's how little I understood about addiction.

Right before Demi started rehearsals for her minitour, I got a phone call from Linda Henrie. We had stayed in touch ever since our days on set for *Wizards*, where I had learned she was a manager in the acting business.

"I just saw an audition notice that would be perfect for Madison," she exclaimed. "It's to play Eva Longoria's daughter on *Desperate Housewives*."

Right, like we have a shot at that! I thought.

After Linda sent me the sides, I sat down and read through the lines. So did Madison. The scene involved Gaby, played by Eva, who discovers both of her children inside a closet eating Twinkies and then proceeds to shame them. I didn't like the drift of the script. One of Gaby's lines—"Skinny girls get husbands, and fat girls get jobs."—left me with a bad feeling. I certainly didn't want my daughter to be labeled as fat.

"Just not sure I like the content," I told Linda afterward, "so I think we'll pass on this one."

Madison was disappointed, but we put the script aside and the two of us headed to Hersheypark, an amusement park in Pennsylvania, where Demi was kicking off her first solo tour. All of the venues on the tour were small stages at either amusement parks or House of Blues locations. Because *Camp Rock* hadn't come out yet, we decided we should make flyers and distribute them inside the park to encourage people to show up. I knew Demi would feel bad if she had to face empty seats. Lisa, already working for us, said she'd help with the flyers and tend the merchandise booth after the show. Demi wasn't a headliner yet, so garnering some excitement about her was all on us. Or so we thought.

The park was packed with families that June day, and we congratulated ourselves for having the foresight to make flyers. But no one would take any. As the sun rose higher in the sky and the heat became unbearable, we doubled our efforts to get a few takers, even resorting to begging. With my hair drooping and mascara melting, I doggedly followed anyone who tried to walk around us.

"Would you please come to see Demi Lovato?" I pleaded, thrusting flyers in their faces. When several people rolled their eyes and shrugged their shoulders, I felt I had to speak up for my daughter. "You know," I pointed out, "she's Disney's newest star—the one who's in *Camp Rock*!"

None of it made a difference. In fact, families started walking farther and farther around us. After an hour, my confidence was shattered. As a smiling grandmother ambled by, I figured she was my last shot. "You probably don't want to go to this show, but here's a flyer anyway," I sighed. But even she walked away empty-handed. I knew then that our efforts were meaningless. "I'm never doing this again," I whined to Lisa. "I just can't take the rejection. Besides, it's too damn hot!"

As Lisa and I walked back to the stage, we contemplated how to break the news to Demi that no one was coming to her show, which is why we were astounded when we rounded the bend to the amphitheater to see several hundred people waiting to take their seats. The second show drew an even larger crowd. Apparently, there were Disney Channel fans in the park that day; they just weren't wandering anywhere near Lisa or me. It was such a relief!

Soon after Madison and I returned home from Hersheypark, another set of sides arrived from CESD. Again, the role was for Eva Longoria's daughter on *Desperate Housewives*. This time, though, Juanita's lines were sassier and more confident, suggesting that the character, although still a bit chubby, was happy with herself and willing to dish it back to anyone who criticized her. I liked the new direction and thought it was important that the character was willing to stand up and say that she liked herself, even though she wasn't perfect like her mother wanted her to be. That message was one I could let my daughter embrace.

But any role with weight issues is touchy, so I took a seat on one of the steps to our staircase and patted the space next to me, asking Madison to sit down. "We need to talk about this," I said.

"Mom, please let me do this," she begged. "Let me try." But I still had misgivings. I pointed out the changes in the script and what had stayed the same. Then we discussed how fans might respond to Juanita's role.

"Maybe you should wait for the next script that comes along," I suggested. But my six-and-a-half-year-old daughter was insistent.

"Pleeeaaase!" she whined again. "Let me try. . . . I can handle it. I promise." But I wasn't ready to concede. "You don't understand," she continued, arguing like a grown-up. "I think this can happen for me!" The more I tried to talk her into waiting for another script to come along, the more she begged to be put on tape. "Please let me try. I have a real shot at this," she insisted.

I doubted that she did, but I went to Dallas and asked if she'd put her on tape. The two worked on the sides together for an hour before Dallas filmed her. That evening the tape was on its way to LA, and once again, we kept our fingers crossed that someone would watch it.

At 10:00 a.m., two days after mailing the tape, Pedro from

CESD called. "How fast can you get here?" he asked. "The audition is Monday morning." He also told me it was a mix-and-match, which meant they'd be putting various people together to read scripts, looking to see whose chemistry worked best together.

"Pedro," I sighed, "it's Friday, and you're telling me to find a flight that will get me in LA before Monday morning. That's going to cost about three thousand dollars!"

"I know," he said, "but it'll be worth it."

"Well, I'm not going to waste that kind of money unless you can guarantee that they're not going to take one look at Madison and dismiss her because she's too tall or too old for the part," I insisted. "So right now, you need to show her picture to everyone and call me back."

A few minutes later, Pedro was back on the phone. Again, he asked, "How soon can you get here?"

Madison and I left that Sunday morning and walked into the audition on Monday only to meet a young girl who acted like the part was already hers. She told us she knew the director because they had worked together before. I tried not to stew about the wasted money, as Madison tried not to act disappointed. "Let's make the best of it and have a good time," I shrugged, hoping to lighten the mood. "After all, we're in LA!"

When Demi's tour bus pulled into our driveway about a week later in early July, the lingering sting of that disappointing trip to LA had already passed. I ran out and snapped photos of Demi in front of her bus like she was going to the prom.

"This is amazing," I squealed when I hopped on board, giving Demi a hug. The bus was far fancier than anything I had ever been on during my career, which made me swell with pride. My plan was to catch Demi's show in Oklahoma, then fly back home. Madison had decided to stay behind and go fishing with her cousins, which meant I'd have Demi all to myself. Just as we started rolling out of the driveway, my phone rang.

"Congratulations!" Pedro shouted. "Madison got the role of Juanita!"

I was speechless. Stunned. And blissfully unaware of the changes about to happen in our lives. I hung up and immediately called Madison, who seemed way too calm about the news. "Madison," I asked, "do you understand what I'm telling you?"

"Nooo," she said. When I blurted out, "You got the part," she responded as nonchalantly as Demi had when she had gotten the *Barney* role. "Oh, cool," Madison replied. "I'm gonna go fishing now." *How can you be so calm?* I thought.

For the next hour, I went over Madison's contract with our attorney and CESD on a conference call. Most of what they said, though, sailed right over my head because all I could hear was this inner voice exclaiming, *Eva Longoria's daughter! Eva Longoria's daughter!*

But I did hear Pedro say, "You're going to need a place to live in LA."

"Oh, no, no, no," I insisted. "We'll stay at our house in Texas and fly out as needed."

Then our attorney jumped in. "Dianna, you don't understand," she said. "You have to be on set by six a.m. most mornings."

"You mean this isn't just a few episodes?" I asked.

"No," Pedro explained, "Madison could be part of the cast for the next several years. We'll get you both a room at the Oakwood for the first month until you can find a place of your own."

And that was that. "Looks like we're moving to Hollywood," I stuttered to Demi.

"Well, you were going to come out in September anyway for the filming of *Sonny with a Chance*," she said, like it was no big deal.

But I was trembling inside. I could feel everything starting to spin faster and faster. I clasped my hands together and gave myself a pep talk. *You can do this! Remember, mind over matter!* Doubting my resolve, I casually reached for my purse and checked to see if my bottle of Xanax was still tucked inside. *Buckle up*, the voice in my head blared. *You're about to take the ride of your life—ARE YOU READY?*

At that moment, I wasn't.

The Hollywood Years

JULY 2008—SEPTEMBER 2014

"It's beauty in the struggle, ugliness in the success,
Hear my words or listen to my signal of distress . . ."

—"LOVE YOURZ" BY J. COLE

CHAPTER TWENTY-THREE

"I liked having people look at us with envy, imagining that they were thinking, 'Oh, they must have the perfect life!'"

"Mom, look!" Madison gasped.

My wide-eyed daughter was mesmerized by the arrival of Eva Longoria. It was a little after 6:00 a.m. on the first day of filming *Desperate Housewives*, although at that hour everyone was just hanging out in a trailer at base camp in the Universal lot, awaiting the day's scripts. Eva, wrapped in a fluffy robe and wearing Uggs, sat nearby in a tall director's chair doing a sudoku puzzle, while Madison stared in adoration. As she continued to gaze without flinching, I grew more uncomfortable.

"Psst! Come over here," I quietly urged, though Madison refused to listen. "Now," I said, a bit louder. Still, she continued her vigil. Finally, I went over and whispered, "We have to give her some space." Heck, I wanted to stare, too, but I couldn't let go of my need to be the perfect stage mom. "Okay," Madison reluctantly agreed.

We had arrived in Los Angeles within a week of Pedro's phone call. It was mid-July of 2008, and my little girl was excited to begin her Hollywood experience. From the moment we stepped off the plane, ABC provided us with everything we needed—a car, executive housing at the Oakwood (which came completely furnished with everything from sofas and televisions to dishes and towels!), and day sheets telling us what we needed to do and where we needed to be each morning. I had to admit, all the pampering and attention made me more receptive to moving so far from home.

At first Madison's schedule was rather light, mostly getting fitted for wardrobe and having some pictures taken, so we spent nearly every free moment binge-watching past episodes of *Desperate Housewives*. We laughed and giggled, "oohed" and "aahed," and fast-forwarded through the sections that weren't appropriate for young kids, all in an effort to get caught up on the storylines that had evolved over the past four seasons. It was too early to determine how big of a role my daughter would have on the show, but that didn't stop me from imagining that she'd become as famous as Eva Longoria. And it didn't stop me from fantasizing that someday friends and family would finally stop thinking that we were crazy, and instead, they'd envy our success.

Less than a week after our arrival, Demi arrived in California, too. She had a show scheduled in Anaheim, and when Madison and I went to see her, the crowds were immense and enthusiastic. She was evolving into a star right before my eyes, and it made me feel so proud and so excited for her future! I was grateful that our wildest dreams were coming true.

Because Demi could now afford to hire all of the help she needed,

I brought Lisa home with me after the show and asked her to be my assistant. Then I assigned her the task of finding us a five-bedroom house to rent as Madison and I spent most of our days on set.

Madison's first days of filming set the tone for all the rest to follow. Shortly after 5:30 a.m., I'd wake my daughter and slip some shoes on her feet, even though she was still in her pajamas. Once she crawled into the car, she'd quickly fall back asleep until we got to the studio. Every morning when I flashed my pass to enter Universal's private lot, it gave me a heady sense of importance to know that I had access to a place where so many others desired to go but couldn't. *We were part of the lucky few—our hard work had paid off!*

Still trying to be the most prepared mom in the business, I brought along a bag filled with necessities such as toothbrushes, toothpaste, extra clothes, Nintendo games, and a bunch of school-work. Her lovely set teacher, Ms. Sandy, would make sure Madison completed three hours of academic work each day before she left for home, as it was a mandatory rule for all children working in the industry.

I quickly learned that a few items in my bag were unnecessary.

"What would you like for breakfast?" the man from craft services asked that first morning, "A potato-egg-cheese burrito? Pancakes? An omelet?"

I looked at the banana and Pop-Tart I had packed for Madison and decided their choices were far better than mine. By late afternoon, someone else was inviting us to a huge gourmet dinner. *I could get used to this!* I decided. Not that I was eating much, but not

239

having to worry about preparing meals for Madison was a huge relief. The best surprise, though, was learning how nice and friendly everyone was, especially Eva Longoria, who would be Madison's mother on the show, and Ricardo Antonio Chavira, who would be her father.

Both had great parenting instincts, and I especially loved how often they wrapped their arms around Madison, telling her she did a great job. I also adored how Ricardo affectionately dubbed Madison *mija*, which in Spanish means "my daughter." Eva, always friendly and upbeat, solidly proved her heart was just as pure as her looks when she insisted one spring that Madison come over to her house and paint Easter eggs. Surprisingly, no one—not Eva, Ricardo, or the directors—knew during those first few months that either of us was related to Demi, which made me realize that Madison had secured her role totally on her own merits. As it turned out, she was such a natural that she rarely had to film a scene twice, earning her the title of "One-Take Wonder."

I was so proud of my youngest daughter, but what I cherished the most was how close we became during those years. Madison, now quite the talker, told me stories every day about what happened on set. I devoured her news like it was the most delicious part of my day. And it was, especially since I often stayed out of the way, rather than hovering around her during filming. One day, she tried to tell me about a scene that she had done with Eva . . . something about a fight . . . with a pencil . . . over a book . . . but Madison was laughing so hard, I couldn't make sense of what she was saying. I laughed with her just the same. I loved that my daughter was so happy.

Life on set was so surreal at times that I wondered if I was dreaming. I loved how magical it all seemed. I loved the people we interacted with. And I loved how attentive everyone was to our needs. I also cherished the perks that came along with the job—invitations to movie premieres, access to award shows, and more financial freedom.

But I wasn't happy. Texas was my home, not Los Angeles. I missed my friends, my family, and my church. Surrounded by strangers, I no longer knew who I was. *Leaving Texas was never part of the plan*, I reminded myself as I tried to adjust to our new circumstance. In fact, we had no plans to sell our home in Colleyville because I knew that someday we'd return. Maybe in a few years, maybe longer, but there was no doubt that we *would* return.

The constant pull between the present and the past put me at odds with myself, causing minor provocations to frazzle my composure. Old fears—like those about getting fired—tugged harder and harder at my self-worth, even as my girls became more and more successful. Doubts lingered at every turn. *Maybe we don't deserve success? Maybe it won't last? Maybe I need to try harder?* As my inner turmoil grew, I longed for escape. I wanted to gaze at familiar faces and listen to voices I recognized. Even Eddie, my rock, wasn't around because he spent most of his days touring with Demi. Every day I felt more scared, more vulnerable, and terribly tired. My heart ached for Texas. I longed for everything that had once been familiar—our favorite restaurants, my former neighbors, and the church we had attended. Most of all, I wanted to jump back onto the roller-coaster excitement of going to auditions and dreaming about the future. It seemed that once the dreaming had stopped, the real work had begun—and there wasn't any end in sight.

I distracted myself by spending hours on my BlackBerry, texting my long-distance friends. And every morning when I showered, I closed my eyes and pretended I was back in the huge master bathroom in our home in Texas, where life had seemed more balanced and my kids had been close by my side.

God, please don't grant us success until we're ready for it, I had prayed for years. Surely we were ready, so why was I always nervous and jittery? Why couldn't I relax? More and more, the mellow, gentle buzz of Xanax made all those concerns slip away. By August, I was popping a pill every morning like it was a vitamin.

CHAPTER TWENTY-FOUR

"In the back of my mind, I thought we were going to ride off into the sunset and be millionaires like The Beverly Hillbillies.*"*

*N*early three weeks after moving into the Oakwood, we still hadn't found a place to live. The search was still in Lisa's hands, as Madison and I came home exhausted most days. Whenever I did have a bit of free time, I tried to take Madison to the pool or the park so she could meet other kids. We also enjoyed doing ceramics at a local shop and arranging play dates with Frankie Jonas. To be honest, spending time with Madison was far more rewarding than house hunting, which always made me feel discouraged. Apparently the price range I had suggested wasn't going to get us anything close to a nice home, and dirty carpets, broken appliances, and dated wallpaper weren't exactly on my wish list! It made me long to be back in Colleyville even more.

"Let me show you the house you'll *want* to live in," our realtor suggested, "and we'll talk about the price later."

I agreed. When we pulled up to the very house in Toluca Lake that I had dubbed "my dream home" the previous year, I couldn't stop exclaiming, "This is the house! This is the house!" My realtor, unaware that I had spied the house the year before, told me that the owners had been unable to sell the property and were now willing to rent it. I rushed inside to find hardwood floors, a balcony overlooking the living room, vaulted ceilings, and a remodeled kitchen with new appliances. It even had a bedroom suite on the third floor that was perfect for Lisa.

"This is how I want to live in LA!" I shouted. When she told me the price, I died a slow, painful death but insisted on calling Eddie, who was on the road with Demi, and urged him to see it for himself. When he did, he agreed that the house met all our needs and that we'd make it work, even though the monthly payment was several thousand dollars higher than we had budgeted. A week later, we moved in, even making a deal to buy all of the staging furniture because we liked it so much. It would be our home for the next two years, a time period I still describe as "the best of times and the worst of times."

As soon as we signed the lease, I sent Lisa back to Texas to start packing. Because I had spent the entire previous year organizing our house, I even made a list detailing where everything was located. "And bring Dallas back with you!" I added.

Living in my dream house temporarily buoyed my spirits. Not only were we living in a fantastic neighborhood, we also had lots of accomplishments to celebrate. Shortly after we moved in, Demi released her first album, *Don't Forget*, and she started filming *Sonny with a Chance*. As Demi's name recognition grew, small groups of fans and paparazzi started lingering on our street. It was as though we had passed some invisible threshold and our lives would never again be the same. Fame and fortune were creeping into our lives, just I had once imagined. But my old joke about riding off into the sunset and being like *The Beverly Hillbillies* never came to pass. Most days were anything but whimsical or comical.

There were cracks in our perfect lives almost from the start. One night when Madison and I were in the house alone, she went into a full-blown asthma attack at two in the morning. I jumped into the car, intent on rushing her to the hospital, only to realize that I had no idea where the closest emergency room was located! *What have we done to our lives?* I groaned. But I also knew there was no turning back. *Better to pretend everything is fine than make a U-turn back to the past.*

That fall, when Demi went to Miley's sixteenth birthday party—a big bash at Disneyland—the paparazzi snapped a photo of Demi that exposed several scars on her wrists. By the next morning, tabloid headlines were accusing Demi of cutting herself. At the time, I didn't really understand what cutting was, even thinking that it was some kind of trend she'd outgrow. But Eddie and I decided that hiring a life coach to help our daughter make better choices might be a good idea. Once again, I reduced the problem to something more manageable and hoped that if I asked Demi to stop cutting, she would.

A few weeks later when Madison and I were at the grocery store, we spied a magazine with Demi's picture on the cover. We both squealed in delight, but my joy faded the moment I started reading. Portraying me as an ambitious stage mom, the article suggested I was responsible for pushing Demi into her rigorous schedule and destabilizing her emotions. As tears welled up in my eyes, I also read how I had forced Madison to play the role of an overweight kid on *Desperate Housewives* because I wanted the money. It completely shocked me. I tried not to show my hurt feelings in front of Madison, but it set my mind on fire. *What if the article was right? Was I a bad person? Would people like me more if I were thinner? Calmer? More protective of my kids?*

Each and every turn of events pushed my thoughts into overdrive. Not a day went by that I didn't worry about other people's opinions. By bedtime, I was usually too restless to sleep. And if I couldn't sleep, I'd be exhausted the next day. There was only one solution. *I need this!* I told myself, reaching for another Xanax. It was the one sure thing that brought me peace in the midst of the storm that had become our lives.

There was one bright spot in all of the chaos and mixed emotions about moving to LA, and that was Meatloaf Wednesdays. I'm not sure whose idea it was, but our Wednesday gatherings quickly became a cherished time of fun and camaraderie. Lisa, who was now running the household and in charge of everything from picking up the mail to cleaning the house, always bought the ingredients to make one of our favorite southern feasts—meatloaf, corn, and mashed potatoes—and Madison loved to help her in the kitchen. Demi's friends—sometimes it was Miley and sometimes it was Selena—joined us on a few occasions and so did various costars from the set of *Sonny with a Chance*, as well as friends of

Dallas's and some of Eddie's coworkers such as Gary, Demi's tour manager.

Mostly, we gathered in the smaller, informal eating area, where we sat at a wooden table, perched on matching wooden benches. If it was a large gathering, we shifted to the formal dining room, where there was more seating. Either way, the laughter and stories abounded, often lasting until 10:00 p.m., when I had to shoo everyone away so that anyone who had to work the next day could get enough sleep.

Demi's behavior continued to swing in opposite directions. Some days she was sweet and enthusiastic, and some days she seemed to brood in darkness. One thing was clear: Ever since turning sixteen that August, she veered toward willful and defiant behavior with increasing regularity. Although teenage angst is normal, I didn't want it to tarnish her career. We had lots of talks about what was acceptable behavior, discussing what she could say on Twitter and where she could go at night, but Demi rarely heeded my advice. To make matters worse, shortly after her birthday, she bought her own car and now was running off most evenings without any explanation. Every night I'd set an alarm for 2:00 a.m. and walk to her bedroom. If she wasn't there, I called her and demanded she return home. And I kept calling until she walked through the front door.

"You're treading on dangerous ground," I warned. "And Disney might get angry and fire you if you can't get to work on time."

Her looks of contempt baffled me. *Where had I gone wrong?* And now that she was so self-sufficient, my rules about curfew seemed unenforceable. What do you say to your child when she is the one paying most of the bills? I couldn't tell her that I'd take her car away when she was the one who owned it. I couldn't take her phone away when she was the one paying to use it. And although I tried to make her follow our rules while she lived under our roof, she was the one paying the rent. When she passed her California High School Proficiency Exam (CHSPE) that same year, her independence really skyrocketed, because then she no longer needed a guardian on set with her.

It was a tough time for both of us and full of contradictions. Although I struggled to curtail Demi's late-night escapades, I cherished every moment when she wanted me by her side. If she invited me to lunch, I went. If she asked me to join her in her dressing room on set to watch a few episodes of *Snapped*, I was there with a smile on my face. And when Demi went on tour, I always relished our connection via video chat so I could be included in the preshow ritual where everyone circled together and prayed. But I also worried that the happy, exuberant little girl I once knew was slowly disappearing. Eddie was worried, too. "She's so tired and cranky," he sometimes told me when they were on the road. "I don't know how to keep her happy." Neither of us did.

I suppose when things become unstable and confusing, it's natural to cling to familiar habits. And I did, putting even more emphasis on looking good and staying thin. Typically, I left the house wearing a ton of makeup and a bright-pink tracksuit. My hair was teased big and high. If that wasn't enough to broadcast that I wasn't a California girl, I also wore a lot of rhinestone jewelry. But I still felt miserable. It took me months to figure out that if I wanted to fit in, I needed to tone things down a bit, as everyone around me was wearing workout gear in shades of gray and black. When I finally put away my teasing comb, I decided it wouldn't come out again until Halloween.

And, Lord! Driving in LA never got easier. I should have known that I needed help when I developed irrational fears about being trapped on the 405 or when I broke out in a cold sweat trying to maneuver through the switchbacks of Coldwater Canyon. Instead, I simply refused to drive on those roads. Regardless, my quirky, illogical fears kept multiplying.

As the pace and upheaval of our lives continued, my inner dialogue about *needing* Xanax slowly shifted. Twice, sometimes three times a day, I soothingly told myself: *I deserve this!* Like it was a reward. I never saw my habit as an addiction. Never saw it as a vicious cycle. I simply wanted relief, and if one tiny pill could give me that, then I was all for it. Of course, my supply wasn't going to last until I returned to Texas, so I found a local doctor to write another prescription. He made it so easy, never asking if I was getting the drug from another source, never asking how often I took it. And the fewer questions, the better, because I didn't want anyone to know.

Resting easy, though, wasn't in my future. Two months shy of her twenty-first birthday, Dallas was arrested for underage drinking.

It became one more secret that I tucked away.

CHAPTER TWENTY-FIVE

"We weren't superheroes. We had to figure it out like everybody else."

There we were, sitting in first class on an overnight flight bound for Madrid in April, watching Gary Marsh and Judy Taylor roam about in their airplane pajamas. Demi and I were dressed for bed as well, but we all kept chatting away in our excitement about the following day's agenda, when Demi would help launch Disney Channel's 2009 TV season in Spain. Considering that two years before I couldn't have even arranged a phone call with the pair of executives, the whole scenario seemed absurd. I reached for my journal and scribbled: *How the hell did I get here?*

It was just another pinch-me moment when life seemed surreal. Demi's work schedule never seemed to slow down. *Sonny with a Chance* had premiered in February to favorable reviews, so taping was underway for the season. In June, the Disney Channel film *Princess Protection Program* would air, and in July, Demi would release her second studio album, *Here We Go Again*, which would debut atop the *Billboard* 200 and became her first number-one album in the country. Then filming *Camp Rock 2* would start in September, after Demi finished touring. All of it was in stark contrast to Dallas, who spent her days riding a bicycle or being driven by me to auditions because her license had been revoked after the underage drinking charge.

In the whirlwind of our daily lives, I never stopped to question how Dallas felt about her sisters' success. *Was she struggling with depression? Was her arrest a sign that something more serious was wrong? Was she dealing with issues of dependency that Patrick or I had passed on to her?* Not one of those questions crossed my mind. To me, Dallas had merely hit a bump on the road to adulthood. The one question I did ask myself was: *Doesn't every teenager flirt with drugs and alcohol?* If my own teenage years were any indication, the answer was a resounding "Yes!" Of course, I wasn't at the point in my own life to ask about when or how experimentation becomes an addiction, especially considering I was still in denial about my eating disorder and my dependency on Xanax.

What I did understand was that we all have different languages of love, and mine was helping my girls succeed. From the moment they were born, I wanted to support their dreams and interests. Not only did I want to be their cheerleader, but I willingly was their organizer and helper, too. My default setting was always goal-centered, which meant that if we stuck to our plan of chasing success, then everything would fall into place.

I never doubted that Dallas would land something big, just as her sisters had done. She was, after all, the one who had started the whole dream-chasing process by auditioning for *Little Rascal*'s Darla, all those years ago. And, she was the one who had booked almost every commercial she'd ever auditioned for. *She's not going to be left out*, I told myself. So, I found her a manager that could help her get to the next level and refocused my attention on Madison. Trying to balance the needs of a twenty-one-year-old and a seven-year-old wasn't easy, but I tried my best. Madison, who needed normal kid activities as well as supervision on set, naturally got the bulk of my time and energy. I figured Dallas was fine with that, considering she was an adult and striving for independence.

But independence wasn't the solution. Neither was better management.

Dallas was dealing with some weighty issues of her own that I'd later learn were related to the trauma she'd witnessed as a child. Regrettably, I was too busy getting Madison to work or flying across the country to join Demi for the weekend to notice. It was an oversight that would haunt me in the days ahead. Family was, and will always be, extremely important to me, but I also was quick to embrace denial when our lives weren't running as smoothly as planned. If anyone ever asked about Dallas, I said she was doing great. It was the story I wanted—and needed—to believe. Besides, when the two of us chatted on the way to auditions, she seemed happy enough. *Why rock the boat and expose something that might make enticing fodder for the media?*

Keeping our lives private, though, was nearly impossible. Even when Demi wasn't around, fans showed up at our house. Sometimes they'd ring the doorbell and snap a photo of whoever answered, and on Saturday nights, large groups of girls would stand outside and sing Demi's songs. It was thrilling for a while, but over time, I began to feel like we were living in a fishbowl. I struggled to get enough air.

One evening around dinnertime, our family came home in a downpour, and we rushed inside to get Madison ready for a play date. Everyone scurried by me as I lagged behind. Alone in the rain, I slipped on a wet tile and smashed my face into a concrete step. The sound of my nose snapping to one side was dreadful. Nearly choking from all the blood running down my throat, I pounded on the back door until someone answered. I'm sure I looked like I had just stepped out of a bad horror film.

"Oh my God," Lisa cried as I raced inside and told her to dial 911. In shock, I kept running in circles, leaving a trail of blood behind me. When the ambulance crew finally arrived, they put me on a stretcher and covered me with a tarp to keep me dry from the rain. As we dashed out of the house, my mind went whirring—not about my broken nose but about the rumors and pictures that might appear the next morning. I could already see the glaring headlines: *Someone Dies in Lovato's Home!*

In reality, pictures of me looking like a corpse were the least of my worries. With all the events and parties we were now invited to, I was once again binge drinking. On more than one occasion, Eddie or whoever was with me had their hands full as they tried to shield me from anyone who might try to get a picture of Demi's mom drunk. Indulging in alcohol wasn't a regular habit because I didn't like to drink, but when I did, I went from zero to sixty fast, often ending up passed out or sick. I weighed only ninety pounds, so it didn't take much to do me in. Although I tried not to take Xanax when I knew I'd be drinking, I never ate much, which didn't help matters. Far worse, I was setting a horrible example for my girls, who often had to take care of me in my debilitated state. By morning, I rarely remembered any details about what I had done.

One of the worst mistakes I made after moving to Hollywood was reading all the gossip about my girls on social media. I even set my phone to receive alerts whenever someone mentioned their names. Some of it was harmless fodder, like rumors about romance or favorite hangouts that Demi frequented, but negativity always won out. The constant scrutiny and criticism about every word we said—or didn't say—didn't help my inner turmoil.

One day as I was reading OceanUp, a teen gossip site, I saw a simple post about Demi visiting Starbucks that day. When I scrolled through the comments, I was shocked. Angry. Hurt.

"Have you heard about the sex tape?" one person commented.

"No, but I think she's a terrible singer," another replied.

"Definitely doing cocaine," said someone else.

Were the rumors true? Did people really hate my daughter? What else was being said? Every day I not only read every bit of gossip I could find, but I read the comments, too. It made me wonder how things had spun so out of control. Was it even possible to turn things around? Instead of confronting Demi, I charged after the girl I thought was a negative influence on my daughter. A girl I'll simply call Jane Doe.

Jane seemed innocent at first, very sweet and polite. But over time she seemed to infiltrate our home like a pestilent cockroach, appearing almost daily and sparking more and more arguments between Demi and me. Every evening the two girls would head out together, which made my stomach churn. Demi rarely returned before the wee hours of the morning. Although I never saw her drunk or high on drugs, I suspected she participated in both activities. As a mom, you just know sometimes. My biggest fear, though, wasn't that my eighteen-year-old daughter was facing issues of addiction, because I never saw the depth of her habits. Once again, I assumed that her experimentation was normal teenage behavior, much like I had done with Dallas.

But I was terribly worried that Demi would ruin her business agreements with Disney, which ultimately affected me because I was considered the gatekeeper to my daughter's behavior. Even after more talks, Demi wasn't interested in curtailing her nightly escapades. At that point, I had a choice. I could lock my daughter in the house and only let her leave for work, or I could set her loose to make her own mistakes. I chose the latter and hoped she wouldn't stray too far from what I had taught her. Making mistakes is part of life and sometimes it's the best teacher, but I also knew that if Demi stumbled and fell, I'd pick her up and help her get on her feet again. I also knew that I wasn't going to tolerate Jane's presence in my house any longer, especially since I was sure she was encouraging Demi to use drugs. (I'd later learn that she was the one who taught Demi how to get Adderall from a doctor, the very drug I had taken years earlier after Madison was born to deal with ADHD, although Demi would misuse it to lose weight.)

"You're not welcome in my house any longer," I finally told Jane, pointing to the door. "Please leave."

She walked out and so did Demi, who screamed at me that I was ruining her life. Although the two would remain friends until the very day that Demi entered treatment, Jane never set foot in our house again. I never regretted my decision, but in the end, it turned out to be a small victory in our efforts to stem Demi's downward spiral.

CHAPTER TWENTY-SIX

"That's a mother's job—to be strong for everyone else."

As 2010 rolled in, the pressures of the industry kept mounting, though none of us suspected that every-thing we'd worked so hard for was about to unravel. Sheer willpower kept me pushing forward, always believing that at any moment we'd find our rhythm and once again become the perfect family I imagined us to be. The newest person who stood in the way of my imaginary life was Wilmer Valderrama, a well-known actor from the sitcom *That '70s Show* who had dated Lindsay Lohan in the past. His sudden interest in Demi worried me, so I arranged a dinner date to ask him a few questions.

"What exactly are your intentions?" I wanted to know, espe-cially considering he was twelve years older than Demi.

"I think she has a bright and promising future," he replied. "Hollywood could use more successful Latinos, and I could be a good adviser to her."

He seemed sincere, but truthfully, I was having trouble trusting anyone in Demi's company. A few months later when Demi told me that she and Joe Jonas had started dating, I should have been happy. But with the *Camp Rock 2* premiere slated for late spring, I knew their budding romance could either be a big win for movie press or a disaster if they broke up. I hoped for the better outcome.

One of the great ironies during this time was that even though I was self-medicating with Xanax, I was also trying to rely more on prayer. I had found a Bible study group in Toluca Lake, thanks to Madison, who now was enrolled at the San Fernando Valley Professional School, a private school that catered to kids in the industry. The parents of one of her classmates led the group, and I loved going there because it reconnected me with the all the staples of my childhood—singing Gospel music, praying, and reading the Bible. It was the first taste of home I'd experienced in quite some time. But as wonderful and kind as everyone was, I never told anyone about any of our problems. It seemed too risky. Who would want to be friends with me if we had so many issues? And wouldn't someone leak our secrets?

By May, the press had plenty to write about without my help.

"Mom," Demi sobbed into the phone, "we broke up." She sounded so distraught that I could barely understand her. In less than forty-eight hours, she was scheduled to appear on *Good Morning America* to sing and promote *Camp Rock 2*. She'd be right next to Joe for all of it. I knew that was going to be tough on her.

"I'm hopping on a plane, and I'll be there as soon as I can," I promised.

I handed Madison off to Lisa and boarded the next flight to New York City. That night as we watched *Grey's Anatomy*, I held her like she was eight years old. I had never seen her so brokenhearted. Although she made it through the performance the next morning, I decided to go with her on the scheduled promotional tour to South America, fearing she wasn't yet over the heartbreak.

After I returned from South America, I put all my attention back on Madison. I had only been gone about a week but it seemed like forever. I missed spending time with my little girl. One night as Madison and I dozed together in bed, I was jerked awake by a loud *BAM*. As the bedroom door flew open, Dallas stormed in.

"HEELLLP!" she shouted. "I'm possessed!"

Horrified and not fully awake, I jumped out of bed and ran toward her, as Madison groggily sat up and watched.

"Help meeee!" Dallas screeched repeatedly as she threw herself to the floor, flailing her arms and legs.

Watching her, I almost believed she was possessed. She looked more like a wild animal than my daughter. I grabbed her and started shaking her shoulders, hoping to dislodge the stranger in front of me. But I couldn't control her, so I slapped her across the face.

"IS THAT ALL YOU GOT?" she bellowed as a twisted grin seeped across her face. Then she started laughing, throwing off a deep, guttural howl that sounded so evil, it made me cringe.

I was horrified. *What had happened to my sweet child? What drug had she taken?* Madison screamed from the bedroom, and Lisa rushed to her side as I chased after Dallas, who was teetering toward the bathroom. Once I grabbed hold of Dallas, I shoved her into the tub and turned on the faucet. With only the cold water running, I blasted her with the sprayer. Then I dialed 911.

Before anyone could answer, Dallas jumped out of the tub and barreled down the stairs, dripping wet. I was sure she would slip and badly injure herself on the slick hardwood floor. When I heard the dispatcher's voice, I begged for help.

"My daughter," I cried. "There's something wrong with her . . . she's going to hurt herself!"

The woman calmly told me to state my name and address and promised help was on the way, while I watched Dallas bolt out the back door with Lisa chasing after her. When they reached the patio, I was stunned to see Dallas pick up a large, heavy clay planter that would have been difficult for three grown men to move. She hurled it to the ground, where it shattered into tiny pieces.

"Oh, God! Please hurry," I pleaded.

When Dallas spied Madison's scooter nearby, she picked that up, too, and marched toward the back door, which was made of glass. "Noooo!" I cried, just as Lisa tore the scooter from her hands and threw it to the ground.

"Hold her down," I shouted to Lisa. "The EMTs are at the front door."

I swiftly guided everyone toward Dallas, while rattling off questions that no one could answer. What had she taken? What would make her act this way? What's going to happen to her? When the ambulance crew approached Dallas, she suddenly seemed calmer.

I gathered she was finally worn out from being pinned down by Lisa, who now sported a split lip. "She probably took drugs and alcohol," one officer said. "She can sleep it off in the hospital, and you can check on her in the morning."

When the ambulance left, I raced upstairs to check on Madison. One wave of terror after another had exhausted me. Glancing at the clock, I saw it was 3:00 a.m.! *Oh, no!* I groaned. In a few hours, Madison needed to be up for a TV interview about her role on *Desperate Housewives*. It seemed terribly unimportant in light of the night's events.

The next morning, I took my Xanax with my coffee and asked Lisa to take Madison to her interview. It was time to focus on Dallas.

CHAPTER TWENTY-SEVEN

"I realized after we had moved to LA that Dallas
had become a little fish in a big pond."

As I drove to the hospital to pick Dallas up, I knew I had let her down. I never wanted to face the fact that she might feel insecure and a bit envious that her sisters' successes overshadowed her own. Nor did I want to admit that I knew how it felt to almost make it big, only to watch others soar past you. *God, fix our family and make us perfect.* That had been my prayer for years, as though the heavens could magically erase all of our shortcomings. Now it was time to face the consequences and work toward a solution.

"I don't know what happened or how I got here," Dallas said when I appeared by her bed, "but I'm okay."

"Nothing at all?" I asked.

"No," she sighed. "But I'm sure you're going to tell me."

My hopes for hugs and apologies vanished. When the social worker arrived, I asked to speak with her privately.

"Can you tell me what she had in her system?" I said, sitting in her office and feeling like I was about to be sent to detention for being a bad parent.

"Oh, we can't tell you that," she said. "She's not a minor."

"But I'm paying for her insurance," I argued, though the woman still shook her head.

"Look," she offered, "maybe you need to get her some help. Somewhere that offers dual diagnosis, which means they'll not only work on getting her sober but they'll also try to get to the root of her problems." She then handed me a list of facilities to consider.

Dallas and I barely spoke on the way home. My mind kept running in circles. *How did this happen? How do I tell Eddie? What should I say to Dallas?* I hated feeling so uncomfortable, and my whole body hurt from feeling guilty.

"I'm sorry," Dallas finally said. "I know I must have done something terrible last night, because both of my legs are bruised and I can barely walk."

"Look," I began, "when I'm able to talk about last night I will, but it's still too raw and scary. What I do want to talk about is finding you some help."

"You mean like sending me away to rehab or something?" she gasped.

"Yes, that's exactly what I mean," I said. "It's time to face this head-on. You need to understand that if you don't get help, you can't be around Madison."

Silence stretched between us. "This is a gift," I added, desperately hoping she'd grasp the lifeline I was tossing her, "and you need to figure out how to take this gift and make the most of it."

Dallas looked at me, alarmed. "Madison means everything to me," she began, "and I know that I need help. Actually, I've been too scared to ask." She paused, then added, "I've tried to stop using several times, but I never make it past a few months."

I was shocked and speechless, but Dallas wasn't waiting for me to say anything. "Now that I know I have your support"—she smiled—"I think I can do this." Her words were like Christmas, Mother's Day, and my birthday all rolled into one.

When we got home, Dallas ran to her room as I turned on the computer to Google every facility on my list. Each one of them was expensive. *How would we afford it? And would Eddie support my decision?* I glanced at the clock, realizing it was twenty-four hours later, and I still hadn't called him. He had his own share of problems trying to keep Demi out of trouble on the road, but I knew he needed to know what had happened.

My hands shook through our entire conversation. I told him about Dallas's horrible ordeal, her suspected drug use, and her need for treatment. My final words were a plea. "I need your support," I told him. "Treatment isn't covered on our insurance plan, and I don't know how we'll pay for it." He assured me that he'd find a way.

"We'll get through this together," he added. "It's going to be all right."

I desperately wanted to believe him.

When Demi called later that night, she added her encouragement. "Don't worry," she said. "I'll help with the costs. I just want

Dallas to get the help she needs." The love and compassion in her voice made me weepy with gratitude.

Forty-eight hours later, Dallas and I were on our way to the Pasadena Recovery Center. And, she was actually excited about going. After exploring the facility's website and learning it was where *Celebrity Rehab* was filmed, she was even more excited. "I'll go there," she had exclaimed, "and I'll think of it as the college experience I never got to have." She even dubbed it her "all-about-me vacation."

Thank you, God! Dallas was ready to turn the experience into a journey of self-discovery. Her enthusiasm was a positive sign. So, too, was the pile of pennies we spied behind our car when we came out of Target after buying all the things that Dallas wanted to take with her. Ever since Lorna's son, Trenton, had died, we often found pennies in our path—never just one or two but lots of them—and we saw it as confirmation that Trenton, who had collected coins, was watching over us. "Thanks, buddy," I whispered into the wind.

The plan was for Dallas to stay four weeks. I called her every evening and went to visit every Wednesday and Sunday. Sometimes I brought Madison or Lisa along; sometimes I went alone. It was my way of lending support, as well as assuaging all the guilt I carried for ignoring the signs that Dallas was struggling. *How many times had she been unable to get out of bed and go to an audition? How many times had I asked her to clean her messy room without seeing results?*

How many days had she refused to get off the couch because she was depressed?

Almost from the start, Dallas was upbeat and positive. "Mom, this is hard work," she told me on one visit, "but I'm getting the chance to be a better person. Who gets a chance like that?" We had a few laughs, too, especially when I caught her staring at some of the more attractive guys in the program. "Things aren't so bad, are they?" I teased. But there were teary conversations as well, like when she got into trouble for fraternizing with those cute guys. "You need to follow the rules," I reminded her during one of our phone calls. "You're not there to make the program fit your needs; you're there to follow the program and stick with it." She took my advice and her cheerful, bubbly self returned in no time.

Some residents seemed to resent being there, but not my daughter. She even raved about some of her therapy sessions, though I never pressed for details. I told myself that I didn't want to pry, but the truth was I wasn't interested in learning what I was doing wrong. Greeting Dallas with a smile each week, buying the things she needed, and relaying news from the outside world were more in my comfort zone. That was how I could help. Exposing the myth that our family wasn't perfect would only damage us all, especially Demi, so I figured protecting everyone was part of my job, too. I also hoped that Dallas's stay would remain a private matter. Fearing an onslaught of bad press for Demi if the news got out, I never told my family or my prayer group. And I never mentioned it to anyone on the set of *Desperate Housewives*. Only my closest friends knew the details.

Week after week, Dallas and I grew closer. Outgoing as always, my daughter did her best to get to know as many of the residents as possible, and she took great pride in introducing them to me. When I found out that some of them never got visitors, I made sure to stop by and chat with them whenever I went to see Dallas, even offering to get things from the store that they might need. Sometimes I had to make several trips to the car to unload everyone's goodies. I never saw it as a bother because it made me feel useful and appreciated. And I loved that no one had a room as bright or cheerfully decorated as my daughter's. Swathed in wild shades of pink, her room cast a glow into the hall whenever the sun's rays came through her window. It made me feel optimistic and hopeful.

One weekend when there was an end-of-summer gathering that parents were invited to attend, I brought along a birthday cake for one of the residents I had gotten to know, even having his name etched in icing. He appreciated my gesture, but one of the counselors didn't. As we sat in a therapy circle outside, that counselor reprimanded me in front of everyone. "You can't do this," she scolded. "A cake is only for a year of sobriety, and these residents have only been here a few months." Everyone turned to stare at me as tears rolled down my cheeks. Feeling embarrassed and humiliated, I stood up and walked a short distance away. A few minutes later, the group moved on to an exercise where residents had the opportunity to share something on their minds. When Dallas stood up, I noticed she was shaking.

"I have something to say," she began. "Life here can be challenging and . . . well, attacking my mother like that was bullshit!" *Oh, no!* I panicked. *She's going to get kicked out for that!* But Dallas continued, sounding more resolute. "My mother is one of the sweetest people you will ever meet, and she came here to do something nice—but she got shot down for it in front of everybody. That wasn't right." When she turned to me and smiled, so did everyone else. And one by one, all those people I had been visiting started clapping. Even though I still feared we'd be packing up and leaving by evening, I couldn't have loved my daughter any more than I did in that moment.

Four weeks later, Dallas asked to stay at rehab a little longer, insisting she had more to learn. I didn't want to deny her the opportunity to get well, but we had already spent thousands of dollars for her treatment, none of which was covered by insurance and at least half of which was funded by Demi.

"Two more weeks," I told her. "We can't afford any more."

About the same time, I learned that the lease on our house couldn't be renewed. When Eddie and Demi popped back into town for a few days, I told them we needed to start house hunting again. Then I suggested to Demi that maybe it was time for her to actually purchase a home with the money from her Coogan Account, which California requires for all child actors, so that a portion of their earnings will be protected until they become adults. It was a preemptive move on my part. In a few weeks, Demi would turn eighteen and have access to those funds, but I feared she'd waste all that money on drugs and alcohol, especially since Eddie had recently called me from the road several times, worried that she wasn't doing well.

Somehow in the blur of Madison's filming schedule, Demi's rehearsals and photo shoots, and Dallas's impending return home, we found a beautiful multilevel home in Sherman Oaks that was built into a magnificent hillside. It had everything our family needed, including enough bedrooms to accommodate everyone, as Dallas and Lisa would continue to live with us. The property also had a separate guesthouse near the pool that would be perfect for Demi now that she was getting older. As we considered making an offer, our family stood on the home's elevated patio and watched the sun set over the valley. The spectacular view cinched the deal. But before we could move in, Demi and Eddie headed back to South America on tour.

Shortly before I was scheduled to pick up Dallas and bring her home, I answered my phone and heard Karen, Demi's former piano teacher, in a panic.

"Is she okay?" Karen asked.

"Who?" I replied, completely rattled by her urgency.

"Demi," she said. "I had a dream. . . . It was awful. She was lying in a ditch and covered with scorpions. . . . I've never been so afraid.

"It was a prophetic dream," she continued.

No, I told myself. *This can't be true. Demi was going to make it through this difficult stage without getting hurt . . . and without anyone knowing the sordid details!*

"Gosh, that sounds awful, but Demi is just fine," I lied. "In fact, she's doing really, really well."

CHAPTER TWENTY-EIGHT

"My world was in jeopardy, and I needed to remain strong
and stoic to keep my family together."

My excitement about returning to Colleyville in late October for my thirtieth high school reunion was so feverish that Eddie contemplated leaving South America so that he could join me for the big event. But when Lorna told me she was going alone, I decided that we should go together. "Stay with Demi," I told Eddie. It seemed a minor detail at the time, and Eddie even joked that I'd probably have more fun without him. Neither of us had any idea how important his presence on tour at that time would be.

The day before the reunion, Lorna showed up at my front door in Colleyville grinning like the Cheshire cat. As we laughed and told stories, I felt the weight of the past two years roll off of my shoulders. *I was finally home with someone who knew and understood me!*

"Look at this," I said to Lorna, presenting an array of Demi's memorabilia, including a silver dress from the *Camp Rock* premiere, a few autographed pictures, and two pairs of Vans that also bore her signature. All were donations for the reunion's auction.

"Oh, nice!" Lorna gushed, just as my phone pinged.

From that moment forward, my life would never be the same. Those five words—*I'm sorry ahead of time*—would forever change the carefully constructed image of our family that I had worked so hard to maintain. Our less-than-perfect track record would soon be an open book. The only thing I was grateful for was that Demi's incident had occurred on a US airplane; otherwise, she could have been thrown into a South American jail.

It always amazes me how when we awaken the world seems fresh and new. I remember opening my eyes that next morning feeling happy and carefree, as though Demi's text had been a dream. Then the whole scene came rushing back . . . the shocking phone call . . . the fear . . . the relief . . . and the crushing realization that my daughter needed help. I longed to go back to sleep, but I knew that people needed me. As I made my way to the kitchen, Lorna greeted me.

"I can stay with you," she offered. "I want to help."

But I told her to go and get ready for the reunion. I had phone calls and decisions to make. Even though I loved her for offering to stay, I knew the work ahead was a family matter. Soon after Lorna left, I was on a conference call with Eddie, Phil, Demi, and her attorney. As a group, we hoped to formulate a plan of action.

When I heard Demi's voice, my heart sank. She sounded so despondent, and her lackadaisical attitude about the future of her career seemed off-key. As a mom, I wanted to erase the pain she was in, but I knew I couldn't. There would be consequences to her actions that she, alone, had to endure.

"Maybe everyone would be better off if I wasn't here anymore," she suddenly sighed, alarming us enough to put her on a suicide watch until we could get her home.

Our conversation ended with everyone agreeing that the only way through the ordeal was to get Demi the help she needed, even though no one really knew the full extent of what she was battling. My overriding desire was to find a treatment facility that would watch out for, care for, and evaluate her to the fullest extent possible. And I wasn't going to wait for someone else to make it happen. Within the hour, I reached out to James Gresham, the owner of Timberline Knolls (TK), a women's treatment center for a variety of mental-health issues that was located near Chicago. I only knew about James because of Phil, who had met him after buying a home in his neighborhood in Texas. Sometime after the two had talked, Phil casually handed me some brochures about TK, saying I should take a look. But I hadn't bothered to read a single page until that morning.

"I think we need your help," I told James, my voice shaking. He sounded so kind, patiently answering every one of my questions. By the time I hung up, I knew it was where Demi needed to go.

When I called and told Phil, he sounded relieved. I could tell he cared about Demi, not just as an artist of his but also as a friend

272

who needed help. Within hours, Demi was let go from the tour, but we saw it as a blessing. She needed time away from work to get better. Unfortunately, the journey home would be a long one for Demi and Eddie, and not just because the trip would involve an entire day of flying from Peru to Miami and then on to Texas.

As soon as I crawled out of bed the following morning, I seemed to know that Demi needed my prayers. I cried and begged God for help while I drank my coffee and even as I showered. But that feeling of peace never materialized, so I did what my God-fearing, Gospel-raised, southern mother would have done—I got down on my knees. Then I went face-first on the floor, pleading for Demi's life. In my mind, I saw all of those terrible signs that I had ignored—the bloody rags, the late-night parties, the forty-eight-hour binges without sleep—and I begged for forgiveness. Then I started quoting every Bible verse I could remember. "Lord," I finally prayed, "I could have lost her, and I don't want to make that mistake again. Help me to find the words that will persuade Demi to get help."

I was still on the floor when the phone rang. It was Eddie.

"She's not coming to Colleyville!" he cried. "She's trying to buy a ticket to LA. . . . I don't know what to do anymore."

There wasn't a trace of control in Eddie's voice. After three days of no sleep, he was exhausted and beside himself with worry. I feared he was ready to throw in the towel.

"Listen to me, Eddie," I insisted. "Bring her to me. Beg her, plead with her, make a deal, whatever it takes! I will do the rest, but you've got to get her to me. Promise me you won't give up!"

Despite all of her teenage rebelliousness, despite all of the arguments we'd had, and despite all of her issues, I knew that Demi loved me. Together, we had been through so much over the years, and I was certain that if I could just look her in the eyes, I could persuade her to go to treatment. Failure wasn't an option.

"I'll try one more time," Eddie said as I hit the floor in prayer again.

A few hours later, Eddie and Demi were at the front door. My heart thumped within my chest. *Could I fulfill the task before me? Would I say the right thing?* Instead, nothing happened. Demi walked in the house, mumbled, "Hi," and walked up the stairs to her room.

After I hugged Eddie, I headed toward Demi. Each step was a chance to rehearse what I would say. *It's time to get you help. You could lose everything if you don't change. Getting angry doesn't solve anything.* All were possible options, but by the top of the stairs, I was ready for drastic measures. I decided I'd tell her that because she had threatened to harm herself, I was calling the police and having her placed in a mental ward under a 5150 hold. It was an option I had learned about earlier that morning when I called the police and asked about my parental rights.

But when I opened Demi's bedroom door, I didn't say any of those things. She seemed too broken. There she was on her bed, curled up in a fetal position. Scattered around her were the remnants of her childhood—the posters, the pictures, the trinkets—that had inspired her during all those endless nights of songwriting. The journey from Colleyville to Hollywood had been hard on her, too. In that moment, I didn't see an eighteen-year-old young woman clinging to her career; I saw a child who was exhausted and afraid. She was still my little girl, and I desperately wanted to turn around and let her rest. But I couldn't.

"Honey," I said cautiously, "we need to talk."

She opened her eyes and looked at me. "Yes," she agreed.

"I found this really nice place for you to get some help," I started. "It's in Chicago."

Silence. I waited, but Demi said nothing.

"I think you know what we have to do," I continued, "but we'll do it together, I promise. And I'll help you every step of the way—but you have to agree to go."

Only more silence. I held my breath, trying to think of what more I could say.

"I guess I don't have much of a choice," she finally said, resigning her fate to my plan.

It felt like a miracle. "Let's pack a few things," I suggested, "and we'll get you an iPod so you can download all your favorite music to take with you." I figured life without her phone or laptop would be hard enough. Without music, she wouldn't survive.

A few hours later, we were making the forty-five-minute trek to Addison, Texas, where James was waiting with a private plane. His firm handshake and warm demeanor assured me we were doing the right thing. When I looked at Demi, though, I could tell something was wrong. I quickly called my sister Kathy.

"I can't tell you all the details," I said, "but start praying for Demi and don't stop until I tell you." Not only did we need to make it to Chicago safely, but we also needed to get Demi signed into treatment before she changed her mind.

Throughout our flight, I silently kept praying, knowing my sister was doing the same. More than once, I reminded God of His promise in Matthew 18:20, which says: "For where two or three are gathered together in my name, there am I in the midst of them." When we landed, I breathed a sigh of relief, thinking the trip had gone much smoother than I anticipated.

Weeks later, though, James would tell me a strange story about our pilot for that trip and how he suddenly had become very ill mid-flight. Sweating profusely and trying not to vomit, he worried that he might have to attempt an emergency landing. When I told Demi about the pilot's troubles, she turned pale and confessed that she was saying prayers of her own that trip—to make the plane crash! So despondent about her situation, she wanted to die rather than face treatment. But God had other plans for her life.

As we drove along the winding, tree-lined road leading to Timberline Knolls, I relaxed a bit, sensing that Demi looked calmer than she had on the plane. I didn't panic until we neared the front door. *Will she go in or try to run away?* But the voice of God stilled my fears. As clearly as I saw the sun shining in the sky, I heard these words: "Demi has great work to do for *me*, but first, she has things to learn here." I wasn't sure what it meant, but I felt certain that Demi was going to follow through on her decision to stay.

––––––

As the intake counselor asked Demi questions and jotted down her answers, I tried to remain calm as I heard more than a few shocking revelations.

"Do you use alcohol on a regular basis?" she asked.

"Yes," Demi replied, which wasn't a total surprise, though I hadn't realized it was a *regular* habit.

When she asked about drugs, my jaw dropped.

"Cocaine, pot, and Adderall," Demi said, after glancing in my direction.

My blood ran cold. *What? Why? Wasn't Adderall for ADHD?* I told myself to calm down. After all, she was being honest and about to get help. But the broken record in my head kept playing. *Cocaine, pot, Adderall . . . cocaine, pot, Adderall . . .* It made me feel sick.

As the intake came to a close, the woman asked for Demi's phone. It was that moment of truth, when I would really know if my daughter was serious about getting help. When she handed it over, I couldn't hold back my tears any longer. Demi looked at me and began crying, too. Neither of us wanted to say good-bye. As I slowly stood up, Demi reached over and handed me a napkin from the table. I thought it was for wiping my eyes, but she whispered, "Read it."

There on the unfolded napkin was Demi's message:

I'm gonna miss you every minute of the day and night. I love you. You're the best mother I could ever ask for. Demi.

I took that little, white piece of love home with me and promptly framed it and hung it on the wall. It's still there today. And it always will be.

CHAPTER TWENTY-NINE

*"As mother and father, we were more concerned about her life
than her career, but there was a storm cloud hanging over
us knowing she could come out of this with nothing."*

*W*hat's he doing here?

A week after dropping Demi off at TK, we
flew back to Chicago to visit her. When Eddie,
Madison, and I walked into the conference room, there was Wilmer
Valderrama, sitting next to my daughter. I knew they had been seeing each other, but I hadn't expected to see him at TK. *This is
family time! Mother-daughter time!* I railed silently. After an intru-
sive week of the paparazzi driving by our house, trailing our car as
I took Madison to school, and surprising us with their cameras and
questions at the airport, I wasn't in the mood to deal with one more
infringement upon our family. Being gracious took every ounce of
energy I could muster.

We all gathered together at one end of the large table that filled
the room and tried to have a normal conversation. Although visitors

typically gathered in the lunchroom, we were given a conference room in an effort to protect Demi's privacy. It was the only exception to the rules that would be granted. Like all the other new residents, Demi had been escorted to the room by a BHS—a behavioral health specialist—and she'd be escorted back to her room when we finished.

"Oooh, we've missed you so much! Everyone is asking about you, and lots of fans are tweeting their encouragement. . . . Everyone sends their love. . . . And the house just isn't the same without you," I rattled on and on in my nervousness. After I hugged Demi again, I told her how good she looked.

It was a lie. Her complexion was sallow. Her cheeks, hollow and sunken. Her eyes, lifeless. Although happy to see us, she didn't say much. More than once, I caught her staring into space like we weren't even there. *Will she ever be herself?* I wondered. The most hopeful thing I saw was when Demi and Madison sat side by side with their heads tipped together in silent solidarity. When we left, I cried all the way back to the hotel. Sunday's visit was a little better, but I still was shaky and uncertain about the future. On the flight back to LA, I kept wondering when the happier, bubblier version of my daughter would return.

Every weekend we flew to Chicago. Sometimes Madison, Dallas, and Lisa came along; sometimes just Eddie and I went. By our third trip, Demi seemed more herself, even putting on a bit of makeup and dressing in nicer clothes. Wilmer, much to my chagrin, was always by her side. Although I still wanted time alone with Demi,

I began to realize that he must care for her or he wouldn't make the effort to be there every week. Eventually, I'd come to love him like he was part of the family and even apologize for my cold reaction back then. When the two broke up years later, his absence from our lives hit me hard, but during those early days of treatment, the mother hen in me wanted Demi to focus on getting better, not on a relationship.

Although Demi had resigned herself to stay for thirty days, she became distraught when TK said she needed to stay longer. It broke my heart to watch her plead with such anguish to return home, knowing full well she wasn't ready, as she was knee-deep in withdrawing from substances and just beginning to conquer an eating disorder. There was also the issue of learning how to manage her bipolar disorder. The setback in her departure made Demi angry and resentful. Once again, she slid into depression. I wondered if she'd ever recover.

I tried to remain strong for Demi and for all of us, but I was growing increasingly weary. Some mornings I struggled to get out of bed, and I often fell asleep midsentence as I sat on the sofa in Madison's dressing room on set. Still refusing to talk about our family's problems, I pretended I was fine. But I wasn't. Not even close. Ominous thoughts looped in vicious cycles through my mind. *How was this all going to end? Would we survive?* Even as my brave front slowly crumbled, I refused to give up the fight. I prayed even more fervently and, at the same time, increased the Xanax I was taking. It wasn't a contradiction in my mind. It was survival.

———

Once Demi got over the fact that she was staying at TK longer than anticipated, we started to see some positive changes. Early on, Dallas had made a great suggestion. "After the first ten minutes of conversation, things can get awkward," she said, "and games are a great distraction." It was something she had learned during her own rehab stay. Her strategy was good for all of us. Sometimes we played Hangman on the whiteboard in the room and sometimes we played Old Maid or Bullshit, a card game that revolves around assessing if someone is bluffing about the cards in their hands. But it was Apples to Apples, a crazy card game that involves categories and a bit of intuitive guessing, that quickly became our favorite. We never finished a round without dissolving into silliness. Once Demi earned some privileges, we even went out to the basketball court to shoot hoops. We tried to keep our visits bright and cheerful.

As time dragged on and Christmas neared, Demi seemed more herself. The kinder, happier daughter I once knew was slowly reemerging, which bolstered my spirits, too. Demi even took up knitting, which seemed completely out of her wheelhouse, but she said it was relaxing. When we opened our Christmas gifts that year, we each found a special, hand-knit scarf in our favorite colors.

Once Christmas was over, we said good-bye to Demi and flew to Texas so we could spend the rest of the holiday season with our relatives. Twitter, at the time, was full of tweets about fans showing their support for Demi by getting little pink heart tattoos, similar to the one that she used in her signature. It got me thinking. "I'm not much for needles or pain," I said to Dallas, "and I've never even liked tattoos, but maybe we should get that heart tattoo on the inside of our wrists. I think Demi would like that."

Dallas said she'd think about it, but since she already had a Dallas Cowboys Cheerleader star tattooed in that area, she thought another would be too much. In the end, Lisa, Marissa (Demi's best friend), and I bravely walked into a tattoo parlor and explained what we wanted.

"Have a seat," said the young, bearded man covered in tattoos. With his ball cap obscuring his eyes, he pointed to a chair. I plopped down and excitedly told him, "Make sure that the heart is pink!" My heart fluttered with excitement as he swabbed my left wrist with alcohol. But at the sound of his machine, I almost lost my nerve. As he drew nearer, I closed my eyes and gripped the chair with my right hand. Then I held my breath. *Oh, my God! It hurt like hell!* The pain was far worse than I had imagined it would be. Ten seconds in, I couldn't take it any longer.

"Are you almost done?" I shrieked. In the end, those sixty seconds of pain to etch a quarter-inch symbol of support seemed endless. "All done," the tattoo artist chuckled at my intolerance for pain.

"No more tattoos for me," I declared when it was over. "Never again!"

On the next visit to Chicago, I strode into the conference room and declared, "Demi, I have something to show you!"

"What?" she asked curiously.

When I proudly held out my wrist, she couldn't believe it. "You did not!" she gasped, her eyes wide with disbelief. And then that big, wide smile of hers spread across her face. I smiled, too, knowing that I had stepped out of my comfort zone for her and she truly appreciated the gesture.

That January, Demi started talking about the future and I was thrilled that she wanted to keep working on her career, even mentioning that she wanted to start working on her next album as soon as she got better. "I want you all to listen to this song that I recorded right before I came into treatment," she said during one visit. "It's called 'Skyscraper.'" The painful lyrics declared that she would rise from the ashes like a skyscraper. By the end, we were all sitting around that conference table bawling. The heartache and determination in her voice touched us all.

"Can you tell me about your eating habits?" the nutritionist asked.

We were sitting in a family counseling session, and the TK staff was training us to be supportive once Demi came home. Comments such as "I'm so full!" or "I can't possibly eat another bite" were to be avoided. And, we needed to watch for signs of relapse, such as frequent trips to the bathroom after meals or obvious weight loss. The nutritionist's sudden interest in my diet surprised me. *Why did she care about me?*

"Oh, I don't eat much," I said. "I just don't get very hungry."

It would be months before I realized that Demi probably had told the staff about my own eating disorder, which I still refused to acknowledge. I was completely oblivious to the fact that if Demi re-entered an environment where someone was participating in an eating disorder, it would make her feel unsafe, which also meant she was far more likely to relapse. Coming back home would be like walking into a lion's den.

At the end of January, that's exactly what she did.

CHAPTER THIRTY

"I didn't think they'd take my Xanax away!"

I
t wasn't a good day. That April I dropped Madison off at
school and turned my car toward home, knowing with
certainty that the demons in my head were ready to
strike. I tried to block out all of my inner noise by turning up the
volume to Reba Rambo McGuire's "Ain't Givin' Up Now," a song
that had been my personal anthem since my teens. From start to
finish, I sang along and tried my best to belt out those final words.
"It's too late now to start this talkin' defeat . . . ain't givin' up now."

But I couldn't summon the strength to believe any of it. Typically,
the lyrics infused me with the determination and conviction that I
could move mountains. That morning, though, I was grasping to
hold on to my own life. Demi had been home for a little more than
two months and was doing well. She was recording music again,
going to support meetings, and agreeing to the supervision of a

sober companion, someone designated to stay with her 24-7 to ensure her sobriety. Now that I no longer had to be strong for her or Dallas, I was free-falling into darkness.

Just drive into that oncoming car! End the pain! Give up!

The dark voice inside my head wanted destruction. While Madison was with me, I refused to give in. But when I was alone, I felt helpless and afraid. As I inched my way home, I kept singing, though my voice was barely above a whisper. After parking my car, I trudged up the six flights of stairs from the garage to the house, telling myself with every step that I had the strength to live another day.

Like most mornings, my plan was to crawl back into bed for a while. Sleep—that soothing, gray fog of nothingness—was my friend. Afterward, I'd spend some time trying to look and feel better, a ritual that usually involved trying on half a dozen outfits until I found the right one that didn't make me feel "heavy." In reality, I was skin and bones, weighing less than ninety pounds. Yet, when I looked in the mirror, I saw a woman who was overweight.

Before I could reach the bedroom, my phone rang. Seeing that it was Eddie, I figured if he wasn't texting, it must be important.

"Hello," I said, trying to sound cheerful.

His voice exploded in my ear. "Did you give Dallas a credit card again?" he roared. "She just spent six hundred dollars at Target! You can't let her do that!"

First suicidal thoughts and now this? I couldn't believe that Eddie was ready to pick a fight. We rarely argued, but his reprimand triggered a landslide of emotions that tumbled out of me.

"What do you want me to do about it?" I shot back. My words

clanged like the bell before a boxing match. All those years of being strong for my kids, dealing with the pressure to be perfect, and feeling so homesick that I could barely breathe ruptured inside of me. "That's it," I screamed. "I'm done! I'm going back to Texas!"

At first there was only silence. Then Eddie softened, "Dianna, you don't mean that. . . . You can't leave Madison behind."

But I couldn't think about that . . . couldn't open the door to staying. I knew if I didn't leave, I would die. It wasn't safe here . . . in this house . . . in this life. I knew that I'd eventually give in to those terrible voices. It might be tomorrow, or it might be next week. My only hope was to get back to Colleyville, the one and only place I had ever felt safe.

I hung up and started packing. And not just for a few days. I grabbed a huge suitcase and threw in everything that I couldn't live without. In went a couple of purses, three pairs of sunglasses, ten pairs of shoes, my makeup, my favorite jeans, my favorite sweatpants, my favorite necklace, my favorite anything I could get my hands on. And, I tossed in my bottle of pills, too. But before I could buy a ticket, I decided to lie down. The Xanax I had taken earlier made it impossible to stay awake.

Sometime later, in the twilight of my nap, I heard Demi's voice. "Mom, wake up," she said. "We need to talk."

"About what?" I asked, opening my eyes to see a hazy crowd of people around my bed. Eddie, Dallas, Lisa, and Demi slowly came into focus.

"We think it's time for you to get some help," Demi said, pointing to the suitcase.

"Oh," I replied, summoning my sweet southern voice. "Okay,

I'll go to a therapist . . . three times a week." But the looks on their faces told me they weren't convinced.

"No, it's time to get some real help, like inpatient treatment," Demi continued.

"I can't do that," I suddenly wailed. "I can't leave Madi—"

But I never finished saying my daughter's name because at that very moment the room began to spin. Visions of my suitcase, everything I had thrown inside, and my plans to run away to Texas swirled around me. The full weight of what I had been ready to do hit me with such force that I thought I would collapse. *What was wrong with me? How sick was I to have considered leaving my child so I could return to Texas?*

Lisa's voice momentarily cut through the whirlwind I was swimming in, but she sounded far away. "Don't worry about Madison," she said. "We'll take care of her."

The next thing I heard was Eddie, who was on the phone, asking for an admissions counselor. When I looked at him, he handed the phone to me. On the other end was a counselor from TK, the very facility that Demi had just left. Within minutes, I was spilling my guts. There, in front of my family, I revealed every dark secret and terrible thought that had stalked me for the past few months. When I was finished, I couldn't look my family in the eyes. *Were they horrified by my revelations? Or worse, disappointed?*

Resigned to the fact that I needed help, I agreed to be admitted. Eddie rushed to purchase airline tickets for the next morning, as Dallas and Demi rifled through my suitcase, removing all the items I couldn't take with me. They took away my shampoo, my conditioner, and anything with alcohol listed as an ingredient. Out went my hairspray and my razors. When someone offered to put all my music onto an iPod, I remembered that I'd be surrendering my phone, too.

That night, we sat down with Madison and explained what was happening. She welled up with tears at the news that I was leaving. It crushed my heart. The poor kid had been through this twice before, but this time was far worse because it was me—her mom—the one who was supposed to love and protect her. There wasn't much more that I could do, so I hugged her and promised to call from the pay phones at TK as often as I could. The next morning, Eddie and I left for Chicago.

Like an instant replay of Demi's drop-off, I didn't panic until we reached the entrance gate. In fact, I had calmly called my parents and a few close friends before our departure to let them know where I was headed. I didn't want the special people in my life learning the details from the media news outlets like so many had after Demi entered treatment. But as I thought about all the people I wouldn't see or talk to in the coming weeks, I began to wonder if my stay would feel more like jail than therapy. *Would I be as strong as Demi and Dallas had been?*

While Eddie and I sat in a small room, seated at a little round table, an intake counselor asked a lot of big questions. "How long have you had suicidal thoughts?" "Were you ready to act on those thoughts?" "Has this ever happened before?" Considering I had answered similar questions earlier, I figured there was no reason to hide anything now, so I answered the counselor as honestly and truthfully as I could. Every word seemed to dislodge more tears.

I slowly became numb and lethargic, probably from the extra

Xanax I had taken on the plane. When I glanced at Eddie, he looked like someone had punched him in the gut. My heart hurt for him. I knew without a doubt that this time I was the one inflicting the pain. The past ten months seemed too bizarre to be real. *How did we get here?* I kept thinking. *Wasn't it just a short time ago that I almost had a perfect life?*

"You're rather thin," the woman suddenly said. "Are you eating normally?"

"Oh," I faltered, "I'm . . . well, I'm just a small person and . . . I've had a high metabolism for years."

When they asked how much I ate, I lied and told them I ate more often than I did. *We can explore my depression*, I thought, *but not my diet!* I knew if they suspected an eating disorder, I'd be put on a meal plan, just like Demi had been. The very thought made me angry. *Don't make me gain weight! That's not why I came here!*

There was one final question: "Do you have Xanax with you?"

I had moved the bottle to my purse before our flight, so I reached in and retrieved it. When she asked me to hand it to her, I objected. "But I need this," I pleaded. "Sometimes I take it three times a day."

She smiled and took the bottle away. "We'll help you with that," she said.

Help me with what? I wondered. *Xanax wasn't the problem!*

With that, it was time to say good-bye to Eddie. I tried to be strong, but I wasn't. Every time I thought of Madison, I started crying even harder. As Eddie walked away, Sheila, a tall, brunette BHS, led me across the parking lot to Oak Lodge, my new home. Rattled as I was, I felt comforted when Sheila placed her arm around my shoulders and looked at me in a way that told me she understood. Her kindness and compassion would see me through a lot of tough days in the coming weeks.

Sheila flashed her badge, and the doors to the lodge parted. When we stepped inside, the finality of the moment hit me: *I'm stuck! I can't get out!* I berated myself for not making a break toward the main entrance when I had a chance. It seemed incomprehensible that I, a forty-eight-year-old mother of three girls who had supervised and guided her children to reach their dreams, was now being told what I could and couldn't do.

"Everything gets started at five a.m., so you should unpack now," Sheila suggested as she led me to my room. Instead, I sat on the bed in my pink warm-up suit and Uggs, staring at her. My hair was perfectly coiffed, but my eyes were swollen shut from crying. I no longer cared about anything—not even meeting my two new roommates. Both were older women who later told me their first impressions of me ran along the lines of "prima donna, trophy wife, and eating disorder."

Faced with my stubbornness not to move, Sheila graciously offered to unpack for me. "Wow, you sure did bring a lot of stuff," she remarked as she emptied the last few items from my bag. Then she held up a purple stone in the palm of her hand. "What's this?" she asked.

"Never saw it before," I said. "Probably isn't mine."

CHAPTER THIRTY-ONE

"Tonight I want to go out with a dance party."

When I look back at the woman who entered treatment that April in 2011, I hardly recognize her. She was fragile and broken in so many ways. And horribly thin and malnourished. There was no light in her eyes, no happiness in her soul. It still makes me sad to think of her. But she didn't dissolve into a pile of dust. Instead, I helped her to grow stronger, though not right away.

Life at TK was very structured. I could no longer reach for my phone when I was lonely or take a nap when I felt exhausted. There were schedules to follow and rules to obey. We got up at the crack of dawn and turned off our lights by ten each evening. Televisions, radios, and newspapers were nonexistent. Morning coffee was offered at 5:30 a.m. and taken away by noon—and there was always a line! Every class, meal, and shower was monitored by a

BHS. And I couldn't leave Oak Lodge, except to eat in the dining room or attend certain classes.

I, like everyone else, had a support team, and we met almost daily. Like dedicated scientists, my team always had piles of notes that detailed my moods, my participation, the meds I took, the comments I made, the food I ate, my grooming habits, the things I worried about, and . . . well, everything. I was a lab rat, of sorts, that they hoped to turn back into a healthy, functioning human being one day. They had their work cut out for them, especially in the beginning. But I came to love my team. The group consisted of Kimberly Dennis, MD, my psychiatrist, otherwise known as Dr. Kim; one regular therapist; a trauma therapist; a nutritionist; and a crew of BHSs. Not one of them ever gave up on me, though at times I wanted to give up on myself.

Those first two weeks at TK were nothing short of a marathon of weeping. When I was asked to make a time line of my life, I cried. When I was asked to make a poster about my future, I sobbed and shook uncontrollably. When I listened to everyone else's stories, I wept and refused to join the conversation. There was simply too much pain and grief inside of me fighting for air. And I didn't have the energy—or guts—to open the wounds of my life for everyone to see. On top of that, I also was muddling through the haze of withdrawal, as Dr. Kim slowly weaned me off Xanax, a complicated process that had to be monitored carefully so that I wouldn't suffer a stroke. All of it put me squarely in the first stage of recovery, which TK describes as "Coming In."

My morning ritual never changed. From the day I started until the day left, I consumed as much coffee as I could before jumping on the treadmill of classes that covered everything from art to nutrition to DBT (Dialectical Behavior Therapy) skills, a group of behavioral skills that addressed mindfulness, distress, tolerance, and emotional regulation. In between classes, I'd attend various therapy sessions. The only breaks in our routines that were allowed came on weekends, during visiting hours, and if we didn't have visitors, someone always found something for us to do.

In order to gain privileges, such as walking to the dining room without an escort or going on shopping trips, I needed to move into stage two, known as "Looking In." To make that leap, I'd have to participate in every class and therapy session, eat all of my food, and turn in my homework assignments on a regular basis. Of course, the challenge of doing all of that made me cry even more.

I learned that there was a reservoir of grief inside of me that had to be emptied. If I was too full of heartache, there was no room for joy. So I wept for the singing career I had never achieved and for the parts of myself that had died during my marriage to Pat. Then I cried for the finger I had lost, the hardships of poverty, and the little girl who had moved too often. I cried for the mistakes I had made and for the mistakes my children had made. And I cried for the friends I had lost, as well as the hopes and dreams that had gone off course. Somewhere in the process, the walls inside of me began to crumble.

On one of those early days, when I was feeling really low, I took the purple rock off my dresser that Sheila had found in my suitcase and carried it with me to art class. It felt comforting to hold on to something. As I sat there listening to the soft music, contemplating whether I should string a few beads together or learn to knit, Rae, the art teacher, wandered past me.

"Hey," she said, picking up my rock, "I've seen this before." She then flipped it over and showed me the sticker that was pasted on the bottom, which I had failed to notice. It said: STRENGTH. "I make a stone for everyone before they leave," Rae explained, "and I gave this one to Demi!"

It was a poignant reminder that Demi and Dallas had been down this path, too, and if they had survived, I figured I could, too. Later, when I asked Demi if she put that stone in my bag, she said she hadn't. But it wound up in my possession for a reason. During those difficult days when I needed an extra boost of comfort or encouragement, I always reached for it and found the "strength" to continue.

One of the most astounding changes to take place during the first week of my treatment came when the nutritionist put a normal plate of food in front of me. I stared at the large cut of steak, the mound of green beans, the heap of mashed potatoes, and the eight-ounce carton of milk and finally admitted that I "might" have an eating problem. The meal before me was more than I typically consumed over several days. My admission of guilt meant more meetings with the nutritionist and adding nutrition classes to my schedule. It also meant agreeing to that dreaded meal plan, which included three meals a day, plus two snacks. Every bite was terrifying.

Since I wasn't used to eating large quantities, my plan at first was simply to eat small amounts with high caloric value. My first meal, a peanut-butter-and-jelly sandwich and glass of milk, made me wince. As I sat in Oak Lodge staring at the challenge before me, some of my comrades in arms felt the urge to help me. "You can do this, Dianna," one woman urged. "It's just food," offered another. Tears were streaming down my cheeks, but I appreciated their encouragement. I tore off the crusts and started eating. Every bite required an eternity of chewing before I could swallow. When I stopped, I still had half a carton of milk and pieces of crust scattered on my tray.

"Not good enough," the BHS said. It was clearly an all or nothing deal, which unleashed a few more tears. The first time I finally finished everything on my plate, everyone around me cheered. I smiled, but wondered how I could possibly do it again in a few hours. At first, I couldn't, which always meant eating the next meal in Oak Lodge with the other "sad sacks," the nickname we gave to those who couldn't comply with the dietary rules, as no one in that situation ever looked happy. The simple fact that I wanted more freedom and the social benefits of eating with other residents finally propelled me to consume greater quantities of food. Eventually, I graduated to grilled cheese sandwiches and pieces of chicken.

But conquering my eating disorder involved more than just a meal plan. In group therapy, I learned that anyone whose life is controlled by food suffers from some type of disorder. Mine was definitely anorexia, as I was fastidious about restricting the amount I ate. This became even clearer in nutrition class when I was asked to draw a life-size picture of myself on a sheet of white paper that was placed on the floor. After I finished, I stared at the crime-scene-like drawing I had made and thought it looked accurate. But when I was asked to lie down while someone else traced my actual figure on top of my sketch, it was clear that I was far tinier than I imagined.

"The syndrome is called body dysmorphic disorder," the teacher said. And we all seemed to have it. But I was thankful that, unlike some of those around me, I never heard voices telling me to throw my food on the wall and I never felt that certain body parts, like my neck or my arms, swelled in size when I ate. As thin as I was, I hadn't yet reached that point of no return. There was still hope that if I found the right tools and motivation, I could change.

Perhaps the most telling sign that I wanted to kick my anorexia came when I learned that all my years of restricting what I ate had affected more than just my outer appearance. In reality, I had been starving my heart, my liver, my kidneys, and my brain as well. And that scared me. I didn't want to be a brittle-boned woman with sagging skin, and I certainly didn't want to die from malnutrition. My children were precious to me, and I desperately wanted to be around for them in the future, especially for Madison, who had so many milestones ahead of her. I dug my heels in and decided to make better progress.

Where did you go? I wrote.

It was the start of an assignment that challenged me to write a letter to my former self and to explain why I thought I was in the shape I was in. At first, I had no idea what to write. Then the words started pouring out of me:

You're not here anymore, and I miss you. You used to be such a cheerleader for me and other people! You used to be so happy all the time! No matter what you came up against, you made it work. You turned every bad situation into something good. And you encouraged me! Why aren't

you here anymore??? Where are those silver linings you always found
behind every cloud??? I'm looking for you, and I hope I find you, because
I miss you. A lot. I know you can help me to heal. . . .

It was a defining moment. I finally was looking at myself with compassion—all of me. That bubbly teenager who had always smiled and dreamed big and that Dallas Cowboys Cheerleader who had proudly represented her team were also the same person who had starved herself, who became a mentally-disease-ridden drug user, and who eventually was a depressed mother fighting for her sanity. They were all pieces of me, and I could no longer pick and choose which ones I wanted the world to see.

One thing was clear: Secrets had made me sick. Now it was time to change my life. I had to find a way to accept all of the weak and imperfect parts of myself and transform them into something stronger. More than anything, I wanted to stop chasing perfection and start creating a life worth living. I wanted to know real joy. Real happiness. Real satisfaction. My letter was a baby step in the right direction.

Another issue I was working on was post-traumatic stress disorder (PTSD). It wasn't something I was even conscious of until I went into therapy. But from my first night on, it was painfully clear that certain situations not only terrified me, they transported me in time to past events. My room situation was a prime example, where my bed, which was located by the door, was an instant trigger. Throughout the night, from midnight to dawn, a BHS stopped by to check on us. And every time that door squeaked open, I jumped up and started climbing the wall next to me. Literally. Each and every time, it was like I was back in my bedroom the night

Dallas came charging in, high on drugs. I was terrified, and my reflex was to escape.

There were other incidents, too. When I'd hear a door slam shut during the daytime, it triggered memories of my fight all those years ago with Pat. *BAM!* The sound was like an alarm that released a physical reaction in my body. All over again, I'd feel the door smashing my fingers. I'd hear the crunch as my bones crumbled. And I'd relive the horror of all that blood spurting in my face. Sweating and panting, I felt like I was going crazy.

It took long sessions with my trauma therapist to change those patterns. And as we worked through the reasons and causes behind such debilitating responses, I began to understand just how many dimensions are involved with treating and understanding mental-health issues. Not just with PTSD, but with everything I was addressing—an eating disorder, depression, anxiety, ruminating thoughts, and addiction to Xanax.

I learned there were possible genetic factors, as well as environmental ones. And telling the difference wasn't always easy. When I learned that my mother had dealt with an eating disorder, and her mother before her, I thought maybe my tendencies were genetic. But my mother suggested that maybe it was more that I had modeled behavior that I had seen, just as she had done. And up until that point, neither of us had ever talked about the topic. Regardless of the cause, I had grown up in a home where dieting was the norm, and that put me in a high-risk situation for developing eating issues of my own. And I learned that early trauma in combination with a parent who has a mental-health issue such as anorexia meant that I was dead center in the perfect storm of conditions likely to produce self-destructive coping mechanisms. All of it made my head spin.

But there was more. I also learned that if we believe at an early age that we are at fault for bad things happening, every future bad thing that happens solidifies the concept. When I looked back, the pattern was clear. Every time I had tried unsuccessfully to obey the pastor's fiery warnings about hellfire and brimstone for so much as a sinful thought, every time I had endured Pat's criticism and his habit of pushing me against a wall, and every time I saw my kids make a mistake—I had blamed myself. Deep down, I had trouble believing that I was a good person . . . a good mother . . . a good anything. It was self-destruction at its worst.

Dr. Kim told me that I had a choice. I could either walk around and wear those old, unhealthy beliefs that told me I wasn't good enough, that I needed to be perfect and that I would only be loved if I was thin—or—I could start paying attention to the beliefs that were ruining my life and consciously choose to change them. It would be some of the most important work I did at TK, because it meant not blaming anyone for my situation but rather taking responsibility for my actions and accepting help to change the way I thought about myself. It was also clear that I needed to change so that I could be a better role model for my kids. It was time to take our family in a new direction!

But trying to let go of perfection, after five decades of striving to attain it, wasn't easy. I was willing to start forgiving myself and to be more compassionate, but I had my limits. I never could get the nerve to break a few rules while I was in treatment, and I never, ever left my room without wearing makeup. At one point, my therapist actually encouraged me to break a rule—like being late or missing a class—just so I could ponder how it felt. She even promised the reward of allowing me to take a short joyride on one of the forbidden golf carts outside. But I couldn't do it. Conquering those challenges would have to wait until I came home.

As I settled into the routines at TK, I started to relax and open up to the people around me. Like most people thrown together for any length of time, we found ways to humor and inspire each other, and we also shared the details of our lives like we were open books. I found it interesting that most people my age didn't know who Demi was, but they all got excited when I mentioned Madison's name. It seemed I was surrounded by *Desperate Housewives* fans, and we all bemoaned the fact that we couldn't stay caught up on the show. Over time, I grew to love the women around me like sisters. And when they opened their hearts and shared their feelings during group sessions, their stories helped me more than they will ever know. Every word taught me something about the incredible journey we were all on to improve our mental and emotional selves.

Sometime, shortly after those difficult first two weeks, I finally earned my white cap, signifying that I had advanced to the second stage of "Looking In." I was over-the-moon excited because it meant two important rewards would be added to my schedule. First, I could hop on the bus in the evenings and go to support meetings like AA that were held off-site. Even though I had never considered myself an alcoholic, I found the group of mostly old men at the local meeting to be charming and sweet, and as I listened to their stories, I realized their battles with alcohol weren't much different from my addiction to Xanax. But if I'm honest, my number-one reason for going was purely selfish: I wanted the free coffee they served at every meeting. It's sad to admit, but when you're in rehab, you look for any motivation you can find, and mine was caffeine!

The second privilege I earned was the opportunity to go shopping. When a trip to Target was announced, I felt a rush of anticipation similar to that of counting down the days until Christmas. Now that I was eating again, none of my clothes fit, and I desperately wanted to buy pretty new outfits, even if they were a size bigger. When they dropped us off in front of the store, I rushed inside like I was on a game show, gathering armfuls of colorful sweatpants in my arms and throwing handfuls of T-shirts into my shopping cart. It felt wildly satisfying. Oh, how I missed normal experiences like going to the mall!

No one ever goes into treatment thinking they'll be there for two or three months. I was no different, especially since I had been working so hard to get better. When someone told me to report to a group meeting with my support team at the end of April, I was elated. *This was my day! My freedom papers were coming!*

"Dianna." Dr. Kim smiled. "We think you need to stay a while longer." The staff around her agreed.

I stared back in disbelief, feeling crushed. Then I ran back to my room and called Eddie, sobbing. He told me that I needed to listen to the experts. "But it's costing a fortune!" I wailed. "They just want our money!" It wasn't true, but I wanted to blame some-one. And the cost of treatment *was* a concern.

Truthfully, I still don't know how anyone without means is supposed to get the appropriate mental-health care they need when insurance companies treat therapy like it's a choice instead of medicine for an illness. My Xanax addiction, my depression, my eating disorder, my PTSD, and my anxiety issues weren't a matter of choice. I wanted to live differently, but I didn't know how to do that without help. Getting help for all my issues was no less important than a diabetic getting medical advice about controlling his sugar, but our insurance company, like most others, didn't see it that way. Although I felt fortunate to have the resources to stay and get better, I also didn't want to exhaust our family's savings in the process.

But the real issue that day was simply the fact that I wanted to go home. Eddie visited regularly and the girls came when they could, but I wanted to be back in their daily lives. *I was ready, damn it! Why were they doing this?* The whole situation made me angry. That afternoon during group therapy, when it was my time to share, I let loose.

"I don't even hear what any of you are saying today, because I thought I was going home," I ranted. "But I'm not! And now I'm pissed. I'm pissed at the therapists. I'm pissed at the doctors, and I'm pissed at everyone who's involved in this place, because I don't want to be here—and that's my thought for the day!"

The BHS politely thanked me for being honest, while someone else smiled. "Good for you! Express your feelings," one woman cheered. I wanted to slap each and every one of them. It took about forty-eight hours to calm down and realize that the staff was right. If I went home too early, I'd relapse, just like many did once most insurance companies refused to pay for another dime of their stay. I understood that I was one of the lucky ones who didn't have to

303

listen to the mental-health directives of some CEO making policy decisions, and I wanted to make the most of my opportunity. Besides, I didn't want to leave until I could uphold my promise to be a better role model for my kids. My new goal was to stay until I completed the program and earned my certificate proving that I had done the work. But I also wanted to do it in record time. Again, I dug my heels in. About two weeks later, I moved into TK's final stage, "Looking Out."

A highlight of my time at TK was on Mother's Day that May, when Madison, Demi, and Dallas came along with Eddie to visit. When everyone strolled into the conference room, I noticed they had brought a gift.

"For you, Momma," they said in unison.

They placed a box on the table before me that bore an emblem I knew too well. It was the Rolex emblem, something I had seen years before when Eddie had decided to use his Christmas bonus to surprise me with a special watch to commemorate Madison's birth. I had always wanted one, but two years later, I had decided (without his approval) to sell it so that we could keep our girls' dreams alive.

"It's okay," I had told everyone. "It's just a watch. One day you girls will be successful, and you can buy me another one."

Now, as I sat there in treatment, tears filling my eyes, I was overwhelmed. When I lifted the new watch from the box, the girls helped me to put it on.

"Happy Mother's Day," they shouted. "It looks so pretty." Dallas beamed and Demi sweetly added, "We're so proud of you!"

I thought my heart would explode. My family had kept their promise to me for all the sacrifices I had made for them during the past, and their gesture meant so much because they gave it to me during one of the toughest times of my life.

As I neared my seventh week in therapy, I was moved out of Oak Lodge and into transitional living at Magnolia House. For two weeks, I'd be totally free to come and go as I pleased. It was a big step, considering I easily could have headed straight to a liquor store or tried to find a source for Xanax. But I didn't. I felt too good to even consider it. My weight was stable. My anxiety was controllable. And my depression had lifted. Although I still took a mild antidepressant, my thoughts no longer cycled around despair or self-harm. In fact, the longer I was off Xanax, the lighter and happier I felt. And I had more energy, which probably was due in part to the fact that I was finally eating normal, healthy meals. I still went to AA meetings at night and still went to all of my classes and therapy sessions during the day, but I also added activities such as going grocery shopping and learning to cook. I also took the important step of asking a woman to be my AA sponsor, and we met regularly at a local coffee shop.

My goals had shifted. Now instead of chasing perfection, I wanted to make better choices about my health and happiness. A few days into my ninth week, there was still one more hurdle to clear: I needed to say good-bye. I had earned my certificate and was finally going home!

Considering that I had come to TK not wanting to share my life with anyone, I was now facing the hard task of having to leave my new friends. I had come to think of everyone, from the residents to the staff, as family. We had cried on each other's shoulders, picked one another up when times got tough, and shared more than a few laughs together. The last thing I wanted was to be a blubbering fool as I handed out my final hugs.

The Wednesday of my departure, I packed my bags in the morning and took them to the front of the building so they'd be there when Eddie came to get me that evening. The remaining twelve hours were for final reflections and expressing my gratitude. My first opportunity to do so was after lunch, when I would make the traditional farewell speech to staff and residents. I promised myself that I would make it a happy and upbeat occasion. Just to make things interesting, Dr. Kim challenged me to make the speech without fixing my hair or wearing makeup. For weeks, everyone had been teasing me about my penchant for always dressing up and wearing big hairdos, especially since there was no one I needed to impress, but I still wasn't ready to let go of those habits. Though, I did manage to add an element of surprise that made everyone cheer.

Most of what I said was one long thank-you. I praised and thanked the people on my team, my roommates, the teachers, everyone in Oak Lodge, everyone who wasn't in Oak Lodge, Jesus. . . . The list went on and on. I truly was grateful for each and every person who had supported me in any way. As my emotions threatened to overflow, I caught myself and threw out a couple of final words that hit home. A few weeks before, one of the girls with eating issues was so exuberant after finally finishing her meal, she had blurted out: "I just made that breakfast my bitch!" Every single one of us knew exactly where she was coming from. I figured she wouldn't mind if I borrowed and tweaked her expression.

"I just made treatment my bitch," I declared with a smile. It brought the house down. People laughed and cheered, hooted and hollered. And just as I had hoped, there wasn't a sad face in the bunch.

A few hours later, before evening meditation, I made one more announcement.

"Tonight I want to go out with a dance party," I said, "and everyone *must* participate!" The staff had agreed to give me five minutes at the start of the evening meeting after everyone gathered in Oak Lodge.

First, I put on CeeLo Green's "Forget You" and cranked up the volume. With my hips swaying and arms waving, I encouraged everyone to join me. To my surprise, a BHS turned off the lights, and someone started handing out flashlights. In no time, we had a full-blown disco party going on. While the music blared, bursts of light streaked across the darkness, and the energy in the room became contagious. No one dared to stay seated.

As more and more people got pulled into the middle of the dance floor, elbows and hands flashed before my face. We laughed and jiggled, gyrating like teenagers. Out of the corner of my eye, I even caught a glimpse of a few wild participants—residents and counselors alike—jumping off the couches! By the time I switched to Lady Gaga's "Born This Way," all hell was breaking loose. And we sank our teeth into it, turning those final minutes of frantic movement into our own personal declarations of "I came in here thinking life was daunting" to "I got this!"

This is life! I thought. It was a powerful moment when I realized deep in my soul that I was not only taking all the memories of these people that I had met with me, but I was also taking home their joys, their sorrows, and their tears. *This was what a life worth living felt like!* And I knew that if I could stay connected to these rich feelings of emotion and hold on to the significance of this culminating moment, then I'd stay inspired in the future to live without behaviors, without drugs, and without the burdens of inferiority or guilt that had shackled me for so long. My heart was full and my spirit was free.

When the music stopped, I waltzed toward the door, hugging the people I passed along the way and brushing happy tears from my face. Then I paused. Took a bow. And ceremoniously shouted, "You're welcome!"

When I walked out, I never looked back.

CHAPTER THIRTY-TWO

"Life really began after treatment—
there was a lot of soul-searching to do."

I realized rather quickly that life outside of treatment was
far different than inside. Now I was on my own without
the rigid structure of classes and therapy sessions to
attend, and it frightened me more than I wanted to admit. Those
first few weeks back at home I barely left our property, choosing
instead to spend hours outside, surrounded by our palm trees and
lush, tropical plants. It was the perfect space for meditating and
writing in my journal.

As I pondered how I had grown and changed in the past nine
weeks, I jotted down the key takeaways from my stay in therapy:

1. I could no longer pretend that things were perfect.
   It was better to share my emotions, talk about my
   problems, and ask questions.

2. I could no longer be afraid of food. Nutritious meals were necessary for a healthy life.

3. I could no longer alleviate anxiousness or distress with drugs or alcohol. I needed to practice the DBT skills I had learned instead of ruminating on the "what-ifs" and "maybes" of life.

4. I could no longer make my whole life about my kids. It was time to find some activities and pursuits that made *me* feel passionate and fulfilled.

Everyone has barriers they need to break through, and those were mine. If I could stay focused on my list, I'd remain on a healthier path. But, it was a daily struggle at first. I felt weak and shaky, as though I had just recovered from a long bout with the flu and now needed to get out of bed and be around people again. I didn't trust myself.

Soon after I returned home, Madison's private school held its graduation celebration. Since it was a small school, all students, regardless of grade, were encouraged to invite their parents, relatives, and close friends. Even though I knew it wouldn't be like walking into Times Square on New Year's Eve, I was terrified. But I couldn't back out, as Madison was graduating from fourth grade, and it was a big deal to her. Not wanting to disappoint her, I wondered how I'd manage not only the ceremony, but also the festivities afterward, which included a big auction and a meal with tons of food and lots of wine. Thankfully, Eddie reserved a table for us with our best California friends, Rod and Amy, who were nondrinkers, but I was still so nervous that I barely let go of Eddie's arm the entire evening. We both sighed in relief when it was over.

I also was uncomfortable with how much weight I had gained during my stay at TK. The twenty-five extra pounds I now carried seemed too much, but I didn't want to swing back in the other direction. Initially, though, there wasn't much danger of that, because suddenly I couldn't stop eating. It was as if someone had given me carte blanche to eat as much as I pleased. I alternated between figuring out which new restaurant to try next and following my favorite food trucks around LA, even downloading an app to alert me when they were close by.

One evening, Eddie and I joined a group of friends at a food-truck convention, where tables and chairs were set up in a parking lot. We all ordered these "grilled cheese burgers" that consisted of alternating layers of grilled cheese sandwich, a burger, another grilled cheese sandwich, and fries. I gobbled mine up and dug into someone else's, just as I caught Eddie staring at me in disbelief.

"Are you okay?" he asked.

The concern on his face alerted me to the fact that what I was doing wasn't the healthiest thing for anyone, even though I was *really, really* enjoying myself. So, I put myself on a meal plan. It was—and still is—the best way to make sure that I stay on an even keel, as resisting the urge to diet will always be my biggest challenge. I also started working out with a group of my friends at a class led by our trainer, Ronin Boushnak. Once a championship MMA titleholder, he ignited our passion for kickboxing and mixed martial arts. And as friends, we all continue to hold each other accountable for showing up to class, even on days when we don't feel like it. These days, I'm proud to say that I'm more concerned about developing my muscles than stepping on a scale.

There's nothing like a good workout with Ronin to make me feel like I can conquer the world.

One of the best decisions our family made during that time was to bring home two new Shih Tzu puppies. Although we had planned on doing it all along, the timing was perfect. I sat for hours stroking Bentley and Oliver, who often cuddled in my lap. The lovefest was good for all of us.

But not all of our decisions were wise ones. Like always, Eddie and I decided to go to Vegas to celebrate our wedding anniversary. Our little getaway started out fine, but one night while Eddie was busy gambling, I wandered away and thought I'd treat myself to a celebratory glass of wine. Several hours later, Eddie found me dazed and confused, roaming the Strip with a collection of photos on my phone that chronicled my bizarre encounter with someone dressed as Barney, the purple dinosaur. Although most details about the night were sketchy, I did remember throwing my arms around the purple beast and declaring: "My daughter Demi was on your show, and I LOVE YOU!"

It was hardly a proud moment. But it was a realization that once they took my drugs away, my addictive personality made me vulnerable to whatever I could get my hands on. From that night forward, I started attending AA meetings, cleared our home of alcohol, and called my friend Amy whenever I needed to be talked out of doing something foolish like buying a drink. I had worked too hard to go back into those behaviors. Unfortunately, there was no remedy to "un-see" those ridiculous selfies I had taken with Barney.

———

As the fall of 2011 slid into winter, I was thankful that our family was on the mend. Dallas, still auditioning, found voiceover work on *Snowflake, the White Gorilla*, while Demi released her third studio album, *Unbroken*, which peaked at number four on the *Billboard* 200. Madison continued her role on *Desperate Housewives*, and I settled into my role as mother without the crutch of Xanax. All in all, it seemed like everyone was committed to living healthier, happier lives. Although relapsing after treatment isn't uncommon, I didn't see any signs that anyone was in trouble.

Demi was still living at home with her sober companion, and at Thanksgiving we all headed to Texas, where MTV filmed our whole clan gathered at my aunt's house. It was part of the footage they would use for *Stay Strong*, the station's documentary about Demi's recovery, which unbeknownst to me was teetering on the edge of collapse. Eddie and I even flew to New York City that New Year's Eve to watch Demi promote the documentary's upcoming release. Not once did I notice that Demi was in trouble. But I also wasn't looking. My own recovery was so important and tenuous at that point that I couldn't focus on anyone else.

A few days into 2014, Eddie pulled me aside one evening and shattered my belief that all was well. "Phil wants us to have an intervention with Demi to make it clear that she needs to take her sobriety seriously," he said, looking sad and weary. I was stunned. *Really? Again? Even with a sober companion?* The news was devastating, but I also knew that confronting Demi was absolutely necessary.

Within forty-eight hours, everyone who had a stake in Demi's future was seated at the table in her manager's office. Front and center was my daughter. Gathered around her were Phil McIntyre; Eddie and I; Mike Bayer, who ran CAST, a recovery center in West Hollywood, and who was supervising Demi; her sober companion; and her attorney. Her business manager joined us by phone. We all knew Demi's life was at stake, not just her career. One by one, we each explained what she needed to do and what would happen if she didn't. It was an outpouring of love and concern, followed by hard realities. We later dubbed the gathering "Demi's come-to-Jesus meeting."

One thing was very clear. Everyone present was rooting for Demi's sobriety, but no one would support her career if she continued using substances. Her record label, the press, her loyal fans, and her management team had already given her a second chance. Asking any of them to endure much more was flirting with disaster. As parents, Eddie and I knew that our love for Demi would never waver, but we desperately wanted our daughter to turn things around before she lost everything she had worked so hard to attain. It was time to play hardball.

"If you're going to be using drugs and drinking," I said, "then I can't have you around Madison. She looks up to you."

We locked eyes for a moment, and I knew I had touched on something dear to her heart—her little sister. Suddenly, she exhaled and said, "Okay, what do I have to do?"

She looked weary, as if she was tired of fighting. "Complete surrender," Mike determined. "You give up your car keys, your credit cards—everything—and you turn them over to your sober companion." He hesitated, knowing the next part wouldn't be easy. "And your cell phone," he added.

I winced at that one as I watched her contemplate her decision. The ball was now in her court. I silently prayed, *Lord, let her surrender to getting well.*

Demi looked down at her phone and slowly picked it up. But instead of handing it to Mike, she suddenly smashed it on the table, causing all of us to jump. Then she dropped it into the glass of water sitting in front of her.

"That's so I don't change my mind and try to get my phone back," she said before finally declaring, "I'm ready to get sober now."

"Thank you, God," I whispered.

I'll never forget Demi's words or the cheers that went around the table that night. We celebrated and congratulated her like she had just won a Grammy. But we also knew she had a lot of tough work to do, and we vowed to support her. And that, I believe, was the night she turned her life around for good.

Demi immediately moved into a sober house in Santa Monica where she was under constant supervision and encouraged to attend therapy sessions and AA meetings. Without access to her car, phone, or credit cards, she no longer was tempted to beat the system. Instead, she started rebuilding her resolve to address the mental and emotional issues that had undermined her recovery. Every week or so, I'd go visit her. We spent our time hanging out with some of the other girls there, watching movies, and gossiping about the latest Hollywood scandals. It wasn't healthy for either of us to dwell on the past or talk about personal issues. We saved that for family therapy sessions. Occasionally, Demi and I ventured to a few AA meetings together, but mostly, she worked on herself and I worked on my issues. We both understood how fragile recovery could be.

After only a few months at the sober house, Demi decided that it was time to refocus on her career. She started writing music again and she landed a spot on the *X Factor* as a judge, but she continued to live at the facility in Santa Monica. This time she wasn't taking any shortcuts. In fact, Demi's stay lasted more than a year. When she finally declared that she was ready to live in her own apartment the following March, I trusted that she was ready. By then, we were all branching out in new directions, but each of us took special pride in Demi's blossoming career as well as her vocal commitment to mental health awareness. If the issue needed a public spokesperson, there was no one more prepared to talk about it than my daughter. Hiding from the truth was no longer our family's strategy.

CHAPTER THIRTY-THREE

"There she was—standing in front of more than fourteen thousand fans—and it began to dawn on me just how badly our youth need someone to show them that being sober is cool."

On September 27, 2014, I was backstage at the Staples Center in LA with Lisa, Dallas, Madison, and Madison's friend Jayde. We were rummaging through Demi's dressing room, trying to find some snacks to eat while we waited for her to finish rehearsing with Travis Barker on stage. He was scheduled to play drums on the opening song, "Really Don't Care," which seemed like a good fit as I remembered how Demi and Dallas used to watch his reality show *Meet the Barkers* way back when they were younger. We were always amazed at his drum-playing.

"Hi, Momma," Demi cried when she saw us. "Joe Jonas is here . . ." she started to say, then trailed off. I figured the playlist that night included a surprise.

"Travis Barker *and* a duet with Joe?" I whispered.

"It's a big night," she said, smiling.

For a second, we both locked eyes and didn't say anything. Memories flooded past in nanoseconds. I saw Demi at five, singing "My Heart Will Go On" at the school talent show; at seven, belting out "You're Never Fully Dressed Without a Smile" during her first pageant; and just a few years ago, singing "This Is Me" in *Camp Rock*. And there were flashes of that first solo tour she kicked off in Hershey, Pennsylvania, and her first live award-show appearance after rehab, when she sang "Skyscraper." All roads had led to this night.

"You're gonna do amazing," I told her. And with that, she thanked me and disappeared.

Even though I was excited, I felt a twinge of disappointment. The one person who should have been with us wasn't. Eddie, still working in the music industry, was back in Texas, helping his new country artist, George Navarro, get ready for a round of record label visits in Nashville. But I knew Eddie deserved to be here, and it was breaking my heart that he wasn't around to see Demi playing before a sellout crowd at the Staples Center. I shot off a text telling him: "It's just not the same without you here!"

He responded by telling me to shoot videos and send them to him. I felt like crying, but I wouldn't let it ruin my evening. About five minutes later, Demi's security guard, Sugar, a sweetheart of a teddy bear and total New Yorker, burst through the door.

"Look what I found," he shouted. Right behind him, carrying a small travel backpack and dressed in his favorite light-blue shirt and jeans, was Eddie. I screamed and pounced on him. "But you just texted me . . ." I protested.

"Did you really think I'd miss this night?" He grinned.

The backstage area was filled with people from Hollywood Records, and I quickly spied Stacy and Lillian, two of my favorites because we always talked about each other's latest pieces of jewelry or Lillian's latest Louis Vuitton item. That night we laughed and giggled like kids, sharing stories about the early days, when Demi was only fifteen. There was a lot of jubilation about how far she had come. And the visitors kept arriving. Phil McIntyre and his family, Judy Taylor from Disney, Cathryn Sullivan and Jennifer Patredis from Texas, and Sarah Jones, a longtime friend of the family since our *Camp Rock* days, were just a few. In all, some fifty people showed up to visit that night before the show. There were so many memories and so much love that it felt like family. Before Demi took the stage, we all held hands and prayed.

"Dear God," Demi began, "touch our voices, our bodies, and our instruments. Let us inspire. Let us entertain. Let us relay your message to those who need it tonight. And let us help people forget their problems for a while. In Jesus's name, amen."

After she finished, we all placed our hands in the center, one on top of the other, and shouted, "STAPLES CENTER!!!"

As Eddie and I walked to take our seats in the sound booth, located in the middle of the audience, I couldn't help but utter my own silent prayer of gratitude. *Thanks, God, for seeing her through the fire.* When I looked up, I saw a montage of photos and videos flashing on the big screen. It ended with the words: ARE YOU READY? My spine tingled. I quickly scanned to make sure Dallas and Madison were there, too. It seemed important that we, as a family, watched together.

This was not just Demi's crowning moment. We all had made the journey with her; we all had suffered and grown along the way. Each of us was a winner, and that night I was just as proud of my other two daughters, who were discovering new dreams of their own to follow. Dallas was thriving in voice-over work and becoming a sought-after acting coach, while Madison, still pursuing acting roles, also aspired to be a writer, producer, and director. None of us had given up on each other or ourselves.

Demi and Travis opened as planned, but that wasn't the highlight of the night. Song after song, the crowd sang along, and during "My Love Is Like a Star," everyone activated the lights to their phones and waved them in the dark. I felt like I was floating under the stars. But the most memorable moment came when Demi sang "This Is Me." After she finished the first verse, Joe Jonas suddenly walked onstage. As he burst into the line, "You're the voice I hear inside my head," the crowd exploded with cheers. Off to my right, next to the sound booth, I spied a young girl waving a *Camp Rock* backpack at me. I couldn't resist slipping out of my seat and giving her a big hug. She, like so many others, had made our family's wild and crazy adventure possible.

As the crowd continued to roar, I tried to take it all in. The screaming, the applause, the flashing cameras—it was so genuine, so heartwarming. And I knew in that moment that life had come full circle. Oh, I knew there would be challenges ahead, but tonight was worth celebrating. After all that we had been through, we had survived. Our family bond was unbroken. Our faith was still strong. And our mental health, thanks to therapy, was better than it ever had been. Despite falling so hard and so low, we had restored our wings and were ready to fly toward a better and brighter future.

AFTERWORD

*A*fter sharing my story, I sincerely hope that families everywhere, especially mothers and daughters, begin a dialogue about mental-health issues. It's time to lift the stigma and banish the secrets about issues like anorexia, anxiety, cutting, addiction, depression, and bipolar disorder. And it's certainly time to start treating such issues with the same urgency and care that medical communities do when fighting cancer or other life-threatening disorders. In the end, whether one is a housewife or a Hollywood star, treatment should be available to everyone who needs it. The well-being of our nation and the world depends upon it.

I am thankful and proud to say that everyone in our family is doing amazingly well, thanks to the help we have received from treatment centers, ongoing therapy, our faith, and the support of friends and family. After all the trials and tribulations we've been through, we all have come through as winners. My greatest joy is seeing that we have remained strong as a family unit, and we continue to gather to celebrate holidays and personal achievements. As a proud mom, I'd like to share that Demi's career continues to unfold in new directions, which include her 2017 Grammy nomination and her appearances at various mental-health symposiums. Dallas, still coaching, has also completed some course work in fashion and costume design and hopes to grow her new business venture of embellishing clothes with colorful splashes of glitter, sequins, and feathers. And Madison, still pursuing acting, now has a presence on AwesomenessTV and is writing a digital media series for YouTube. While Eddie continues to break new ground for his country artist, George Navarro, I'm branching out to embrace my love of public speaking and pursue my interest in movie production.

To aid you in your own search for assistance with many of the mental-health issues mentioned in my book, I've compiled the following list of resources. It is my wish that you, too, may find help and healing on your journey.

Xoxoxoxo,

Dianna De La Garza

RESOURCES

ALCOHOLICS ANONYMOUS
www.aa.org

CAST CENTERS
(Therapy, case management, crisis management,
interventions, and sober companions)
www.castcenters.com
1-866-283-9885

DEPRESSION AND BIPOLAR SUPPORT ALLIANCE
www.dbsalliance.org
1-800-826-3632

HELPGUIDE.ORG
(Information and resources on various mental and emotional health topics)
www.helpguide.org

MENTAL HEALTH AMERICA
www.mentalhealthamerica.net
1-800-969-6642

MENTAL HEALTH SERVICES
(Learn about the basics of mental health, treatment options,
disorders, symptoms, and how to get help)
www.mentalhealth.org

NAR-ANON FAMILY GROUPS
(Meeting lists and literature for relatives and friends who are
concerned about the addictions or drug problems of another)
www.nar-anon.org

NARCOTICS ANONYMOUS
www.NA.org

NATIONAL ALLIANCE ON MENTAL ILLNESS (NAMI)

www.nami.org

1-800-950-NAMI (6264)

NATIONAL ASSOCIATION OF ANOREXIA NERVOSA AND
ASSOCIATED DISORDERS

www.anad.org

630-577-1330

NATIONAL EATING DISORDERS ASSOCIATION (NEDA)

www.nationaleatingdisorders.org

1-800-931-2237

NATIONAL INSTITUTE ON DRUG ABUSE

www.drugabuse.gov

NATIONAL SUICIDE PREVENTION HOTLINE

1-800-273-TALK (8255)

THE NATIONAL DOMESTIC VIOLENCE HOTLINE

www.thehotline.org

1-800-799-SAFE (7233)

SUBSTANCE ABUSE AND MENTAL HEALTH SERVICES
ADMINISTRATION

www.samhsa.gov

1-877-726-4727

TIMBERLINE KNOLLS

(Treatment center for women with eating disorders, addictions,
mood disorders, trauma, and/or PTSD)

www.timberlineknolls.com

1-844-335-1932

SUICIDE PREVENTION RESOURCE CENTER

www.sprc.org

ACKNOWLEDGMENTS

Years ago, I had a dream that one day I would publish a book so that I could share my family's journey with the world. Today, that dream has come true, thanks to so many people. Never let anyone tell you that you are "too young," "too old," "too busy," or "too inexperienced" to do anything, because I am living proof that you can accomplish any goal you choose in life. But I had a lot of help along the way, and I want to thank these people sincerely from the bottom of my heart.

Thank you, Phil McIntyre, my daughter Demi's longtime manager at Philymack, for jump-starting this project by introducing me to Simon Green at CAA, who became my amazing literary agent. Without the two of you, this book would never have happened. You were the start of my story becoming a real, tangible manuscript, not just an idea. And I am grateful to you both. Also thank you, Danielle McMonagle, Simon Green's assistant, for your editorial advice, and Reece Pearson, COO at

Philymack, for being my intermediary with CAA. I am sincerely thankful for both of you.

To Vickie McIntyre, my incredibly talented co-writer who agreed to embark on this long, hard process with me. This wouldn't be a book if it weren't for you. How many laughs and tears did we share during those frequent book-writing sessions down in the "dungeon"? I lost track after the first year. You stood by this project, never wavering, even through my losing five close family members in one year, giving me the time I needed to grieve and then get back to work as soon as I possibly could. You were my therapist, my interrogator, and my beloved friend during the process, and I will forever be indebted to you for not giving up on me. You managed to arrange my thoughts and stories into this perfectly shaped memoir that I can now share with the world. I thank you with my whole heart, nothing less. You are incredible. I love you.

I also want to thank you, Jean Feiwel, publisher and senior VP at Macmillan Children's Publishing Group, for believing in my book from the beginning. I cannot tell you how honored I am that someone as accomplished as you thought my story was worthy of your attention and approval. Thank you for your faith in me as a storyteller. I appreciate you so very much. Anna Roberto, editor at Feiwel and Friends, you are amazing, patient, and kind. Thank you for answering my barrage of questions with ease, and for making sure this book is the best it could possibly be. I can't ever thank you enough for your attention to detail and your willingness to help in every aspect. You are amazing.

The hardest part is finding the words to thank my incredible family. To Eddie DeLaGarza, my husband, I first want to thank you for loving us and taking care of us as a family, but I also want to thank you for being so supportive of this book and all my creative endeavors. You are my rock, my soul mate, and my best friend. I hope we are able to push our beds together in the nursing home when we are old and hold hands like Grandma and Papa did—and I'll even let you have the remote! But only on Tuesdays. I love you for the rest of our lives.

Dallas Lovato, my oldest daughter, thank you for your love and kindness, as well as all of your help with everyday things that I couldn't do while I was spending hours on this story. I also appreciate your help with remembering so many details that I couldn't, especially with our family's insanely LONG time line that served as the outline for the book. You've had this incredible spirit of resilience since your first day on Earth that I expect will get you through the roughest of times. You are an inspiration to those around you. Never stop wearing sequins and rhinestones, and never stop being your wonderful self. I love you forever.

Demi Lovato, my middle child, you have come through the fire without even the smell of smoke on your clothing. I am incredibly proud of who you've become. Your life hasn't always been easy, but if it had been, your music probably wouldn't touch so many lives across the world today. Thank you for the love and support you show me every day, and thank you for trusting me to tell this story in hopes of helping people who may be walking the same path we did. They need to know that a happy ending is possible if they are willing to work for it. I love you so very much.

Madison De La Garza, my youngest daughter, I thank you for your love and for your faith in me as a writer, something you aspire to be one day. I have a connection with you because of our love for creating stories, whether for movies or books. Your approval of this memoir means the world to me, as I have been inspired by you to create something that will last through the ages. I know without a doubt that one day you will do the same. Never stop challenging yourself, because there is no limit to what you will accomplish in this lifetime. I love you sincerely.

To my mom and dad, I thank you for instilling in me that thread of faith that has been entwined into every aspect of my life. We didn't always have money, but we had something way more valuable— LOVE. And our faith in God has and will continue to see us through the hardest of times. Without your love and guidance, who knows where my path would have led me in life? I thank you both with all my heart for loving me.

Amy Emory, thank you for being my friend and for supporting this book from the first day. I sincerely appreciate your taking my place at school events when I was writing and unable to volunteer, and thank you for the housework help when I was overwhelmed. I love you, my "Cali BFF."

Lorna Bailey, you have been an inspiration to me during my hardest times. Thank you for your love and support, and for showing me that even in the midst of the most unimaginable tragedies, it's possible to pick yourself up and keep going. Trenton, our angel, would be proud of this book. I love you to the moon and back.

Dawn Burkett, my Louisiana friend and partner in future crimes, you have been such a help to me. Your spirit of giving of your time to help whenever I'm in need is inspiring, and I'm grateful to you forever. Ms. Gayle raised a beautiful soul. I love you dearly.

Thank you, my siblings Joey Hart, Julie Moe, Brandon Hart, and BJ Hart, for your love and support and for being an important part of my story. I'm proud of each of you and your sweet families, and I love you all. Special thanks to my sister, Katherine Barnes, because through-out all your struggles, you have been an inspiration to me. Every time I felt like quitting because we had to attend yet another loved one's funeral, you would call or text, "Hey, how's that book going?" like it was just what I was SUPPOSED to do in this lifetime. You've been through so much, and yet you never stopped encouraging ME. I can't wait for you to hold this book in your hands while we sit by the ocean and read together. I love you more than you know.

To my attorney, Paul Almond, thank you for everything you do for me. You are a superhero without a cape. To Dr. Kim Dennis, thank you for being a huge part of my recovery. I will always be grateful to you. Additionally, thanks to my friends Richard Martinez, Melody Fowler, Kris Smalling, Cindy Howard, and Vanessa Porea for supporting my book. I am truly blessed to have some amazing friends.

I have so many more friends and relatives who have supported my book wholeheartedly, but I just can't name them all here. But you know who you are, and I will be thanking you in person, if I haven't already. And, I want to express my gratitude to all of the parents who have come up to me at events and concerts and asked, "How did you all do it? How did you get through everything you've dealt with as a family and survive, especially in this industry?" You are the ones who inspired me to write this book, because many times I thought to myself, *Oh, I wish I had my book written and I could just hand them one*. I hope that if any of you are reading this, you realize that you are the reason I wrote this story. Thank you all sincerely.